Reconstructing Policy in Higher Education

Reconstructing Policy in Higher Education highlights the work of accomplished and award-winning scholars and provides concrete examples of how feminist post-structuralism effectively informs research methods and can serve as a vital tool for policy makers, analysts, and practitioners. The research examines a range of topics of interest to scholars and professionals including: purposes of Higher Education, administrative leadership, athletics, diversity, student activism, social class, the history of women in postsecondary institutions, and quality and science in the globalized university.

Students enrolled in Higher Education and Educational Policy programs will find this book offers them tools for thinking differently about policy analysis and educational practice. Higher Education faculty, managers, deans, presidents, and policy makers will find this book contributes significantly to their own policy analysis, practice, and discourse.

Elizabeth J. Allan is an Associate Professor of Higher Education at the University of Maine where she is also an affiliated faculty member with the Women's Studies program.

Susan Van Deventer Iverson is an Assistant Professor of Higher Education Administration and Student Personnel at Kent State University where she is also an affiliated faculty member with the Women's Studies Program.

Rebecca Ropers-Huilman is a Professor of Higher Education and an affiliate with the Department of Gender, Women, and Sexuality Studies at the University of Minnesota.

Reconstructing Policy in Higher Education

Feminist Poststructural Perspectives

Edited by
Elizabeth J. Allan,
Susan Van Deventer Iverson,
and
Rebecca Ropers-Huilman

 Routledge
Taylor & Francis Group

NEW YORK AND LONDON

First published 2010
by Routledge
270 Madison Ave, New York, NY 10016

Simultaneously published in the UK
by Routledge
2 Park Square, Milton Park, Abingdon, Oxon OX14 4RN

Routledge is an imprint of the Taylor & Francis Group, an informa business

© 2010 Taylor & Francis

Typeset in Minion
by Keystroke, Tettenhall, Wolverhampton
Printed and bound in the United States of America on acid-free paper
by Walsworth Publishing Company, Marceline, MO

Library of Congress Cataloging in Publication Data
Reconstructing policy in higher education: feminist poststructural
perspectives/[edited by] Elizabeth J. Allan, Susan Van Deventer Iverson,
Rebecca Ropers-Huilman.
        p. cm.
        Includes bibliographical references and index.
    1. Women in higher education—Government policy—United States.
    2. Feminism and higher education—United States. 3.
Poststructuralism.   I. Allan, Elizabeth J., 1964–   II. Iverson,
Susan Van Deventer.   III. Ropers-Huilman, Rebecca.
    LC1568.R43 2009
    378.73082—dc22   2009012071

ISBN 10: 0–415–99776–3 (hbk)
ISBN 10: 0–415–99777–1 (pbk)
ISBN 10: 0–203–87003–4 (ebk)

ISBN 13: 978–0–415–99776–8 (hbk)
ISBN 13: 978–0–415–99777–5 (pbk)
ISBN 13: 978–0–203–87003–7 (ebk)

Contents

List of Contributors

Editors

Elizabeth J. Allan is an Associate Professor of Higher Education at the University of Maine where she is also an affiliated faculty member with the Women's Studies program. Prior to her arrival at UMaine in 2000, she was a Visiting Assistant Professor in Women's Studies and earned her Ph.D. in Educational Policy and Leadership at The Ohio State University (1999). She is the author of *Policy, gender, and education: Constructing women's status* (Routledge, 2008) and has authored articles and book chapters related to gender, diversity, and campus climates in higher education. Her work has been published by the *Harvard Educational Review, The Journal of Higher Education, The Review of Higher Education,* and *Innovative Higher Education.*

Susan V. Iverson is an Assistant Professor of Higher Education Administration and Student Personnel at Kent State University where she is also an affiliated faculty member with the Women's Studies Program. Iverson earned her doctorate in higher educational leadership, with a concentration in women's studies, from the University of Maine (2005) where she also served as an instructor in higher educational leadership and women's studies. In April 2006, Iverson was honored with the Outstanding Dissertation Award, presented by the American Educational Research Association, Division J (Postsecondary Education) for her dissertation research, "A policy discourse analysis of U.S. land-grant university diversity action plans." Her scholarly interests include diversity, gender equity, citizenship, and service-learning. Recent work has appeared in *Equity and Excellence in Education, Journal about Women in Higher Education, Educational Administration Quarterly, Review of Higher Education,* and *NASPA Journal.*

Rebecca Ropers-Huilman is a Professor of Higher Education and an affiliate with the Department of Gender, Women, and Sexuality Studies at the University of Minnesota. After completing her doctorate at the University of Wisconsin-Madison in 1996, she served as a faculty member at Louisiana State University for 11 years. She has published three books, all of which related to women's experiences in higher education. Additionally, she has authored more than 30 articles or book chapters focusing on related areas. In her commitment to put theory into practice and policy, she served both as the Director of the Women's Center and as the Director of Women's and Gender Studies while at LSU. She also serves as the editor of the *National Women's Studies Association Journal.*

Contributors

Judith Glazer-Raymo is Lecturer in Higher and Postsecondary Education at Teachers College, Columbia University and Professor of Education Emerita at Long Island University. She is the editor of *Unfinished agendas: New and continuing gender challenges in higher education* (2008) and the author of *Shattering the myths: Women in academe* (1999) and numerous other publications on gender equity, governance, and graduate education.

Suzanne Gordon is a Professor and Chair of the Department of Physical Therapy at Husson University, Bangor, Maine. Dr. Gordon earned a Doctor of Education in Higher Education Leadership from the University of Maine (2006). Her research interests focus on higher education leadership, and multicultural and social justice education of healthcare professionals. Prior research leading to this chapter was reported in *The Review of Higher Education*.

Jeni Hart is currently an Associate Professor of Higher and Continuing Education in the Department of Educational Leadership and Policy Analysis at the University of Missouri. She earned her Ph.D. in 2002 at the University of Arizona. Broadly, her scholarly work focuses on campus climate, faculty, gender, and activism in higher education. Recent publications include a chapter in Lester and Sallee's book *Establishing a family-friendly campus: Best practices*; "Assessing the campus climate for gender: Lessons from the research" with Jennifer Fellabaum in the *Journal of Diversity in Higher Education*; and "Non-tenure track faculty women: Opening the door" in the *Journal of the Professoriate*. She regularly presents her research at the Association for the Study of Higher Education and American Educational Research Association conferences. In addition, she has conducted campus climate research on three campuses and published technical reports and articles related to that research.

Jennifer Hubbard is a Ph.D. candidate in Educational Leadership and Policy Analysis at the University of Missouri. She currently works as a Research Associate for the Maine Higher Education Alcohol Prevention Partnership (HEAPP) and is an adjunct faculty member in the Higher Education graduate program at the University of Maine. Her research interests include the college student experience, social justice issues in higher education, with particular focus on student political ideology, gender, first-generation college students, and social class.

Jennifer Lee Hoffman is a Research Associate in the Intercollegiate Athletic Leadership Program at the University of Washington. Her research focuses on policy in intercollegiate athletics, with a specific interest in gender and ethnicity. Her research has been published in the *Journal for the Study of Sports and Athletes in Education* and appears in the forthcoming *ASHE Reader on the Study of Sports and Athletes in Higher Education* and *Women in Higher Education and Student Affairs: Research and Practice from Feminist Perspectives*, to be published by the

ACPA Standing Committee for Women. Her work has been presented at the American Educational Research Association annual conference. Previously she taught in the Department of Physical Education at Seattle Pacific University. She earned her Ph.D. from the University of Washington (2006), and holds an M.A. from Seattle University (1998) and a B.S. from Washington State University (1989).

Jana Nidiffer is currently an Associate Professor in the Department of Educational Leadership at Oakland University in Michigan. Prior to her appointment, she was the Jean W. Campbell Scholar in Residence at the Center for the Education of Women and on the faculty of the Center for the Study of Higher and Postsecondary Education in the School of Education at the University of Michigan. She teaches courses on current, historical, gender-related, and methodological issues in higher education. She earned her doctorate from the Harvard Graduate School of Education in 1994. Dr. Nidiffer's primary research interest is in access and opportunity in higher education, largely from a historical perspective. She is co-author of *Beating the odds: How the poor get to college* (1996) with Arthur Levine, and author of *Pioneering deans of women: More than wise and pious matrons* (2000), and *Women administrators in higher education: Historical and contemporary perspectives* (2001). She has published in *History of Education Quarterly, American Educational Research Journal, About Campus*, and *Education Policy*.

Nelly P. Stromquist is a Professor of International and Comparative Education in the College of Education at the University of Maryland. She received her Ph.D. from Stanford University in international development education and her M.A. and B.A. from the Monterey Institute of Foreign Studies in political science. Dr. Stromquist specializes in issues related to international development education, globalization, equity, and gender, which she examines from a critical sociology perspective. She has considerable experience in formal and non-formal education, particularly in Latin America and West Africa. Her most recent books are: *Feminist organizations and social transformation in Latin America* (2006), (ed.) *The professoriate in the age of globalization* (2006), and *Education in a globalized world: The connectivity of economic power, technology, and knowledge* (2002). She is currently examining the possibilities and challenges of global citizenship and transnational migration. She is former president of the Comparative and International Education Society and a 2005–2006 Fulbright New Century Scholar.

Tatiana Suspitsyna is an Assistant Professor in the School of Educational Policy and Leadership at the Ohio State University (OSU). She earned her Ph.D. from the University of Michigan, Ann Arbor, in 2004, and was a Visiting Assistant Professor at the University of Illinois, Urbana-Champaign, for a year before joining OSU. Suspitsyna's dissertation, entitled *Adaptation of Western economics by Russian universities: Intercultural travel of an academic field* was published in the Routledge Dissertation Series in Higher Education. Her research interests include narrative approaches to organization studies, gender and race issues in organizations, and poststructuralist methodology.

Susan Talburt is Director of the Women's Studies Institute at Georgia State University, where she teaches courses in youth cultures, youth and sexualities, feminist methodologies, feminist theories, and LGBT Studies. She has published articles related to these topics in such journals as *International Journal of Qualitative Studies in Education, Review of Higher Education, Journal of Higher Education,* and *Educational Theory.* She is the author of *Subject to identity: Knowledge, sexuality, and academic practices in higher education* and co-editor of *Youth and sexualities: Pleasure, subversion, and insubordination in and out of schools.* She is presently working on projects centered on higher education and the spatial in relation to neoliberalism and globalization. She received her Ph.D. in Education and Human Development from Vanderbilt University in 1996.

Foreword

Judith Glazer-Raymo

The growth of policy analysis as a field of study in higher education has paralleled federal and state involvement in the allocation of resources and the regulation of educational institutions. Over the decades, the policy process has taken many forms but as events occurring in the first decade of the twenty-first century continue to make obvious, traditional modes of policy analysis using the tools of micro-economics and decision science have only limited relevance for colleges and universities in a rapidly changing and often volatile global environment. The educational and cultural missions and purposes of public and private higher education are being contested on many levels. Feminist scholars have long questioned the gender-neutral stance of policy-makers. Two major challenges continue to be: first, how to sustain more interpretive ways of conducting policy analyses that heighten public awareness and action on issues affecting women, and second, how to convey the complex interrelationships among multiple factors guiding the implementation and evaluation of higher education policies and programs.

A historic gender policy breakthrough occurred with the passage of the omnibus Higher Education Act of 1972, prohibiting sex discrimination and calling for affirmative action in higher education employment, compensation, and admission of students to undergraduate and graduate programs. The possibility of sanctions for non-compliance and a series of class action lawsuits by women's groups motivated colleges and universities to re-examine existing policies and practices (Glazer-Raymo, 1999). Liberal feminism dominated the discourse throughout the 1970s based on assumptions that if male–female representation and support could be equalized, the underlying problems that characterized discriminatory practices and unequal treatment would be resolved. Women soon learned that protection of the status quo made change difficult in entrenched gender hierarchies, and that statistical and comparative demographic analyses had only limited impact on the policy agenda. Nevertheless, sustained demands by women and other under-represented groups, coupled with external intervention by state and federal regulators, judicial rulings, and support from women leaders led to the adoption of more equitable policies and the implementation of gender-equity programs and practices. The development of women's studies courses and their institutionalization as gender studies, ethnic studies, cultural studies, and gay and lesbian studies paralleled these advances, engaging new generations of students and faculty in the creation and use of theoretical and methodological perspectives that facilitate critical feminist policy analysis.

The Art and Craft of Policy Analysis

In *Speaking truth to power*, Aaron Wildavsky (1979) asserted that policy analysis is both an art and a craft that has as its purpose the clarification of values that inform the decision-making process and the forms of knowledge used to fulfill analytical objectives. In this text, he sought justification for the systematic training of graduate students in public policy analysis as a subfield of political science. Many such schools now operate, variously linked to public administration, public and international affairs, and government (as in the case of the Kennedy School at Harvard University). However, policy analysis continues to be a field in ferment, struggling with the fundamental incompatibility between technocratic (bounded rationality) and democratic (incremental, pluralistic) models of decision-making; the appropriate tools (quantitative or qualitative, cost-benefit or risk-benefit) for conducting policy research and the relative interests and purposes of policy-makers and stakeholders.

It is unlikely that gender plays other than a supporting role in these schools that operate on a national and international stage and are concerned with mainstream economic and political theory and practice. After eight years of experiencing the ungendering of public policy at the federal level (2000–2008), and in a period of deep economic recession, the continuing challenge for women policy analysts in addressing women's issues is how to obtain a hearing for improvements in gender-related policies and practices, and how to reverse the systematic dismantling of programs such as affirmative action. Since 1996, ballot initiatives banning public institutions from using affirmative action programs that "give preferential treatment to groups or individuals based on their race, gender, color, ethnicity, or national origin for public employment, education or contracting purposes" have been approved in four states (California, Washington, Michigan, and Nebraska).[1] Narrower challenges to the consideration of race in college admissions have been mounted in Texas on the grounds that race-neutral alternatives are working.[2]

Higher education decision-making and policy analysis generally occur in environmental contexts that differ from governmental and business organizations. However, governmental intervention into the policies and practices of higher education systems is blurring these distinctions. Public and private institutions now compete for state and federal support through student aid programs, programmatic and research subsidies, and capital construction funding. This competition for resources extends into the global marketplace through student exchange programs, scientific and technological partnerships, and entrepreneurial projects limited only by the imagination of their developers. As Charles Lindblom (1965) observed at the time of passage of the first Higher Education Act, "By operating in the political arena, [institutions] are forced to consider a much broader social reality than [their] own interests" (p. 192). In the current political and economic climate, it is therefore not surprising that critical policy analysis is an inevitable outcome of increased public scrutiny. Persuasive cases will have to be made by feminist scholars in reasserting gender priorities in the face of competing domestic and foreign policy agendas.

Policy as Discourse

The authors of this text recognize this challenge and argue convincingly that the poststructural premise of "policy-as-discourse" can reveal the ambiguities and contradictions of policies emphasizing accountability, productivity, and the status quo, and can facilitate the reconstruction of policies that translate into more equitable practices in the academy. Their case studies and their critiques are grounded in feminist poststructural theory, viewed from the standpoint of women's experiences and how policy shapes "both discourse and, within discourse, lived experience" (Allan, Iverson, & Ropers-Huilman, p. 3). The authors are consistent in their adherence to feminist poststructural concepts and methods, avoiding counterproductive debates that sometimes lead feminists into blind alleys where the theory becomes more important than the problem being addressed. Instead, their analyses demonstrate that when women are the categories of analysis, the ways in which the policy agenda is constructed and issues are represented, reframe both underlying meanings and the policies and practices emanating from them.

In their introduction, Allan, Iverson, and Ropers-Huilman distinguish between the poststructuralist feminist approach to scholarly inquiry and liberal feminist or enlightenment approaches, contrasting "the relationship between discourse and subjectivity" and "how language and meaning produce dynamic and contradictory subject positions" with "the rational, fixed, individual subject(s) of enlightenment humanism." Thus, they acknowledge the multiple, often competing discourses and methodologies that feminists have applied in critiquing existing policy positions and the production of knowledge within their disciplines.[3] Rather than rely on data collection, legal precedent, or universal truths, which, as they state, are generally supported by adherence to traditional practices, these authors draw on feminist poststructural perspectives to inform the readers' understanding of dynamic policy processes.

Allan defines poststructuralism as an academic branch of postmodern thought, or in her words, as "a loosely connected group of theories predicated upon a critique of structuralist approaches" (p. 12). Her observation that language is socially constituted and shaped by the interplay we have yet to discover, lays the groundwork for the essays that follow. Some authors are influenced by Michel Foucault, particularly his work on power relations and resistance, and by Jacques Derrida and the methodology of deconstruction. Both Foucault and Derrida expressed the changeable nature of the meaning of elements in world cultures and the multiple and competing discourses that mutually reinforce one another. It is of some significance that women were not

xiv • Judith Glazer-Raymo

an integral part of their formulation. However, as Harland Bloland observed in his essay on postmodernism and higher education: "Derrida's powerful attack upon hierarchies in the modernist world can be used with great effect in challenging higher education's hierarchies and illuminating its exclusions" (1995, p. 527). Allan and other contributors demonstrate in their poststructural analyses that "[d]econstruction provides reasons and arguments supporting the accusations that excluded groups make against institutions of higher education" (Bloland, p. 528).

The ensuing chapters of this text show how feminist poststructural critique can be a productive mechanism for contesting, disrupting, and illuminating programs, policies, and commentary about women in higher education. It can also be a useful tool for ameliorating conflicts that arise from adherence to identity politics in feminist thought, bringing greater clarity to gender discourse and its intersections with race, ethnicity, social class, and sexuality. In working within the frame of feminist poststructuralism, critical policy analysts view policies not as linear stages from issue definition to agenda setting, selection of alternatives, and problem resolution. Rather, they reveal four clusters that highlight the issues raised in this text: (1) the ambiguities and contradictions of the language used to propose or evaluate institutional policies and practices by external arbiters with limited stakes in the long-range consequences of their words and actions; (2) the inadequacies of decontextualized analyses and methodologies that focus on costs and benefits, means and ends, goals and objectives; (3) the multiple meanings of theoretical constructs that (perhaps unintentionally) perpetuate partial solutions or untenable situations; and (4) the significance of power relations and resource dependence in determining the extent of political influence on institutions and their constituencies. In Chapter 2, Allan proposes a series of questions as "prompts" for chapter authors, asking them to consider the "subject positions" emerging from policies, the underlying assumptions of problem selection, the regulation of discourses and subject positions, and the outcomes of policy-making and policy analysis.

Policy Issues

How and why policies are selected for analysis has been a frequent subject of debate among scholars of public policy. Wildavsky (1979) somewhat facetiously likened the selection of problems for analysis as occurring in a crowded space where existing policies collide with each other, vying for attention from decision-makers. Carol Bacchi applies a "What's the Problem?" approach to issues affecting women as a means of thinking about "the interconnections between policy areas" and policy issues that may be excluded from the discourse, depending on how problems are defined or represented (1999, p. 2). This interpretive approach to policy analysis is defined by Bacchi as "the language, concepts, and categories employed to frame an issue" (p. 2).

The methodology of deconstruction is employed effectively in the chapters that follow this Foreword, revealing the contradictory, ambiguous, and exclusionary discourses of organizational statements (Iverson, Suspitsyna, Stromquist); the decontextualized use of theoretical constructs (Gordon et al., Talburt); the unanticipated consequences of policy on women students (Hart & Hubbard, Hoffman et al.) and the silences about women's role as change agents (Nidiffer, Ropers-Huilman). In their analyses, these scholars reveal the ambiguity permeating institutional statements which illustrate organizational inattention to gender in official documents about diversity, globalization, and accountability in higher education. Contradictions also arise in the disjuncture between policy premises and formulations. Some exemplars follow.

In her discourse analysis of 21 diversity action plans, Iverson displays the problematics of designing and implementing "diverse, inclusive campus communities" in crowded policy spaces where diversity has multiple meanings and applications that can be measured through a variety of approaches. Her critique illuminates the contradictory discourses of "access" and "disadvantage" in portraying minority students as at-risk victims of discrimination and/or outsiders to "particular arenas within the institution, and the dominant culture" (p. 200). She also reveals the ambiguities of the market model of education with its emphasis on competition and students as commodities, at the same time that universities assert their commitment to change, inclusivity, and equality. In revealing the unquestioned assumptions of policy problems, she highlights the multiple meanings of diversity and the unanticipated consequences for students as objects of implementation.[4] Suspitsyna's analysis of 144 official statements by the Secretary of Education and her staff between 2005 and 2007 focuses attention on the conservative discourse of the federal bureaucracy, and its preoccupation with the language, but not the substance, of access, affordability, and accountability. In this context, she reveals contradictions implicit in the dominant themes of quality assurance, student consumerism, and institutional competitiveness at a time when the unanticipated withdrawal of resources by the states and by private loan agencies increases institutional vulnerability to political intervention.

The market model that is so prevalent in higher education, blurring the lines between non-profit and for-profit universities, is highlighted in the chapter on Title IX policy and intercollegiate athletics (Hoffman et al.). Here again, operating below the radar screen, the Department of Education has sought to deregulate the one piece of legislation that has made it illegal for educational institutions to discriminate on the basis of sex "under any education program or activity receiving Federal financial assistance"[5] (Carpenter & Acosta, 2005, p. 3). In their analysis of the impact of Title IX policy on intercollegiate athletics, Hoffman et al. show how the market model of "big-time sports" contradicts the equitable use of resources for women's athletics. A recent report issued by the American Association of University Professors (AAUP) compares salaries of full professors and football coaches of Division IA institutions. In commenting on the disproportionate base salaries and other income of head football coaches (all male), the AAUP reports that "head football coaches, on average, earn more than twice the salary of full professors in every conference" and that "the base salaries and other income of 50 head coaches are $1 million and higher" (Committee on the Economic Status of the Profession, 2008, p. 12). As Hoffman et al. state in their chapter, the marketplace discourse of Title IX policy "gives rise to images of the athlete as a commodity" (p. 139).

Gordon et al. pose an interesting question in their chapter on the discursive framing of gender and leadership in the *Chronicle of Higher Education*. They ask whether "dominant discourses" eclipse alternative conceptualizations of leadership precisely because normative models are not "sufficiently exposed and disrupted." Here again, the market model is part of the discourse on women and leadership, a possible consequence of the fact that the dominant discourse on leadership is derived from scholarship conducted mainly in male-dominated schools of business, organizational management, and public administration. The chapters I have cited make visible the "marketplace discourse" that creates tensions in the support and continuation of gender-sensitive policy-making.

I continue to believe that we are witnessing the ungendering of public policy in higher education and in the larger society. The potential demise of affirmative action policies constitutes a critical turning point in coordinated efforts to reverse many decades of exclusion and under-representation. Women are now the majority of undergraduate and graduate students, and are achieving parity with their male counterparts in executive and managerial positions. Glass ceiling metaphors and feminism writ large are discredited by those who assert that gender equality has been achieved and it is time to "move on" to more immediate concerns. And while we can list accomplishments, large and small, that have been made by women in higher education and in the larger society, much work remains to be done. As the essays in this text show, feminist poststructural policy analysis provides fresh perspectives on taken-for-granted assumptions of existing policies and practices. The strength of their arguments on gender-related policy issues warrants close attention from every reader with a stake in the outcomes.

Notes

1 The language cited here is contained in the Michigan Civil Rights Initiative, a state constitutional amendment approved as a ballot initiative in November 2006 (Glazer-Raymo, 2008, p. 14).

2 *Hopwood v. University of Texas Law School* (1995) was overturned in 2003 when the Supreme Court ruled in *Grutter v. Bollinger* that "the educational benefits of diversity constitute a compelling interest that can justify the consideration of race as a factor in admissions" (electronic communication with Janice Robinson, February 27, 2009).

3 See, for example, Alcoff and Potter (1993) on the intersection of feminist philosophy and epistemology.

4   The discourse of diversity played a prominent role in the *Grutter* decision; see Gurin, Dey, Hurtado, and Gurin (2002) for a discussion of their research on the positive outcomes of diversity policies under affirmative action in contributing to students' academic experience.
5   See Glazer-Raymo (2008, pp. 17–22) for a discussion of recent efforts to deregulate Title IX.

References

Alcoff, L. & Potter, E. (Eds.). (1993). *Feminist epistemologies.* New York: Routledge.

Bacchi, C. L. (1999). *Women, policy and politics: The construction of policy problems.* Thousand Oaks, CA: Sage.

Bloland, H. (1995). Postmodernism and higher education. *Journal of Higher Education,* 66(5), 521–559.

Committee on the Economic Status of the Profession (2008). Where are the priorities? Report on the economic status of the profession. *Academe,* March/April. Retrieved January 8, 2009, from http://www.aaup.org/AAUP/comm/rep/Z/ecstatreport2007–08/survey2007–08.htm.

Glazer-Raymo, J. (1999). *Shattering the myths: Women in academe.* Baltimore, MD: Johns Hopkins University Press.

Glazer-Raymo, J. (2008). The feminist agenda: A work in progress. In J. Glazer-Raymo (Ed.), *Unfinished agendas: New and continuing gender challenges in higher education.* Baltimore, MD: Johns Hopkins University Press.

Gurin, P., Dey, E. L., Hurtado, S., & Gurin, G. (2002). Diversity and higher education: Theory and impact on educational outcomes. *Harvard Educational Review,* 72(3), 330–366.

Lindblom, C. (1965). *The intelligence of democracy: Decision-making through mutual adjustment.* New York: Free Press.

Wildavsky, A. (1979). *Speaking truth to power: The art and craft of policy analysis.* Boston, MA: Little Brown.

Acknowledgments

A book is always a collaborative process. While we (Elizabeth, Susan, and Rebecca) take full responsibility for the final form of this book, we would like to thank many people who helped us in big or small ways to collaborate on our vision. Specifically, we were inspired by those whose work urged us to think differently about educational practice and policy. Some of these people have contributed their own writing to this volume. Others include Estela Bensimon, Patti Lather, Catherine Marshall, Chris Weedon, Deb Britzman, Elizabeth Ellsworth, Wanda Pillow, Elizabeth St. Pierre, Petra Hendry, MaryAnn Danowitz Sagaria, Carol Bacchi, Jill Blackmore, and Judy Glazer-Raymo. We are also indebted to policy-oriented colleagues who provided feedback about how we might best craft this book for an audience that was invested in understanding, analyzing, and developing educational policy. These included David Weerts, Robert Poch, Susan Gardner, and Gertrude Steuernagel. As well, the volume benefited greatly from the supportive and critical feedback we received from three esteemed colleagues: Amy Scott Metcalfe, Wanda Pillow, and Mary Ann Danowitz Sagaria, who carefully read and commented on the full manuscript in its final stages. Also, our contacts at Routledge, Sarah Burrows and Alex Sharp, have been very supportive in turning earlier visions into a reality. Finally, we would like to acknowledge Katherine O'Flaherty, a doctoral student in Higher Education and History at the University of Maine, whose competent assistance and patience with the editing process for this book was invaluable.

Individually, Elizabeth would like to thank University of Maine colleagues including Sue Estler, Susan Gardner, Mary Madden, Anne Pooler, Connie Perry, Mazie Hough, and Ann Schonberger, who have helped make space for my engagement in feminist scholarship and the compilation of this volume in particular. As well, I am grateful to UMaine graduate students, especially Julie-Ann Scott, Lynn Atkins, Elizabeth Barry, Lisa Hallen, Stuart Swain, and Andrea McGill-O'Rourke who took the time to carefully read and provide feedback on my chapters for this book. To my partner, Brian, our children, and our extended families, I extend sincere gratitude for your love, patience, support, and daily doses of good humor.

I, Susan, greatly appreciate the intellectual contributions, professional advice, and the friendship of peers, mentors, and colleagues who have fostered my work. My foray into feminist poststructural research began at the University of Maine, where I benefited from feedback, encouragement, and thought-provoking questions from many, enabling me to view my work from multiple perspectives. Heartfelt thanks to Elizabeth Allan from whom I have learned much; she has mentored, inspired, and guided me, and facilitated many opportunities. I also thank Sue Estler, Mazie Hough, Renate Klein, Suzanne P. Gordon, and Marwin Spiller who each provided support and from whom I learned firsthand the work of a community of scholars. To my colleagues at Kent State University, especially Jennifer H. James, Mark Kretovics, Stephen Thomas, and Kathe Davis, I offer thanks for their positive contributions, interests, and willingness to support my work; they have strengthened my abilities to make a contribution. For my husband Yale's support and encouragement, and my daughter Mia's patience and humor, I extend my deep gratitude. Finally, I acknowledge my parents, George and Arlene Van Deventer, who made the start of this journey possible. I dedicate this project to the memory of my mother.

I, Rebecca, extend my thanks to colleagues both at Louisiana State University as well as at the University of Minnesota. In both places, my thinking has been immeasurably enriched by relationships with students, staff, and faculty who come together regularly to support, challenge, and expand each other's ideas. I found LSU to be a generative place where ideas and "making a difference" were taken seriously. From my time at LSU, I specifically thank Petra Hendry, Roland Mitchell, Nina Asher, Laura Choate, and Susan Gardner (who is now at the University of Maine). At the University of Minnesota, I have found colleagues whose kindness and intellect provide a climate of scholarly energy and passion that informs my work. To my new colleagues, especially Darwin Hendel, Melissa Anderson, David Weerts, Cryss Brunner, Joan Dejaeghere, Peter Demerath, and Fran Vavrus, I offer enthusiastic thanks. Finally, to my family, both immediate and extended, who buoy any contributions I am able to make to this world. Brian, Anson, Aaron, and Ray and Rosa Ropers, a heartfelt thanks.

1

Introduction

ELIZABETH J. ALLAN, SUSAN V. IVERSON,
AND REBECCA ROPERS-HUILMAN

Higher education, like any complex educational or social system, encounters problems that need solutions. Policy is one vehicle through which colleges, universities, and systems of higher education work to sustain and improve as they strive to enact their missions, goals, and objectives. Policy researchers and analysts are frequently called upon for expertise in assessing the effectiveness of extant policy and making recommendations for improvement. Yet, despite the implementation and refinements of policy, some problems – such as those associated with access, equity, and diversity – continue to plague postsecondary/ individual campuses and higher education systems. Moreover, the very language through which policy (and power relations within systems) is created continues to be both value-laden and contentious.

Catalyzed by a growing awareness of feminist poststructural perspectives and their potential to enhance understandings of policy and professional practice in postsecondary education, this volume responds to the need for a text that illustrates how these perspectives can help researchers and practitioners think differently about policy issues and policy analysis in the context of higher education. The research highlighted in subsequent chapters examines a range of topics of interest to scholars and professionals in higher education, including: purposes of higher education, administrative leadership, athletics, diversity policy, student agency, social class, the history of women in postsecondary institutions, and quality and science in the globalized university.

The majority of the chapters examine policy-related issues in the context of U.S. higher education; importantly however, the analytic approaches employed are transferable to policy investigations in varied contexts. As well, two of the chapters bring a more global perspective to this volume by detailing research related to student engagement in New Zealand (Chapter 9) and transnational implications of discourses carried by educational policy reports of the World Bank (Chapter 11). In addition to the scope of policy-related issues and contexts examined, the chapters also range widely in their focus on different aspects of sociopolitical identity, including: sexual identity, socio-economic status, geographic home, gender, race, and status within university organizational hierarchies.

This text joins together the work of scholars who draw upon theories of feminist poststructuralism (FPS) to examine policy issues within the context of postsecondary education. While the chapters included in this volume shine a spotlight on different issues related to higher education, they share two themes: (1) they all investigate issues relevant to policy, and (2) they draw upon FPS perspectives to analyze and understand the issues in new ways with a focus on struggles for social justice. Our use of the plural terms, theories and perspectives, is intended to emphasize the fluidity of FPS and to highlight that such approaches do not conform to a singular methodological protocol. FPS approaches provide a lens through which to analyze what has come to be taken-for-granted as "normal" everyday practice. When applied to research and policy analysis, FPS approaches foreground assumptions embedded in the naming of problems and examine the discourses that may produce unintended consequences of policy solutions.

To set the stage for the ensuing chapters, we offer a few definitions of key concepts associated with FPS. First, what is theory? Theory has various meanings depending upon context and methodology. As noted by Creswell (2009), quantitative researchers, generally, test theories as an explanation for answers to their questions, whereas typically for qualitative researchers, theory provides a "lens that shapes what is looked at and the questions asked" (p. 49). For our purposes, we draw upon the latter understanding of theory. This "orienting lens" (Creswell, p. 62) serves as an explanatory framework through which to analyze and understand a given phenomenon. For instance, drawing upon feminist perspectives as a theoretical lens may illuminate policy issues with particular effects for women in specific contexts (Allan, 2003) or knowledge about oppressive situations for women (Olesen, 2000). We ascribe to Ozga's (2000) view that "there is no such thing as theory in itself, divorced from a standpoint in time and space. When any theory so represents itself, it is important to lay bare its concealed perspective" (p. 45).

This project – guided by the notion that inquiry leads to change – is informed by feminist theory, which is defined by a commitment to eliminating subordination and oppressive conditions in social institutions (e.g., education) and a liberatory belief in a more just and equitable society (Ladson-Billings, 2000; Lather, 1991; Tierney, 1992). The term feminism is often treated as a unitary category, yet there are actually many feminisms, each informed by different theoretical underpinnings (Tong, 1998). All, however, share the concern with gender relations and women's emancipation (Tisdell, 1998). While feminist perspectives foreground the examination and inclusion of women's experiences and contributions, we ascribe to versions of feminism that draw upon the concept of intersectionality. Such perspectives acknowledge ways in which women's experiences are not monolithic and highlight how gender is shaped by sociopolitical identity forces like race, social class, physical ability, sexuality, and cultural context to name a few. Inspired by a range of feminist perspectives (e.g.,

Collins, 2000; Ladson-Billings, 2000; Lather, 1991; Olesen, 2000; Wing, 2003), this project joins feminism with poststructuralism to retain, yet also problematize, a critical approach to policy studies that helps raise important questions about the control and production of knowledge, and the ways policy can be used to empower individuals to act within unique sociopolitical contexts to challenge dominant ideology (Ball, 1994; Marshall, 1999).

An FPS lens is important because it can help policy analysts and scholars studying policy-related issues trace the discursive shaping of policy problems and identify how the embedded assumptions may contribute to consequences of policy solutions that may not have been explicitly intended. Specifically, as Susan Iverson's analysis of diversity plans in Chapter 10 poignantly illustrates, policy solutions can employ discursive images that are meant to be liberatory and yet are restrictive to those the policy is meant to serve.

The identification of policy shortcomings, limitations, or inherent contradictions is not new (see Berman & McLaughlin, 1974). Darling-Hammond and McLaughlin (1995), in their examination of policies that support professional development, call for critical examination of practice and rethinking of policy-making so that policies do not support rigid systems. Yet, absent in their calls for change is an interrogation of the taken-for-granted assumptions that make a policy problem a problem. The use of FPS as an analytic lens affords new ways of thinking and seeing that work to dismantle the "givenness" of policy issues and goals and a means of examining ways in which the taken-for-granted policy discourses may reinforce the problems they seek to alleviate.

A primary objective of this book is to provide readers with a useful overview of feminist poststructural perspectives as well as a range of examples demonstrating how FPS offers helpful lenses for analyzing policy and policy development processes in the context of higher education. In this sense, the book is part of several ongoing conversations about higher education policy, feminist, and poststructural research approaches, and the ways in which governing policies are developed, enacted, and interpreted. Perhaps most importantly, the book focuses on the role of policy in shaping both discourse and, within discourse, lived experience.

To this end, *Reconstructing policy in higher education* has several purposes. Specifically, through policy analysis, theoretical discussion, and the presentation of original empirical research, the book:

1. Describes key tenets characterizing FPS and how this theoretical framework can support the analysis of policy and policy development processes.
2. Promotes understandings of how policy serves to both transmit and produce realities affecting higher education.
3. Highlights how hidden assumptions embedded in policy may serve to undermine intended goals of policy-makers.

4. Showcases feminist poststructural perspectives and methods applied to a range of policy issues in higher education.
5. Informs more effective development of policy and change strategies advanced by groups committed to promoting more equitable experiences for historically disadvantaged groups in postsecondary education.

Important Concepts

As will be made clear in Chapter 2 of this volume, FPS draws from and relies on concepts and approaches that emerge from multiple sources and across disciplinary domains. In the following section, we provide a brief overview of key concepts and approaches to set the stage for engaging with subsequent chapters.

Policy

The term "policy" can be understood differently depending on the disciplinary context. According to Fowler (2009), distinctions and disagreements about the ways in which policy is defined emerge from philosophical differences about the nature and roles of society, power, and government. As an academic field of study, public policy emerged in the 1960s as a subfield of the discipline of political science (Cochran & Malone, 1999). In general, public policy refers to

> the dynamic and value-laden process through which a political system handles a public problem and the policy process is a sequence of events that occurs when a political system considers different approaches to public problems, adopts one of them, tries it out, and evaluates it. (Fowler, 2009, pp. 4, 13)

For some, the study of policy is limited to the realm of government and is concerned primarily with the development and implementation of laws or statutes, associated rules and regulations, court decisions, and their implementation via elected and appointed officials and those working within government agencies and bodies (Conway et al., 2004; Fowler, 2009). For others, policy is more broadly defined to also include the dynamic and value-laden process through which political systems operate to solve problems at the institutional level (e.g., college/university policy, school policy, hospital policy).

The two arenas, public policy and institutional policy, are connected in many ways and the study of either can involve analyses of policy environments and dynamics including power, demographic trends, political culture, ethics, values, and discourse (Fowler, 2009). This volume is framed with a broad understanding of policy in mind; readers will find chapters focus on policies and policy-related issues within both public and institutional policy arenas. As well, the volume is intended to provide insights for a range of policy stakeholders including scholars, analysts, and practitioners who implement and often assess outcomes of policy.

Feminist Poststructuralism (FPS)

While FPS does not carry a single fixed meaning, we build on the work of Bacchi (1999), Baxter (2003), Lather (1991, 2007); Ropers-Huilman (1998), St. Pierre and Pillow (2000), Weedon (1997), and others to characterize feminist post-structural approaches to scholarly inquiry as providing the following:

- An understanding of discourse as a dynamic constellation of words and images that legitimate and produce a given reality (Allan, 2003).
- A focus on the relationship between discourse and subjectivity – providing a theory for understanding how language and meaning produce dynamic and contradictory subject positions.
- An explanation of identity and sense of self as inevitably fluid, in-process, and contingent upon discourse. Poststructural feminism works to destabilize the rational, fixed, coherent subject of enlightenment humanism.
- An explanation of both methodological and political assumptions embedded in questions asked and answered by other forms of feminist theory (Weedon, 1997).
- An emphasis on and understanding of power as a productive rather than repressive force.
- An imperative for examining how particular educational realities have been constituted and regulated through discourse, asking: What social effects are produced and with what consequences?
- An ethic of activism central to feminism while also acknowledging subjectivity as an effect of discourse.

Discourse

Discourse is a term often used but without simple definition (Mills, 1997). Considered broadly, "discourse refers to both spoken and written language use, and the study of discourse (discourse analysis) includes the examination of both talk and text and its relationship to the social context in which it is constructed" (Allan, 2003, p. 47). Discourse, for the purpose of our book, generally refers to "the way in which language, or, more broadly, bodies of knowledge, . . . define the terrain and consequently complicate attempts at change" (Bacchi, 1999, p. 40).

Language – spoken and written words – enables us to give meaning to the world and act to transform it, since "through language, we actively construct our experience" (Wilkinson & Kitzinger, 1995, p. 35; also Mills, 1997). Language is not simply descriptive, or a reflection, of the world; it "doesn't just mirror reality; it actively shapes the way we perceive and understand it" (Fischer & Forester, in Hajer & Wagenaar, 2003, p. 14). Consider, for example, a university student handbook. On the one hand, such a document is descriptive of an institution's behavioral expectations for students, a procedural guide, and an archival document useful for historical purposes. On the other hand, such a document is "a set of tacit rules that regulate what can and cannot be said, who can speak with the blessings of authority and who must listen, whose social constructions are valid and whose are erroneous and unimportant" (Kincheloe & McLaren, 2000, p. 284). As such, the discursive practices set forth in a student handbook have some institutionalized force, which means that "they have a profound influence on the way that individuals act and think" (Mills, 1997, p. 62). Applied to this project, "an interest in discourse becomes an interest in the ways in which arguments are structured, and objects and subjects are constituted in language" (Bacchi, 1999, p. 41).

Subject Positions

Subjectivity and subject positions are central to discourse theory and post-structuralism. According to Weedon (1997), subjectivity refers to "the place where our sense of ourselves . . . is constructed" (p. 21) and subject positions are the social identities that can be taken up or inhabited by individuals. One's subjectivity is "neither unified nor fixed," as assumed in humanist discourses; rather, the individual is viewed as a "site of disunity and conflict," and discursive fields offer a range of modes of subjectivity, often producing conflicting subject positions for the individual (Weedon, 1997, p. 21). For example, a woman who is the primary caretaker of her child and works outside the home in a white-collar job may be referred to as a working mother. The working mother must negotiate competing discourses that produce conflicting subject positions: woman as mother, a subject position produced by a discourse of motherhood, and shaped by a dominant discourse of femininity, and woman as white-collar worker, a subject position produced by a discourse of professionalism, and shaped by a larger dominant discourse of masculinity. The working mother, thus, is "subjected" to the contradictions and double-bind that often occur within a range of conflicting discourses (Weedon, 1997, p. 34).

Discourses, then, as the above example illustrates, do not occur or circulate in isolation; rather, multiple and competing discourses exist simultaneously, propagating often conflicting subject positions. Yet, some discourses emerge as dominant and are supported more readily than others, masking alternatives; these dominant discourses are supported by institutional practices (Mills, 1997) that constitute and conceal, produce and "constrain the possibilities of thought" (Ball, 1990, p. 2; also Allan, 2003). This project illuminates ways in which policy discourses come together to make particular perspectives or subject positions more prominent and accessible than others (Allan, 2003).

Chapter Descriptions

Drawing on the concepts and approaches described above, each of the contributors to *Reconstructing policy in higher education* suggests new ways of thinking about the construction and effects of policy through feminist and poststructural lenses. To better contextualize subsequent chapters, Elizabeth Allan provides in Chapter 2 a more thorough discussion of the strengths and limitations of FPS as an analytic tool.

In Chapter 3, Jana Nidiffer illuminates the contrast between college women's participation in the suffrage movement as activists from 1900 to 1920 and the dominant historical narrative in the history of American higher education. Then, through an FPS perspective as a corrective lens, she illustrates how policies related to women's participation in both higher education and the broader social sphere affect the various interpretations of women's involvement in social change movements.

In Chapter 4, Tatiana Suspitsyna examines discourses of U.S. Department of Education speeches and press releases produced over a two-year period in an effort to answer three interrelated questions: What is the purpose of higher education? Who are the stakeholders in higher education? What is the desired and desirable vision of the U.S. as an educated nation? The findings of this study reveal that discourses related to citizenship and democracy have been eclipsed by economic and social mobility discourses.

Suzanne Gordon, Susan Iverson, and Elizabeth Allan's analysis of the discursive framing of women leaders represented in *The Chronicle of Higher Education* is presented in Chapter 5. Their chapter illuminates how expectations of leaders rooted in (taken-for-granted) assumptions about masculinity and femininity may contribute to marginalizing female leaders and serve to shape masculine norms for what constitutes a "real" leader. In addition to dominant discourses of masculinity and femininity, Gordon et al. illuminate ways in which tension between these gender discourses produces a "double-bind" for female leaders. Finally, they discuss how a social justice strand of the liberal humanism discourse constructs female leaders as social justice leaders.

Chapter 6 presents Susan Talburt's qualitative study of the inter/actions of student members of a Gay Lesbian Straight Alliance (GLSA) at a public university. In this chapter, Talburt explores the potential for knowledges created through qualitative inquiry to illuminate the categories that frame university policy and practice. Beginning with a rejection of two commonsense discourses: (1) that lesbian, gay, bisexual, and transgender (LGBT) students are primarily at-risk and in need of social and academic support, and (2) that universities must support the development of "successful students" by promoting campus "involvement" and "belonging," Talburt argues that these discourses create a normalizing technology that assumes who and what students are and who and what they need to become.

In Chapter 7, Jennifer Hoffman and colleagues provide an analysis of the role Title IX policy plays in shaping our understanding of athletics in higher education and reveals a tension between marketplace and developmental discourses that produce competing subjectivities for student-athletes. Through an examination of historical and contemporary context for women's and men's sports, the authors consider the potential for a discursive shift to promote gender equity in athletics.

Jeni Hart and Jennifer Hubbard, in Chapter 8, examine how policies regarding social class in a women's college contribute to reproducing a cycle of oppression at one women's institution. Through analysis of interview data, they show how the policies created to ensure access unwittingly replicate and reinforce the very structures those policies were intended to minimize.

In Chapter 9, Rebecca Ropers-Huilman's analysis of student change agents describes discourses associated with students as consumers, students as change agents, and students as citizens, and suggests that these competing discourses structure students' experiences. Following from the literature suggesting that women and men tend to have different experiences in leadership situations, Ropers-Huilman asks: How are women and men in different contexts motivated to be student change agents? She suggests that students articulate their motivations in gendered ways, and that those gendered motivators have potential effects on students' civic engagement and understandings of their experiences as student leaders.

In Chapter 10, Susan Iverson's policy discourse analysis of diversity action plans generated at U.S. land-grant universities reveals four predominant discourses shaping images of diversity: access, disadvantage, marketplace, and democracy, respectively constructing images of people of color as outsiders, at-risk victims, commodities, and change agents. In her discussion of dominant discourses taken up to depict diversity in diversity action plans, Iverson draws upon the work of Foucault to illuminate "techniques of power," such as surveillance, (self)regulation, normalization, and classification, operating in diversity action plans.

Nelly Stromquist, in Chapter 11, employs a feminist poststructural perspective to illuminate the linkages between gender and the global knowledge society with its emphasis on accreditation and quality control. Through her analysis of two important policy documents on higher education with global implications, she identifies three main patterns: (1) a premium on quality, defined as that which generates revenue and prestige for the university; (2) the absence of serious examinations of how social equity may be affected by the emergence of selective research universities and the parallel set of marginal institutions of higher education that attend to the massification of higher education; and (3) how gender issues are rendered mute or invoked to argue that they have been resolved.

Finally, in Chapter 12, we discuss the questions and complexities associated with FPS analysis and policy in higher education. We draw attention to the potential of FPS approaches for reconstructing policy problems and solutions; yet we also consider the tensions associated with such approaches, especially as they are articulated by the contributors in this volume. In the spirit of "working the ruins" (St. Pierre & Pillow, 2000) of policy analysis, we take a FPS approach to considering what has been produced by this text – including subjectivities, power, presences, and absences – and the implications these may have for scholarship and approaches to policy that seek to improve the quality of practice while avoiding the reinscription of grand narratives that normalize ways of thinking that limit, constrain, and ultimately undermine the very goals some policies seek to attain.

While each of the chapters in this volume draws upon FPS perspectives, the authors engage with the theories and enact their analyses in different ways. In keeping with the spirit of poststructuralism, we caution against a reading of this text that anticipates a coherent and universalizing approach to "doing" FPS. Rather, we expect the chapters to leave open many possibilities as they expose readers to diverse examples of the author's engagement with FPS. This volume highlights ways in which the research/policy nexus and the FPS merger can indeed be messy. As Lather (2008) notes, "research for policy is not so much about providing answers as about changing the way questions are understood, so that people can begin to think differently" (p. 362). It is our hope that the diversity of chapters and approaches highlighted in this text will speak to readers in different ways and spark fruitful dialogue toward unthinking, rethinking, and thinking differently about the topics and analytic perspectives of policy analysis in higher education.

References

Allan, E. J. (2003). Constructing women's status: Policy discourses of university women's commission reports. *Harvard Educational Review*, 73(1), 44–72.
Bacchi, C. L. (1999). *Women, policy and politics: The construction of policy problems.* Thousand Oaks, CA: Sage.
Ball, S. J. (1990). *Politics and policy making in education: Explorations in policy sociology.* New York: Routledge.
Ball, S. J. (1994). *Education reform: A critical and post-structural approach.* Buckingham: Open University Press.
Baxter, J. (2003). *Positioning gender in discourse: A feminist methodology.* New York: Palgrave Macmillan.
Berman, P. & McLaughlin, M. (1974). *Federal programs supporting educational change, Vol. I: A model of educational change.* Santa Monica, CA: Rand Corporation.
Cochran, C. L. & Malone, E. F. (1999). *Public policy: Perspectives and choices.* Boston, MA: McGraw-Hill.
Collins, P. H. (2000). *Black feminist thought: Knowledge, consciousness, and the politics of empowerment,* 2nd ed. New York: Routledge.

Conway, M., Ahern, D., & Steuernagel, G. (2004). *Women in public policy: A revolution in progress,* 3rd ed. Washington, DC: CQ Press.

Creswell, J. W. (2009). *Research design: Qualitative, quantitative, and mixed methods approaches,* 3rd ed. Thousand Oaks, CA: Sage.

Darling-Hammond, L. & McLaughlin, M. W. (1995). Policies that support professional development in an era of reform. *Phi Delta Kappan,* 76(8), 597–604.

Hajer, M. A. & Wagenaar, H. (Eds.). (2003). *Deliberative policy analysis: Understanding governance in the network society.* New York: Cambridge University Press.

Fowler, F. C. (2009). *Policy studies for educational leaders,* 3rd ed. Boston, MA: Pearson.

Kincheloe, J. L. & McLaren, P. (2000). Rethinking critical theory and qualitative research. In N. K. Denzin & Y. S. Lincoln (Eds.), *Handbook of qualitative research* (pp. 279–313). Thousand Oaks, CA: Sage.

Ladson-Billings, G. (2000). Racialized discourses and ethnic epistemologies. In N. K. Denzin & Y. S. Lincoln (Eds.), *Handbook of qualitative research* (pp. 257–277). Thousand Oaks, CA: Sage.

Lather, P. (1991). *Getting smart: Feminist research with/in the postmodern.* New York: Routledge.

Lather, P. (2007). *Getting lost: Feminist efforts toward a double(d) science.* Albany, NY: SUNY Press.

Lather, P. (2008). New wave utilization research: (Re)imagining the research policy nexus. *Educational Researcher,* 37(6), 361–364.

Marshall, C. (1999). Researching the margins: Feminist critical policy analysis. *Educational Policy,* 13(1), 59–76.

Mills, S. (1997). *Discourse.* London: Routledge.

Oleson, V. L. (2000). Feminisms and qualitative research at and into the millennium. In N. K. Denzin & Y. S. Lincoln (Eds.), *Handbook of qualitative research,* pp. 215–255. Thousand Oaks, CA: Sage.

Ozga, J. (2000). *Policy research in educational settings: Contested terrain.* Philadelphia, PA: Open University Press.

Ropers-Huilman, R. (1998). *Feminist teaching in theory and practice: Situating power and knowledge in poststructural classrooms.* New York: Teacher's College Press.

St. Pierre, E. A. & Pillow, W. S. (Eds.). (2000). *Working the ruins: Feminist poststructural theory and methods in education.* New York: Routledge.

Tierney, W. G. (1992). *Official encouragement, institutional discouragement: Minorities in academe – the Native American experience.* Norwood, NJ: Ablex Publishing Corporation.

Tisdell, E. (1998). Poststructural feminist pedagogies: The possibilities and limitations of a feminist emancipatory adult learning theory and practice. *Adult Education Quarterly,* 48, 139–156.

Tong, R. P. (1998). *Feminist thought: A more comprehensive introduction,* 2nd ed. Boulder, CO: Westview Press.

Weedon, C. (1997). *Feminist practice and poststructuralist theory,* 3rd ed. Cambridge, MA: Blackwell Publishers.

Wilkinson, S. & Kitzinger, C. (Eds.). (1995). *Feminism and discourse: Psychological perspectives.* Thousand Oaks, CA: Sage.

Wing, A. (Ed.). (2003). *Critical race feminism: A reader,* 2nd ed. New York: NYU Press.

2

Feminist Poststructuralism Meets Policy Analysis

An Overview

ELIZABETH J. ALLAN

Building on the introduction and key terms provided in Chapter 1, I turn here to a closer examination of feminist poststructural (FPS) perspectives and their application to policy and policy-related matters. Familiarity with theories informing an FPS approach is vital to understanding their application and their potential for policy analysis. Since FPS is a relatively new approach to policy analysis, this chapter is written with the novice in mind. Readers with a more sophisticated understanding of feminist poststructuralism will likely find this chapter review familiar ground as it provides a common conceptual backdrop for the remaining chapters in this volume.

While I intend for this review to be introductory in tone, an important caveat is in order: any attempt to "introduce" FPS may run the risk of working against itself, imposing a modernist frame of reference by reducing poststructuralism and feminism to singular and fixed definitions or simplistic schemas. Indeed, as St. Pierre (2000b) notes, "postmodernism [and poststructuralism] *does not and cannot* provide essentializing answers to questions about its meaning" (p. 26). Therefore, as I propose to introduce the concepts, I work to cautiously navigate the tensions produced when modernist desires for intelligibility collide with the necessary complexity, multiplicity, and fluidity of postmodern or poststructural approaches.

Poststructuralist[1] theory and some feminist theories have been criticized for being too theoretical and esoteric to be of much practical use (Baxter, 2003; St. Pierre, 2000b). As well, poststructural scholars point to the non-innocence of transparent language, arguing that perceptions of clarity are rooted in particular discursive systems that render some things more intelligible than others in certain contexts (Lather, 1996; St. Pierre, 2000b). Thus, readers will find that even while this text is intended to be useful to a wide range of readers, including those with minimal familiarity with FPS theories and perspectives, it is also intended to highlight complexity and encourage a plurality of discourses that may, at first glance, appear to lack clarity and coherence.

Bearing this tension in mind, my intent for this chapter is to provide a platform for building understandings about ways in which FPS approaches can inform policy analysis. Toward that end, this chapter moves from general to specific, starting with theory and tracing its application to policy. The chapter proceeds from the basics – elaboration of key terms introduced in Chapter 1 – to provide an introduction to poststructuralism and its key tenets, including: discourse, difference, subjectivity, and how power/knowledge operate via discourse to dynamically shape images and realities that are continually revised and reconstituted. Subsequently, the chapter provides a closer look at feminism with an examination of why some feminists have taken up poststructural perspectives despite challenges inherent in this merger. From there, the chapter concludes with an overview of FPS perspectives in relation to policy analysis more specifically.

Discourse Theory

Poststructuralism, like feminism, does not carry a singular or fixed meaning, and theories considered to be poststructural vary; yet there are a number of common premises that loosely connect these theories. Foremost among these is the premise that language and discourse produce sociopolitical realities. This premise characterizes poststructural discourse theory, a term that describes a group of theories largely influenced by the works of Michel Foucault (e.g., 1978, 1979) and other poststructural thinkers including Derrida (e.g., 1976, 1982), Kristeva, and Irigaray to name a few of the most well known and cited (Baxter, 2003). In my experience, many students and colleagues new to this theoretical field confess they find the world of "posts" mystifying at first. The terms *poststructuralism* and *postmodernism* are sometimes used interchangably and discerning the distinctions can be confusing. Since poststructuralism is a key focus for this text, I begin with a brief overview of this term.

Poststructuralism can be understood as an academic branch of post-modernism where the postmodern refers to larger cultural and philosophical shifts (reflected in art, architecture, politics, and new media, for example). Postmodern perspectives highlight a skepticism of universal causes, absolutes, and truths (Baxter, 2003; Lather, 1991, 1992) that undergird modernist views of reality. In so doing, postmodern perspectives also challenge modernist visions of an essential, autonomous, and rational subject. In place of these universal truths and fixed/stable identities, postmodernism posits a vision of reality and subjectivity that is dynamically constituted via discourse.

Against the backdrop of postmodernism, *poststructuralism* refers to a loosely connected group of theories predicated upon a critique of structuralist approaches to the investigation of language. Structuralist approaches to lin-guistics proceed from the premise that language, as a meaning-making system, carried fixed or intrinsic ideas that provided an ultimate correspondence to the world (Scott, 1988) and could thus discern the true meaning of a text by analyzing its deep structures and motivations of the author. In contrast, poststructuralist theories assert that language is socially constituted and shaped by the interplay between texts, readers, and larger cultural context rather than carrying any kind of fixed or inherent meaning that can be "discovered." In sum, poststructuralism moves away from structural assumptions of essential and fixed meanings in language to provide for an approach that views language and/or discourse as the "site for the construction and contestation of social meanings" (Baxter, 2003, p. 6).

Some of the approaches described in the chapters of this text are influenced by poststructuralist discourse theories shaped by Foucault's configuration of power and subjectivity and feminist appropriations of this (e.g., Allen, 1999; Bailey, 1993; Baxter, 2003; Blackmore, 1995, 1996, 1999; Butler, 1990, 1993; Mills, 1997; Pillow, 2003; Ramazanoglu, 1993; Ropers-Huilman, 1998; Sawicki, 1986, 1991, 1994; Weedon, 1997, 1999). While Foucault did not explicitly position himself as a discourse theorist or a discourse analyst, through his work he advanced particular ideas about discourse that have since influenced methodologies across a range of disciplines.

As well, some approaches in this volume are influenced by the work of Jacques Derrida (e.g., 1976, 1982) and those who have appropriated the analytic approach of *deconstruction*. In its usage relative to poststructuralism, "deconstruction" refers to a specific approach to analyzing text that understands language as more than simply words on paper. Instead, words are symbolic of power relations that *construct* culture as well as reflect it. Importantly, and reflective of poststructuralism, deconstructive approaches "do not attempt to identify one, true meaning within a text, but recognize the plurality, multivocality, and non-fixity of all meaning" (Baxter, 2003, p. 6). Further elaboration about the methods of deconstruction is provided later in this chapter.

Many books and papers have been written about poststructural theory and feminist theory; and about particular theorists within that context. The nuances among the range of theories considered to be poststructural and/or feminist are too numerous and complex to detail within the space of a single chapter. However, a working knowledge of the basic premises of each can provide a helpful framework for understanding and learning more about these important conceptual approaches. The following pages provide a glimpse of some key tenets and issues vital to poststructuralist and feminist thought.

Discourse Produces Reality

Rather than understanding language and discourse as static entities that can stand in isolation and be investigated as such (e.g., a stretch of text or collection of words on paper), poststructuralists contend that language and discourses are dynamic sites for the construction of meaning. From a poststructural perspective, discourse not only reflects culture, but also actively produces it. Further, and especially important to thinking about policy issues, poststructural theory contends that discourse is the place "where our sense of ourselves, our subjectivity, is *constructed*" (Weedon, 1997, p. 21).

It is this productive property of discourse (i.e., discourse *produces* reality rather than simply reflecting it) that shapes the development of particular kinds of research questions highlighted in this text and in other scholarship influenced by poststructuralism. For example, researchers who employ a poststructural lens often ask, *What is being produced or constructed* through a particular policy or practice?; and *What are the discourses shaping* particular perspectives, images, and cultural practices?

A common critique of discourse analysis is that it is a purely cerebral exercise lacking in any practical utility. Poststructural thinkers point out that such criticisms are made possible through modernist frames of thinking that foreground dichotomous approaches (e.g., masculine/feminine, white/black, true/false) and tend to mask complexities by producing either/or debates like the theory vs. practice debate that tends to captivate endless attention in education (Lather, 1996; St. Pierre, 2000a). For instance, while poststructural perspectives contend that realities are shaped via discourse, Mills (1997) reminds us that even while making this claim, theories of discourse acknowledge material conditions in our daily lives. In other words, conditions like poverty and discrimination are not simply discursive or linguistic effects – they are real conditions with real and damaging consequences for human beings. Nonetheless, such conditions are produced by, and understood through, a particular confluence of discourses and power relations that create "conditions of possibility" (Foucault, 1979). Certainly, a range of theories exists to offer lenses through which to understand conditions like poverty. For example, Marxism offers a distinct perspective from a capitalist or meritocratic approach. However, a distinguishing feature of a poststructural lens from other explanatory lenses is the foregrounding of discourse and the contention that we come to understand material aspects of our daily lives through discourse (Mills, 1997; St. Pierre, 2000a; Weedon, 1997). In other words, "realities" are produced through the discursive shaping of materiality. Bordo (1993) comments on this aspect of poststructuralism, saying:

> [W]orks of art and literature, like styles of architecture and forms of governance . . . are products of a temporal imagination negotiating its embodied experience; the point therefore is not to refute such notions, but to demystify them . . . [as Foucault said] "because they are made they can be unmade." (p. 180)

To summarize, key introductory concepts for understanding poststructural discourse theory include: (1) discourses are more than words on paper – they are constellations of words and images that produce meaning; (2) discourses are dynamic and not only reflect, but also produce culture; and (3) it is through discourse that we gain a sense of ourselves and come to interpret the physical and social aspects of the world in which we live.

Discourse Constructs the Self

The dynamic properties of discourse – the ways in which discourse *constructs and produces* not only reality, but also our sense of self (subjectivity) in relation to these realities – are key to understanding poststructuralist thought. Thus, it is through discourse that one learns "to recognize, represent, and 'be,' for instance a 'rapper,' a 'learning disabled,' a 'loyal American'" (Luke, 1995, p. 14). According to feminist scholar Chris Weedon (1997), "subjectivity is produced in a whole range of discursive practices – economic, social and political – the meanings of which are a constant site of struggle over power" (p. 21).

While critics argue that some aspects of the subject are determined or constituted in advance of discourse, many assert that biological sex and race can be added to this list of identity[2] markers as well as other material realities (Bordo, 1993; Butler, 1990, 1993; Pillow, 2003; St. Pierre & Pillow, 2000). For example, Baxter (2003) explains:

> While someone's death is an inescapable biological and material fact, the ways in which a culture construes that person's death through competing discourses constitutes the lived reality for the friends and family of the deceased . . . . Thus experience of material or social realities is always produced discursively. (p. 9)

If we accept the poststructural premise that discourse is dynamic and bound to its historical moment, then subjectivity constituted through discourse is also not fixed or stable. Rather, according to poststructuralism, each of us is continually engaged in a process of locating ourselves within discursive fields and drawing upon discourses to represent ourselves. From this perspective, subjectivity is not fixed, unified, or essential (determined in advance of discourse) as a modernist view of personhood would suggest. Rather, poststructuralism contends that subjectivities are shaped through multiple discourses that mutually reinforce and/or compete with one another. In the process, subject positions are produced and subjectivity is continually revised and reconstituted as discourses are contested, disrupted, and/or coalesce. As St. Pierre (2000a) notes, "poststructural theories of discourse . . . allow us to understand how knowledge, truth, and subjects are produced in language and cultural practice as well as how they might be reconfigured" (p. 486). This opportunity to reconfigure knowledge and truth has attracted many scholar-activists to learning more about discourse theory as a powerful lens for analyzing and promoting social change.

In sum, poststructural discourse theories seek to destabilize the "humanist essence of subjectivity and propose a subjectivity that is precarious, contradictory and 'in process,' constantly being reconstituted in discourse each time we think or speak" (Weedon, 1997, p. 32). Poststructuralism seeks to "disintegrate the notion of the unified subject" and replace it with an understanding of subjectivity contingent upon discourse (Mills, 1997, p. 34). The shift away from modernist assumptions of an essential or pre-determined self and toward a subject-in-process produced via discourse, opens up new avenues for thinking about many important concepts like agency, empowerment, and change-making.

Discourse and Power/Knowledge

A more complete delineation of the ways in which discourse constructs subject positions and subjectivities requires a discussion of power, truth, knowledge, and difference as they operate via discourse from a poststructural perspective. Again, the work of Foucault has been instrumental in reconfiguring these concepts in ways that depart from traditional "limited supply" models of power. Since a thorough analysis of Foucault's delineation of power/knowledge is beyond the scope of this chapter, only an introduction to this key concept and its implications is provided here.

Productive Power

Foucault's explication of power/knowledge and its theoretical implications have been considered as being among his most notable contributions to feminism (Diamond & Quinby, 1988). A key aspect of Foucault's (1978, 1980) work in this regard is an understanding of power as a *productive* force rather than a primarily *repressive* one.[3] In contrast to traditional configurations of power as omnipotent, coercive, and prohibitive, Foucault (1978) delineates creative functions of power and its relation to knowledge; power is produced and transmitted through knowledge and discourse at the micro- or local levels of any society. So, rather than understanding power as primarily rooted in people and places with structural authority, Foucault emphasized the ways in which social change occurs through a myriad of local power exchanges and negotiations within a complex system of discourses (discursive fields).

A poststructural understanding of local, productive, and relational forces of power serves to challenge a binary understanding of power relations focused on "those with power" and those "without power" (Ropers-Huilman, 1998). When considered in a poststructural frame, power is not possessed as much as it is *exercised* as it circulates via discourse between and among individuals and groups. For instance, in describing femininity as discourse, Mills (1992) writes:

> Discourse theory does not locate the origins of femininity in patriarchy, a rather amorphous agentless term. Rather, it sees femininity as a system of discursive frameworks. Although it is obviously in some people's interests

for it to continue, men as well as women . . . it is a discursive system within which we operate and each act adds to or questions its constitution; it is always changing, *but it is not controlled by anyone.* [italics added] (p. 281)

From a poststructural perspective then, the position of women in a patriarchal order is shifted from merely *resisting* dominant and coercive forces of power to *participating* in the production of power (Diamond & Quinby, 1988; Mills, 1997).

In contrast, modernist theories of social relations, rooted in a configuration of power as a repressive force, typically position women activists as resisting oppression within a patriarchal order. One reading of this configuration is that women activists represent the subjugated power(less) working against the dominant power(ful). For feminists, the poststructural shift away from this dualistic powerful/less configuration of power provides an analytic advantage in that the potential for women to share in power relations is more clearly recognized (Allan, 2008).

A major emphasis related to power in Foucault's work is his assertion that power and knowledge are inseparable – hence, his use of "power/knowledge" to convey the link between them. In his words, "it is in discourse that power and knowledge are joined together" (Foucault, 1978, p. 100). Thus, discourse, power, and knowledge are inextricably linked in structuring our sense of reality as well as our sense of self (Mills, 1997). Also important to the power/knowledge configuration is the contention that truth is produced through their interplay. In other words, truth is an *effect* of power/knowledge operating through discourse. As such, there is no singular transcendent truth "out there" waiting to be discovered as a modernist view might suggest. Rather, for poststructuralists, truths are discursively constructed and legitimated. Related to this is the Foucauldian conceptualization of power/knowledge – a concept that emphasizes how power is dispersed as it operates through discourse to *produce* certain forms of conduct.[4] According to Foucault, it is productive power, operating through knowledge formation, truth claims, and disciplining through self-surveillance that is *most potent, and most overlooked* in theories of politics and society (Mills, 1997). Together, power/knowledge and discourse provide conditions of possibility – the conditions necessary to think of ourselves, and our world, in particular ways and not in other ways. Taking up subject positions and living them is a process continually repeated and revised throughout one's life.

Difference is another key concept that is closely tied to understandings of discourse and power within a poststructural frame (Ellsworth & Miller, 1996; Ropers-Huilman, 1998). Emerging from the work of Derrida, *difference* draws attention to the binaries and oppositions (e.g., male/female, straight/gay, rational/emotional) that tend to dominate Modernist interpretations of reality. "The acceptance of these dualisms as commonsense without problematizing the power relations they establish is a concern of those engaging in poststructural thought" (Ropers-Huilman, 1998, p. 8). The method of deconstruction provides a way to recognize the constructedness of dichotomies and the ways in which multiple complexities are present within, among, and between the terms that are positioned as such.

In sum, poststructuralism operates from the premise that discourses both produce and circumscribe possible formations of the self in ways of which we are not always fully aware. These key ideas about discourse, power, knowledge, subjectivity, and difference are crucial to understanding why poststructural perspectives provide a different kind of approach to policy analysis. These ideas are woven throughout this collection and provide an opportunity for readers to consider the range of ways in which they can be applied to understand important issues facing those studying and working in higher education. Readers can begin to draw upon these concepts and premises by asking different kinds of questions about policy-related issues. For instance, what are the subject positions produced by this policy? And, what truths or realities are produced through a particular policy discourse? Later in this chapter, I turn to discussing policy theory from conventional and FPS perspectives including the idea of policy as discourse. First, I turn to a closer look at the interplay of feminism and poststructuralism.

Feminist Theory Meets Postructuralism

Exceedingly diverse in focus and scope, feminism and feminist theory encompass a range of interdisciplinary approaches to the problems of discrimination and oppression (Fonow & Cook, 1991; Reinharz, 1992).[5] In this book, authors draw upon feminist theories for their shared acknowledgment of socially constituted sex- and gender-based inequalities in society as well as similar networks of power and stratification systems rooted in other forms of identity difference including race, social class, citizenship, sexuality, and disability. While there are many strands of feminism with different emphases, they share in their embodiment of the following premises: (1) sex/gender inequality exists and is central to social relations and the structuring of social institutions; (2) sex/gender inequality is not "natural" or essential but a product of social relations; and (3) sex/gender inequality should be eliminated through social change (Allan, 2008).

A number of theoretical approaches share feminist goals of analyzing discriminatory practices and promoting more egalitarian social relations (e.g., critical theory, postcolonial theory). However, a *feminist* approach to inquiry more specifically describes research that seeks social change while also placing an emphasis on women and gender as key analytic categories. Importantly, placing an emphasis on women does not imply the exclusion of other important aspects of identity. The feminist approaches featured in this volume work to emphasize the intersections of gender and sex with other identifiers (e.g., race, social class, disability, and citizenship) and join other feminist research that highlights the relationship between identity, privilege, and oppression (Lugones, 2003; Mohanty, 1991; Weedon, 1999).

Feminist policy analysis, like feminism, is not new; feminist critiques of sex discrimination and bias in law date back to the early nineteenth century in the U.S. Over the years, feminist scholars have "expanded the range of their investigations" within numerous policy arenas by "exploring gender privilege and gender disadvantage, distinguishing disparate treatment from disparate impact, and examining 'benign' discrimination in relation to long histories of invidious discrimination" (Hawkesworth, 1994, p. 98). According to Marshall and Bensimon (in Marshall, 1997b), a policy analyst applying a feminist critical perspective engages in policy formulation by asking, "who benefits, who loses and how do females fare here?" (p. 17). More specifically, they propose the following goals for policy analysis:

1 Critique or deconstruct conventional theories and explanations and reveal the gender biases (as well as racial, sexual, and social class biases) inherent in commonly accepted theories, constructs, methodologies, and concepts.

2 Conduct analysis that is feminist both in its theoretical and methodological orientations . . . reading policy studies with a critical awareness of how androcentrism is embedded in the disciplines, theories of knowledge and research designs that are foundational to policy analysis and which are ostensibly neutral (Bensimon & Marshall, 1997, p. 6).

3 Understandings of subjectivity are inextricably linked to con- ceptualizations of agency and strategies for social change. From many feminist and critical theory perspectives, the subject is oppressed through dominant ideology, which is defined as systems of thought serving to reinforce the status quo. In other words, individuals are subject to power through ideological hegemony. This perspective contends, however, that the status quo can be changed, if individuals learn to see these ideological systems and actively work against/resist them. This model of agency – or political activity – differs markedly from agency conceptualized within a poststructural frame. With a focus on the discursive shaping of subjectivity, models of agency within poststructuralism are necessarily messy and complex (Mills, 1997). St. Pierre (2000a) elaborates:

Poststructural feminists believe the struggles of women are local and specific rather than totalizing. Relations of power are complex and shifting. Resistance and freedom are daily, ongoing practices.

> Humanism's totalizing understanding of power, resistance and freedom seem to allow less room to maneuver, fewer possibilities for social justice than that of the poststructural critique. In education, these understandings of power, resistance, and freedom have produced more complex and subtle analyses of desires, relationships, strategies, and structures. (p. 493)

As St. Pierre notes, poststructuralist discourse theories account for political change. However, they remain unclear about how much (if any) control individuals can exercise over their own actions, and they emphasize the multiple effects of action – *and* the unintended consequences of political action (Mills, 1997). So, in order to maintain a theory of agency – the capacity to act with intentionality – poststructuralism requires some degree of modification. It is at this juncture that feminist and postcolonial scholarship has been particularly instrumental (Mills, 1997). A number of feminist theorists have offered perspectives on this tension over the years. For instance, Linda Alcoff (1988) has proposed "positionality" as a means by which feminists can adopt poststructural perspectives of non-essentialized identity, yet not diminish the shared realities of gender/sex-based oppression. She writes:

> [W]ith the conception of the subject as positionality, we can conceive of the subject as nonessentialized and emergent from a historical experience and yet retain the ability to take gender as an important point of departure. Thus we can say at one and the same time that gender is not natural, biological, universal, ahistorical, or essential and yet still claim that gender is relevant because we are taking gender as a position from which to act politically. (p. 435)

Nevertheless, feminist theorists continue to debate the potential dangers of poststructural subjectivity, the decentering of the humanist subject in favor of a subject in-process and constituted through discourse. In particular, some feminists point to "the timing of the popularity of poststructural theory in Western academia, pointing out that they prefer not to be decentered and, therefore, silenced once again" (St. Pierre & Pillow, 2000, p. 7). Another key concern among some feminists is the assertion that FPS may be more concerned with language and discourse than with working to remedy daily acts of discrimination for women.

However, rather than "bewailing inconsistency and incompatibility," some feminist scholars remain energized by the tensions produced by poststructural versions of subjectivity and the "ethic of activism" and agency that are central to feminism (Diamond & Quinby, 1988, p. xvi; see also Ramazanoglu, 1993). While Foucauldian theories describe subjectivity as an effect of discourse, feminist adaptations work from here to highlight the process by which this occurs, focusing on the ways in which we engage or interact with discourse to construct ourselves (Mills, 1997). As feminist education scholar Jill Blackmore (1999) reminds us:

> To be *constituted* by discourses is not to be *determined* by discourse however. Subjectivity conceptualizes identity formation as an ongoing contradictory, precarious, and complex process. It imparts a sense of agency, reflexivity, and contradiction often lost in theories of the unitary self. (p. 17)

Drawing upon Dorothy Smith's (1990) feminist work in the field of sociology, Mills (1997) posits, "since discourse is something you do, rather than something to which you are subjected, engaging with discourses constitutes an interactional relation of power rather than an imposition of power" (p. 88). Rather than understanding women as passive products of discursive fields, or as having assumed a false consciousness rendering them victims of male oppression (as in a Marxist interpretation of ideology in language), discourse theory posits that women are active and can intervene on their own behalf (Mills, 1997). Within discourse then, participants are both subjects and agents within a sphere that is pre-constituted and, while ever-changing, affects choices for expressions of power, knowledge, language, and difference.

In summary, FPS embodies key feminist premises to provide an analytic framework that highlights the power of discourse yet also sustains an awareness of how gender and other forms of identity differences shape our daily lives and serve as mechanisms of social stratification. At the same time, poststructural feminists also work to uncover how liberatory discourses may serve as regimes of truth and potentially undermine the very problems they seek to alleviate (Allan, 2003, 2008; Gore, 1993; Iverson, 2008; Ropers-Huilman, 1998). While there are important critiques to consider within feminism, St. Pierre and Pillow (2000) point out that one of the strengths of the proliferating category of FPS "is that it continues to reinvent itself strategically, shifting and mutating given existing political agendas, power relations, and identity strategies" (p. 8).

For policy analysts and scholars examining policy-related problems, an FPS perspective provides a lens for understanding how policy problems and assumptions undergirding these problems are constructed within a complex discursive web. Such an understanding of the ways in which policy issues are discursively constituted and contested enables the examination of policy problems in different and promising ways. The next section of this chapter builds on this framework to situate poststructural policy approaches within the field of policy studies and to delineate policy as discourse.

Policy Studies

A range of analytic approaches exists in the field of policy studies. In general, key differences can be understood in terms of how the frameworks acknowledge (or fail to acknowledge) the role of human values in relation to policy, and by how they approach policy problems. A brief review of these approaches is provided here.

Rational Scientific Perspectives

The positivist scientific approach tends to emphasize a value-free or value-neutral process of policy analysis. Commonly referred to as the *rational scientific* model of policy analysis, this approach generally treats problems according to a step-by-step procedure where facts are examined in order to arrive at the best policy solutions for a given problem (Bacchi, 1999; Cochran & Malone, 1999; Hawkesworth, 1988; Lindblom, 1980, 1993; Stone, 1988, 2002).

In writing about this approach, Stone (2002) describes the fields of political science, public administration, law, and policy analysis as having "a common mission of rescuing public policy from the irrationalities and indignities of politics, hoping to make policy instead with rational, analytical, and scientific methods" (p. 7). Proponents of the rational scientific approach contend a best collective decision can be attained by following an apolitical and objective process that involves formulating resolutions to the policy problem, implementing them, and then evaluating them (Bacchi, 1999; Cochran & Malone, 1999; Stone, 1988, 2002). Stone (2002) regards this approach as a consequence of the "rationality project" which she argues "has been at the core of American political culture since the beginning" and "remains at the turn of the twenty-first century in full bloom in the disciplines of political science and law" (p. 7).

In response to perceived shortcomings of the rational scientific approach (e.g., failure to account for bias in the framing of policy problems), alternative models have been advanced to acknowledge policy as a political and value-laden process. These models, often described as incrementalist or pluralist approaches, argue against policy analysis as an expertise-based, formulaic, and objective process of arriving at straightforward solutions to readily identified problems. For instance, Lindblom (1980) describes policy-making as an "untidy process" that is "an extremely complex process without beginning or end and whose boundaries remain most uncertain" (pp. 4–5). Lindblom and others advocate an approach that blends expertise with political participation. The result is a more open, pluralist, and flexible analytic process where the complexities of human values are taken into account and a wide range of constituents are included in the policy process. In general, these theorists are referred to as *political rationalists* because they apply a rational approach to dealing with values inherent in the policy process (Bacchi, 1999; Cochran & Malone, 1999; Lindblom, 1980; Stone, 2002).

Dominant approaches to policy analysis have also been criticized for their failure to acknowledge *assumptions* undergirding the articulation of policy (Bacchi, 1999; Ball, 1990, 1994; Baxter, 2003; Marshall, 1999; Pillow, 1997;

Scheurich, 1994). Typically, these critiques suggest that traditional policy approaches are embedded in a modernist frame that implicitly advances particular perspectives about efficiency, productivity, and individuality. Guba (1984) has argued that even the policy analysis literature has typically assumed a common understanding of the very meaning of the term "policy." He contends:

> The particular definition *assumed* by the analyst shapes (determines, constrains) the kinds of policy questions that are asked, the kinds of policy-relevant data which are collected, the sources of data that are tapped, the methodology which is used, and, finally, the products which emerge. [italics added] (p. 3)

Adding to this, other scholars have asserted that conventional approaches to policy-making and policy analysis are constructed through a lens that privileges rational/scientific logic, which often results in policy perspectives that are narrow, linear, and managerial in focus (Ball, 1994; Carlson, 1993).

Feminist Policy Perspectives

When considering whether or not politics and values are legitimate components of the policy process, the differences between rational scientific and the political rationalist models are significant. However, feminist policy scholar Carol Bacchi (1999) argues that both approaches operate within a "problem solution" orientation (p. 19). In other words, they share the common goal of working toward better ways of solving an identified policy problem. In contrast, recent scholarship from critical and poststructural feminist perspectives suggests that these established policy studies methods fall short because they typically proceed from an acceptance of policy problems and tend not to analyze the assumptions undergirding the articulation of those problems (Bacchi, 1999; Ball, 1990, 1994; Blackmore, 1999; Marshall, 1999, 2000; Pillow, 1997, 2003; Scheurich, 1994; Stone, 2002). More specifically, Stone (1988, 2002) argues that traditional approaches to policy are embedded in particular assumptions about decision-making and a marketplace model of society. In this model, "society is viewed as a collection of autonomous, rational decision-makers" who work to maximize their well-being through rational calculation devoid of community life, emotional bonds or traditions influencing their choices (Stone, 2002, p. 9). Emerging from this model are human capital theories that contend, for instance, that education, voting patterns, political leadership, and even marriage can be explained in terms of maximizing self-interest through the rational decision-making process.

The marketplace model of society shapes perspectives about social problems and, according to Stone (1988, 2002), is connected to a production model of policy-making that suggests policy can be formulated in an orderly sequence of steps akin to the rational decision-making process. In contrast, she posits that "ideas are the medium of exchange and a mode of influence even more powerful than money and votes and guns" (Stone, 1988, p. 7). Accordingly, it is in this realm – the struggle over ideas and the formation of shared meanings – where approaches to policy analysis may fall short.

The work of other scholars resonates with Stone's thesis. For example, Hawkesworth (1988, 1994) overviews feminist policy studies and points out that such approaches examine the "seldom scrutinized . . . beliefs concerning the nature of facts and values, the powers of reason, the structure of science, and the possibilities for scientific knowledge – beliefs so widely accepted by practitioners in the field that they are no longer perceived as issues" (Hawkesworth, 1988, p. 2). In considering policy related to women's health, Griffin (1994) provides the following perspective not typically attended to by conventional policy theorists:

> It is impossible to discuss issues of public policy without reference to the terms in which they are articulated. Such terms have profound symbolic value. When policy issues are imbued with moral meanings, the terms that are used and the symbols that attach themselves to both words and issues can redefine them. (p. 205)

Thus, despite a traditionally held view that policy theory and analysis can somehow stand apart from the political, these critiques suggest policy study and practice are value-driven endeavors that serve particular political interests (Bacchi, 1999; Ball, 1990, 1994; Marshall, 1997a).

Feminist policy perspectives foreground power dynamics related to gender and other identity formations (e.g., race, sexual identity, social class) and examine how these are implicated in social policy (e.g., Blackmore, 1999; Collins, 1991; Conway, Ahern, & Steuernagel, 1995, 2004; Fraser, 1989; Fraser & Gordon, 1994; Hawkesworth, 1994; Pillow, 2003; Smith, 1990; Williams, 1991, 1997; Winston & Bane, 1993). Feminist policy analysis has historically emphasized ways in which policy produces uneven effects for men and women. As well, feminist policy analysts in general, and especially those from post-structural perspectives, have worked to illuminate the ways in which power operates through policy by drawing attention to hidden assumptions or policy silences and unintended consequences of policy practices (Allan, 2003; Bacchi, 1999; Blackmore, 1999; deCastell & Bryson, 1997; Conway, Ahern, & Steuernagel, 2004; Fine, 1988; Pillow, 1997, 2003; Stone, 2002; Tyack & Hansot, 1988). For instance, feminist policy analysts have pointed to policy silences about women's experiences and assumptions about gender roles that are implicit in the framing of policy problems and solutions (e.g., Bacchi, 1999; Bensimon & Marshall, 1997; Fine, 1988; Marshall, 1997a, b, 1999; Pillow, 2003; Stivers, 1993; Stone, 2002).

Policy as Discourse

We need to appreciate the way in which policy ensembles, collections of related policies, exercise power through a production of "truth" and "knowledge." Discourses are [not only] about what can be said, and thought, but also who can speak, when, where, and with what authority (Ball, 1994, p. 21).

Conventional approaches to policy analysis typically position policy as regulating social relations through a repressive process of proscribing certain behaviors as unacceptable, unwanted, and prohibited. In contrast, poststructural understandings of policy-as-discourse view policy as regulating social relations primarily through positive or productive means. In other words, policy is a means by which subjectivities, hierarchies, and taxonomies for understanding the social world are produced (Bacchi, 1999; Ball, 1994; Griffin, 1992; Shore & Wright, 1997). For instance, policy discourses in education support the production of normative behavior through policy initiatives like total quality management, educational standards, efficient use of resources, faculty/teacher productivity, and calls for more scientific rigor.

In her book on policy research in educational settings, Jenny Ozga (2000) suggests that policy texts and the discourses shaping them serve as important resources for considering "the story about what is possible or desirable to achieve through education policy" (p. 95). A narrative approach to policy foregrounds analysis of the source of the policy, the scope of the policy, and the pattern of the policy. However, a narrative or textual approach to policy analysis is not necessarily poststructural. Lather (2004) points out that in Foucauldian terms, policy serves to "regulate behavior and render populations productive via state intervention in and regulation of the everyday lives of citizens in a 'liberal' enough manner to minimize resistance" (p. 25). As such, Foucault frames policy as a technology of governmentality that operates within complex discursive networks to produce disciplined bodies that regulate themselves as much as they are regulated by external influences (Lather, 2004).

As discursive formations, policies produce subject positions that contribute to shaping identities. Ball (1994) explains, "we are spoken by policies [and] we take up the positions constructed for us within policies" (p. 22). As such, poststructural policy analysis examines subject positions constructed via policy as a means of learning how policy contributes to shaping subjectivity. For instance, in my analysis of policy efforts to promote gender equity in higher education, I found that the discourses drawn upon to describe gender/sex-based discrimination tended to reinforce images of women as *vulnerable, fearful,* and *in need of protection* (Allan, 2003, 2008).

As Ball (1994) delineates, policy can be considered both "*as* [discourse] and *in* discourse" (p. 21).

Importantly, a focus on policy *as and in* discourse does not overlook concrete experiences of daily lives. Rather, it provides an opportunity to view materiality through a different lens – a lens that sharpens our focus on ways in which policy *produces* possible action through discourses it makes available to us. (Ball, 1994)

As Marshall (1999) contends:

Debates over education policy are power conflicts over which knowledge is the "truth." Those who control the discourse discredit or marginalize other "truths." Thus, debates over required curriculum, the canon and requirements for professional credentials are power/knowledge struggles. (p. 65)

Thus, from a poststructural perspective, policies are not static entities implemented to shift the balance of power in one direction or another. A view of policy-as-discourse shapes understandings of policy as actively circulating, intervening, and intervened upon at micro-levels of society and enmeshed in a complex and contradictory process of negotiation. This perspective serves to disrupt and displace traditional approaches to policy analysis by highlighting how policy actively produces subjects, knowledge, and perceived truths.

A primary task of a poststructural approach to policy analysis is to describe the process by which discourses become inscribed within individuals and social relations (Smith, 1990). Thus, a poststructural approach to policy analysis seeks to: (1) describe subject positions produced through policy discourses; (2) highlight assumptions embedded in the framing of policy problems and solutions (Bacchi, 1999; Baxter, 2003; deCastell & Bryson, 1997; Humes, 1997; Pillow, 1997; Scheurich, 1994); and (3) re/consider the modernist ameliorative missions embedded in humanist discourses that inhere in traditional (and critical) policy theory and practice (Ball, 1994; Lather, 1991; Pillow, 1997, 2003).

In sum, an understanding of policy-as-discourse illuminates how policy produces conditions of possibility for thought and action (Ball, 1994; Walker, 1997). Given this, we may only be able to conceive of possible policy solutions through the knowledge and subject positions that discourses make available to us. Poststructural approaches to policy analysis acknowledge how policy reinforces an ensemble of normative judgments about the correct way to solve "social problems" (Ball, 1994; Connolly, 1993; Marshall, 1997a, b; Scheurich, 1994; Shore & Wright, 1997). In working to expose the discursive framing of policies while displacing the taken-for-grantedness of policy problems, poststructural approaches to policy shift the focus from finding answers to examining what is improved via policy (Lather, 2008).

Analyzing Policy as Discourse

Traditional approaches to policy analysis do not provide for a focus on the discursive shaping of subject positions, or on the assumptions embedded in the naming of policy problems and solutions. Further, they typically do not consider gender as central to the analysis, nor do they specifically focus on the role of policy in the promotion of emancipatory goals (e.g., Ball, 1994; Marshall, 1997a, b; Scheurich, 1994). In contrast, FPS approaches insist that policy analyses include examination of: (1) the process by which policy problems are defined; (2) the influence of identity differences in the shaping of policy problems and solutions; (3) the ways in which policy as discourse not only reflects, but also contributes to producing subjectivities and sociopolitical realities (Allan, 2003, 2007; Bacchi, 1999; Marshall, 1999; Pillow, 1997).

Methodologies in FPS Analysis

Researchers drawing upon FPS perspectives have borrowed, developed, and refined a range of specific approaches to the analysis of policy-related issues. Deconstruction, geneaology, discourse analysis, and policy discourse analysis are among some of the noteworthy approaches. However, due to space limitations, and since the authors of subsequent chapters draw upon and describe various FPS methodological approaches, I provide a brief review of each here.

DECONSTRUCTION

As noted earlier, deconstruction as a form of analysis can be traced to the work of French philosopher Jacques Derrida who is noted for developing this approach to critiquing humanist assumptions embedded in structuralist approaches to literary theory and criticism. A few key aspects are highlighted here with the caveat that philosophical and methodological differences exist among various methods widely considered to be poststructural.

Deconstruction, as proposed by Derrida, is predicated upon the rejection of singular meanings in texts and therefore works to illuminate the plurality of meanings and the discursive webs from which they emerge. From this perspective, "the tentativeness and partiality of meanings in legitimated knowledge, as well as the constant shifting of power relations within social systems, lead to language that is also tentative, partial and permanently in flux" (Ropers-Huilman, 1998, p. 7). Derrida also emphasized the salience of binary oppositions (e.g., male/female, nature/nurture, ability/disability, white/non-white) where status hierarchies are reflected and reinscribed. This occurs as "one side of the opposition serves as the key concept in relation to which the other is defined negatively" (Weedon, 1997, p. 159). Thus key goals of deconstruction are to highlight and reverse these oppositions to demonstrate how discourses achieve their effects, and in the process, work to interrupt and destabilize them, thereby opening up space for different ways of thinking (Weedon, 1997).

Some feminists are drawn to deconstruction for its utility as a means of disrupting binary oppositions that undergird hierarchical practices in social relations. In the process, feminists have augmented the purely textual approach of deconstruction by drawing attention to the social context and power dynamics within which texts are located. Gayatri Spivak, Luce Irigaray, and Helene Cixous are some of the early and most prominent feminist thinkers who appropriated deconstruction to analyze questions related to women, gender, and sexuality (Weedon, 1997).

Examples of deconstruction in feminist analysis related to policy can be seen in Estela Bensimon's (1995) "Rebellious Reading" of Total Quality Management (TQM) in the context of postsecondary education and Wanda Pillow's (2000) "Exposed Methodology: The Body as Deconstructive Practice" where she analyzes programmatic and educational policy implications of teen pregnancy and demonstrates how the dominant discourses drawn upon to articulate educational policies related to teen pregnancy have located the social "problem" of teen pregnancy within girls themselves. The acceptance of this problem as a starting point for related policy initiatives then associates these girls with various deviant behaviors including illegitimacy, delinquency, and poverty. This interpretation serves to construct the girls as deviant and ignores the role of fathers in the making of teen pregnancy. Further, Pillow points to how the complexities of race, social class, and sexuality are obscured by policy that uncritically accepts the discursive constitution of social problems and the subject positions offered by them (Pillow, 1997).

GENEALOGY

Emerging from Foucault's work to study history through the lens of discourse, genealogy is another prominent analytic approach within poststructuralism. As a method, genealogy is predicated upon the Foucauldian configuration of power/knowledge as exercised rather than possessed and was "designed to explore not who had power, but rather the patterns of the exercise of power through the interplay of discourses" (Ramazanoglu, 1993, p. 18). Thus, genealogy seeks to examine the "conditions of possibility," understanding how it has become possible to think or act in particular ways by illuminating how knowledge, truth, and social practices have been shaped via discourse.

Importantly, from a Foucauldian perspective, the point of genealogy is "not where discourses come from, nor what interests they represent, but what 'effects of power and knowledge they ensure' and what makes their use necessary" (Ramazanoglu, 1993, pp. 19–20). According to Foucault (1978) in his *History of sexuality* volume I, discourse analysts using a genealogical approach "must not imagine" a world divided between accepted and excluded or dominant and dominated discourses, but rather:

> a multiplicity of discursive elements that can come into play in various strategies . . . discourse transmits and produces power; it reinforces it, but also undermines and exposes it, renders it fragile and makes it possible to thwart it. (p. 100)

Appropriations of Foucault's geneaological method are many and varied. Feminists have also been drawn to the approach because of its emphasis on subjectivity and its potential for theorizing the body. For instance, in Foucault's *Discipline and punish* (1979), he illuminates the discursive shaping of criminality over time and, in *History of sexuality* (1978), the discursive constitution of sexuality as well as normalcy and deviance in this context. As Bailey (1993) summarizes, in Foucault's genealogical work, "bodies are understood in relation to the production, transmission, reception and legitimation of knowledge" (p. 102).

An example of feminist use of geneaology for policy analysis is Nancy Fraser and Linda Gordon's (1994) analysis of welfare policies as reported in their article, "Genealogy of dependency: Tracing a keyword of the U.S. welfare state." Other examples of a genealogical analysis in education include Labaree's (1992) study *Power, knowledge and the rationalization of teaching: A genealogy of the movement to professionalize teaching,* and Lenzo's (1995) *Looking awry: A genealogical study of pre-service teacher encounters with popular media and multicultural education.*

DISCOURSE ANALYSIS AND POLICY DISCOURSE ANALYSIS

The study of discourse manifests itself in a variety of forms inspired by fields as diverse as anthropology, communication, history, psychology, and theology to name a few. Modes and styles of analysis vary significantly. Many involve the study of structures and strategies of text and talk (van Dijk, 1997) and do not necessarily challenge humanist understandings of the unified autonomous subject challenged by poststructural thinkers. In contrast, poststructural discourse analysis foregrounds dynamic subject and truth claims that are continually shaped and reshaped as they are constituted through multiple, shifting, and at times competing, discourses. Discourse analysis that is both feminist and poststructural does not adhere to a singular definition; however, generally speaking, some common questions and strategies characterize such approaches. These include: (1) tracing the discursive shaping of policy problem(s) by asking questions like, "what discourses make it possible for this issue to be identified as problematic? what discourses make it possible for this approach to be identified as high-quality?"; (2) identifying the subject positions that emerge from policy discourses; and (3) applying a feminist lens to the analysis.

Building on shared tenets of poststructuralism and feminism, policy discourse analysis is described as a "hybrid methodology" (Allan, 1999, 2003, 2008) specifically for the study of policy. This approach emerges from the conceptual tensions that inhere in models of policy analysis across several paradigms. While it is most profoundly influenced by feminism and poststructuralism, it also incorporates specific methods and approaches from interpretive and critical theory frames of inquiry. Cutting across these inquiry paradigms, policy discourse analysis incorporates a range of investigatory approaches with the goals of understanding, liberation, and destabilization (Allan, 2008; Lather, 1991).

Policy discourse analysis proceeds from the premise that policy-making and analysis are discursive practices that both reflect and produce culture. Influenced by textual analysis, critical discourse analysis, and poststructural methods of deconstruction, archaeology, genealogy, and feminist appropriations of these, policy discourse analysis provides a specific method for examining policy discourses and the subject positions produced by them. As a method, policy discourse analysis was inspired by the feminist desire to examine how well-intentioned attempts to advance equity policy may unwittingly perpetuate discourses and practices that reinforce *in*equity. Typically, dominant discourses embedded in policy are normalized to such an extent they are rarely called into question. Policy discourse analysis illuminates these discourses to examine policy problems and solutions in new ways (Allan, 2008).

For example, in an examination of university women's commission reports published over three decades, these policy-focused documents were found to highlight policy problems for women in higher education that included such issues as: access, representation, professional development, and safety to name a few. Through the method of policy discourse analysis, the study revealed that the problem of "safety," produced through discourses of femininity, constructed the *vulnerable woman* subject. In so doing, women's fear was foregrounded as the problem to be solved – rather than behaviors and circumstances known to create unsafe spaces and relationships that give rise to fear. Thus, the vast majority of policy solutions proposed in reply to the problem defined as "safety" focused on helping women feel more safe through the provision of protective measures (e.g., better lighting, wallet cards with emergency numbers, escort services, pepper spray) rather than measures focused on eliminating the sources of unsafe environments by, for example, naming, challenging, and transforming violent masculinity (Allan, 2008).

Some examples of discourse analysis and policy discourse analysis from feminist perspectives are featured in this volume. Susan Iverson's chapter, "Producing Diversity," employs policy discourse analysis to examine the discursive shaping of policy problems and solutions and the subject positions produced through university Diversity Action Plans issued at research universities throughout the U.S. In Tatiana Suspitsyna's chapter, "Purposes of Higher Education and Visions of the Nation in the Writings of the Department of Education," she uses poststructural discourse analysis to uncover assumptions embedded in U.S. federal education policy. Also, in the Gordon, Iverson, and Allan chapter on "The Discursive Framing of Women Leaders in Higher Education," the authors employ poststructural discourse analysis to examine gendered subject positions produced through the discourses carried by textual representations of leaders and leadership in *The Chronicle of Higher Education* over a one-year period.

Reconstructing Policy

This chapter has described a number of key concepts salient to poststructuralist and feminist theories including: discourses and subjectivity; power/knowledge; the assertion that power is exercised rather than possessed; the importance of analyzing the discursive constitution and regulation of gender and other identity categories; difference; and maintaining an ethic of activism central to feminist thought and practice. The overview of policy studies described how feminist poststructural approaches offer different ways of thinking about policy-related issues and new ways of thinking about old and new problems.

Policy-making and policy analysis are discursive practices that contribute to the production and regulation of truth claims and the construction of subject positions. Given this, approaches and methods are needed to illuminate policy discourses and consider their implications. Research from FPS perspectives demonstrates how policy assumptions may carry exclusionary consequences, and hence limit policy effectiveness or even reinforce the very problem(s) the particular policy seeks to eliminate (Allan, 2003, 2008; Bacchi, 1999; deCastell & Bryson 1997; Marshall, 1997a, b, 1999; Pillow, 2003; Scheurich, 1994). Further, FPS approaches to policy call for researcher reflexivity to consider how our subjectivity enters and shapes policy analysis and to work toward inter-rupting and destabilizing the modernist impulse to produce fixed truths or conclusions as a result of our analyses.

While this chapter has worked to describe FPS in terms of some common characteristics, such a delineation risks being read as reductive – an erasure of the fluidity and complexity of FPS. Even while common threads can be identi-fied, researchers who employ FPS may vary in the ways they take up post-structural premises. Tensions produced by the merger of poststructural versions of the discursive constitution of subjectivity and feminism's commitment to agency are evident across chapters of this text. Consequently, readers will not experience uniformity of engagement with FPS, but will likely note how authors have read discourses through policy relationships, institutional norms, and socio-cultural identities.

Rather than accepting policy problems at face value and analyzing policy effectiveness in relation to these problems, FPS approaches to policy prompt researchers to ask different kinds of questions such as: What subject positions emerge from a particular policy or group of policies? What are the conditions of possibility – what discourses give rise to the subject positions? What are the assumptions inherent in the naming of the policy problem? What is produced through the policy text? What are the effects? How are gender and other aspects of identity implicated? How are the discourses and subject positions regulated? What is produced through the process of policy analysis? (Bacchi, 1999; St. Pierre & Pillow, 2000). These and other provocative questions have catalyzed the scholarship featured in the remaining chapters of this text.

32 • Elizabeth J. Allan

Notes

1 I use *poststructuralist* here primarily as it has been appropriated by feminist theorists who draw largely on theories of discourse and power as informed by the work of Foucault (e.g., Baxter, 2003; Diamond & Quinby, 1988; McNay, 1992; Mills, 1991, 1992, 1997; Sawicki, 1986, 1994; St. Pierre & Pillow, 2000; Weedon, 1997, 1999). However, the term "poststructuralist," like "feminist," is plural. Poststructuralism does not have a single fixed meaning, nor is it specific to one school of thought or academic discipline; rather, it reflects a plurality of theoretical positions (Baxter, 2003; Weedon, 1997). Generally, approaches described as poststructuralist may reflect theoretical positions developed in or from the work of Barthes, Derrida, Lacan, Kristeva, Althusser, Baudrillard, and Foucault (Baxter, 2003; McNay, 1992; Weedon, 1997). Much of my work in this volume is informed by the work of Foucault (1972, 1977, 1978, 1979, 1980) and feminist scholars like Weedon (1997, 1999), Mills (1991, 1992, 1997), Sawicki (1986, 1994), and others who have appropriated his work.

2 I use the term "identity" in this context to mean social and cultural aspects of individual and group identities such as race, sex, sexuality, social class, and ability. In using these terms however, I do not mean that these aspects of identity are necessarily determined or foundational. Rather, I align my thinking with postfoundational accounts like that of Judith Butler (1993) who, while she describes gender as a repetitive performance, acknowledges the complexity of identity that fails to be conveyed through an either/or constructed or determined logic.

3 Ideology is a Marxist-inflected term widely used by theorists across the social sciences and humanities and describes particular ways of looking at the world – sets of perspectives, organized representations of experiences. Ideology is thought to mediate between individuals and the material conditions of their lives (Mills, 1997; Weedon, 1997). In their research on academic women in research universities, Moore and Sagaria (1991) describe ideology as "reality as it is defined by a given society . . . beliefs about how the world functions, and articulates the values, expectations, and standards which are intended to inform and orient people's behavior" (p. 188). The concept of "ideological hegemony" draws from Marxist and neo-Marxist perspectives that describe an understanding about how people come to participate in their own oppression by acting in ways that are not in their best interest (Mills, 1997). This complicity is sometimes delineated through the Althusserian theory of interpellation, which contends ideology functions through a very specific process to interpellate individuals – or constitute one's subjectivity through language (Weedon, 1997). This process relies on the individual's recognition of her/himself as a subject, but also the *misrecognition* that s/he is author of the ideology s/he is speaking. In other words, "she 'imagines' that she is the type of subject humanism proposes – rational, unified, the source rather than effect of language" (Weedon, 1997, p. 31).

4 Importantly, Bordo (1993) contends that while Foucault's genealogical approach to explaining the deployment and "scientization of sexuality" was innovative, his theory of productive power, "power that works not through negative prohibition and restraint of impulse but proliferatively, at the level of the production of bodies and their materiality . . . was not itself new" and had been the subject of "extensive feminist literature (from the 1960s and 1970s) on the social construction and 'deployment' of female sexuality, beauty and femininity" (p. 183).

5 For example, some feminist approaches argue for social change through legal reform, others place an emphasis on women's empowerment through separatism, and others emphasize language as the site of social change (Fonow & Cook, 1991).

References

Alcoff, L. (1988). Cultural feminism versus post-structuralism: The identity crisis in feminist theory. *Signs*, 13(3), 405–436.

Allan, E. J. (1999). *Constructing women's status: Policy discourses of university women's commission reports*. Unpublished doctoral dissertation, The Ohio State University.

Allan, E. J. (2003). Constructing women's status: Policy discourses of university women's commission reports. *Harvard Educational Review*, 73(1), 44–72.

Allan, E. J. (2008). *Policy discourses, gender, and education: Constructing women's status*. New York: Routledge.

Allen, A. (1999). *The power of feminist theory: Domination, resistance, solidarity*. Boulder, CO: Westview Press.

Bacchi, C. L. (1999). *Women, policy and politics: The construction of policy problems*. Thousand Oaks, CA: Sage.

Bailey, M. E. (1993). Foucauldian feminism: Contesting bodies, sexuality and identity. In C. Ramazanoglu (Ed.), *Up against Foucault: Explorations of some tensions between Foucault and feminism* (pp. 99–122). New York: Routledge.

Ball, S. J. (1990). *Politics and policy making in education: Explorations in policy sociology*. New York: Routledge.

Ball, S. J. (1994). *Education reform: A critical and post-structural approach*. Buckingham: Open University Press.

Baxter, J. (2003). *Positioning gender in discourse: A feminist methodology*. New York: Palgrave-Macmillan.

Bensimon, E. M. (1995). Total quality management in the academy: A rebellious reading. *Harvard Educational Review*, 65(2), 593–611.

Bensimon, E. M. & Marshall, C. (1997). Policy analysis for postsecondary education: Feminist and critical perspectives. In C. Marshall (Ed.), *Feminist critical policy analysis: A perspective from post-secondary education* (pp. 1–21). Washington, DC: The Falmer Press.

Blackmore, J. (1995). Policy as dialogue: Feminist administrators working for educational change. *Gender and Education*, 7(3), 293–313.

Blackmore, J. (1996). Doing emotional labor in the educational market place: Stories from the field of women in management. *Discourse*, 17(3), 337–352.

Blackmore, J. (1999). *Troubling women: Feminism, leadership, and educational change*. Philadelphia, PA: Open University Press.

Bordo, S. (1993). Feminism, Foucault, and the politics of the body. In C. Ramazanoglu (Ed.), *Up against Foucault: Explorations of some tensions between Foucault and feminism* (pp. 99–122). New York: Routledge.

Butler, J. (1990). *Gender trouble: Feminism and the subversion of identity*. New York: Routledge.

Butler, J. (1993). *Bodies that matter: On the discursive limits of "sex."* New York: Routledge.

Carlson, D. (1993). The politics of educational policy: Urban school reform in unsettling times. *Educational Policy*, 7(2), 149–165.

Cochran, E. F. & Malone, C. L. (1999). *Public policy perspectives and choices*. New York: McGraw-Hill.

Collins, P. H. (1991). *Black feminist thought: Knowledge, consciousness, and the politics of empowerment*. New York: Routledge.

Connolly, W. E. (1993). *The terms of political discourse*, 3rd ed. Princeton, NJ: Princeton University Press.

Conway, M. M., Ahern, D. W., & Steuernagel, G. A. (1995). *Women in public policy: A revolution in progress*. Washington, DC: CQ Press.

deCastell, S. & Bryson, M. (1997). En/Gendering equity: Paradoxical consequences of institutionalized equity policies. In S. deCastell & M. Bryson (Eds.), *Radical in<ter>ventions: Identity politics, and difference/s in educational praxis* (pp. 85–103). Albany, NY: State University of New York Press.

Derrida, J. (1976). *Of grammatology*. Baltimore, MD: Johns Hopkins University Press.

Derrida, J. (1982). *Margins of philosophy*. London: Harvester.

Diamond, I. & Quinby, L. (1988). *Feminism and Foucault: Reflections on resistance*. Boston, MA: Northeastern University Press.

Ellsworth, E. & Miller, J. L. (1996). Working difference in education. *Curriculum Inquiry*, 26(3), 245–263.

Fine, M. (1988). Sexuality, schooling and adolescent females: The missing discourse of desire. *Harvard Educational Review*, 58(1), 29–53.

Fonow, M. M. & Cook, J. A. (1991). Back to the future: A look at the second wave of feminist epistemology and methodology. In M. M. Fonow & J. A. Cook (Eds.), *Beyond methodology: Feminist scholarship as lived research* (pp. 1–15). Bloomington, IN: Indiana University Press.

Foucault, M. (1972). *The archaeology of knowledge and the discourse on language*. New York: Pantheon Books.

Foucault, M. (1977). *Discipline and punish: The birth of the prison* (A. Sheridan, Trans.). New York: Vintage Books. (Original work published 1975).

Foucault, M. (1978). *The history of sexuality: Volume I: An introduction* (R. Hurley, Trans.). New York: Vintage Books. (Original work published 1976.)

Foucault, M. (1979). *Discipline and punish: The birth of the prison.* New York: Vintage Books.
Foucault, M. (1980). *Power/knowledge: Selected interviews and writings, 1972–1977.* Brighton, Sussex: Harvester Press.
Fraser, N. (1989). *Unruly practices: Power, discourse, and gender in contemporary social theory.* Minneapolis, MN: University of Minnesota Press.
Fraser, N. & Gordon, L. (1994). A genealogy of dependency: Tracing a keyword of the U.S. welfare state. *Signs: Journal of Women in Culture and Society,* 19(2),309–336.
Gore, J. M. (1993). *The struggle for pedagogies: Critical and feminist discourses as regimes of truth.* New York: Routledge.
Griffin, A. I. (1992). Educational policy as text and action. *Educational Policy,* 6(4), 415–428.
Griffin, A. (1994). Women's health and the articulation of policy preferences: Setting the terms of discussion. *Annals of the New York Academy of Sciences,* 736, 205–216.
Guba, E. G. (1984). *The impact of various definitions of "policy" on the nature and outcomes of policy analysis.* Paper presented at the Annual Meeting of The American Educational Research Association, New Orleans, LA, April.
Hawkesworth, M. E. (1988). *Theoretical issues in policy analysis.* New York: State University of New York Press.
Hawkesworth, M. E. (1994). Policy studies within a feminist frame. *Policy Sciences,* 27, 97–118.
Humes, W. M. (1997). Analysing the policy process. *Scottish Educational Review,* 29(1), 20–29.
Iverson, S.V. (2008). Capitalizing on change: The discursive framing of diversity in U.S. land-grant universities. *Equity and Excellence in Education,* 41(2), 1–18.
Labaree, D. (1992). Power, knowledge and the rationalization of teaching: A genealogy of the movement to professionalize teaching. *Harvard Educational Review,* 62(2), 123–154.
Lather, P. (1991). *Getting smart: Feminist research with/in the postmodern.* New York: Routledge.
Lather, P. (1992). Critical frames in educational research: Feminist and post-structural perspectives. *Theory Into Practice,* 31(2), 87–99.
Lather, P. (1996). Troubling clarity: The politics of accessible language. *Harvard Educational Review,* 66(3), 525–545.
Lather, P. (2004). Scientific research in education: A critical perspective. *Journal of Curriculum and Supervision,* 20(1), 14–30.
Lather, P. (2008). New wave utilization research: (Re)imagining the research/policy nexus. *Educational Researcher,* 37(6), 361–364.
Lenzo (McCoy), K. E. (1995). *Looking awry: A genealogical study of pre-service teacher encounters with popular media and multicultural education.* Unpublished doctoral dissertation, The Ohio State University, Columbus.
Lindblom, C. (1980). *The policy making process.* Upper Saddle River, NJ: Prentice-Hall.
Lindblom, C. & Woodhouse, E. J. (1993). *The policy making process.* Upper Saddle River, NJ: Prentice-Hall.
Lugones, M. (2003). *Pilgrimages/peregrinajes: Theorizing coalition against multiple oppressions.* Lanham, MD: Rowman & Littlefield.
Luke, A. (1995). Text and discourse in education: An introduction to critical discourse analysis. *Review of Research in Education,* 21, 3–47.
Marshall, C. (Ed.). (1997a). *Feminist critical policy analysis I: A perspective from primary and secondary schooling.* Washington DC: The Falmer Press.
Marshall, C. (Ed.). (1997b). *Feminist critical policy analysis II: A perspective from post-secondary education.* Washington, DC: The Falmer Press.
Marshall, C. (1999). Researching the margins: Feminist critical policy analysis. *Educational Policy,* 13(1), 59–76.
Marshall, C. (2000). Policy discourse analysis: Negotiating gender equity. *Journal of Educational Policy,* 15(2), 125–156.
McNay, L. (1992). *Foucault and feminism: Power, gender and the self.* Cambridge: Polity Press.
Mills, S. (1991). *Discourses of difference: An analysis of women's travel writing and colonialism.* London: Routledge.
Mills, S. (1992). Negotiating discourses of femininity. *Journal of Gender Studies,* 1(3), 271–285.
Mills, S. (1997). *Discourse.* London: Routledge.
Mohanty, C. (1991). Cartographies of struggle: Third world women and the politics of feminism. In C. T. Mohanty, A. Russo, & L. Torres (Eds.), *Third world women and the politics of feminism* (pp. 1–50). Indianapolis, IN: Indiana University Press.
Moore, K. & Sagaria, M. D. (1991). The situation of women in research universities in the United States: Within the inner circles of academic power. In G. P. Kelly & S. Slaughter (Eds.),

Women's higher education in comparative perspective (pp. 185–200). Netherlands: Kluwer Academic Publishers.

Ozga, J. (2000). *Policy research in educational settings: Contested terrain.* Philadelphia, PA: Open University Press.

Pillow, W. S. (1997). Decentering silences/troubling irony: Teen pregnancy's challenge to policy analysis. In C. Marshall (Ed.), *Feminist critical policy analysis: A perspective from primary and secondary schooling* (pp. 134–152). Washington, DC: The Falmer Press.

Pillow, W. S. (2000). Exposed methodology: The body as a deconstructive practice. In E. A. St. Pierre & W. S. Pillow (Eds.), *Working the ruins: Feminist poststructural theory and methods in education* (pp. 199–219). New York: Routledge

Pillow, W. S. (2003). "Bodies are dangerous": Using feminist genealogy as policy studies methodology. *Journal of Education Policy,* 18(2), 145–159.

Ramazanoglu, C. (1993). Introduction. In C. Ramazanoglu (Ed.), *Up against Foucault: Explorations of some tensions between Foucault and feminism* (pp. 1–25). New York: Routledge.

Reinharz, S. (1992). *Feminist methods in social research.* New York: Oxford University Press.

Ropers-Huilman, B. (1998). *Feminist teaching in theory and practice: Situating power and knowledge in poststructural classrooms.* New York: Teacher's College Press.

Sawicki, J. (1986). Foucault and feminism: Toward a politics of difference. *Hypatia,* 1(2), 23–36.

Sawicki, J. (1991). *Disciplining Foucault: Feminism, power, and theory.* New York: Routledge.

Sawicki, J. (1994). Foucault, feminism, and questions of identity. In G. Gutting (Ed.), *The Cambridge companion to Foucault* (pp. 286–313). Cambridge: Cambridge University Press.

Scheurich, J. J. (1994). Policy archaeology: A new policy studies methodology. *Journal of Education Policy,* 9(4), 297–316.

Scott, J. (1988). Deconstructing equality-versus-difference: Or, the uses of poststructuralist theory for feminism. *Feminist Studies,* 14(1), 33–50.

Shore, C. & Wright, S. (1997). Policy: A new field of anthropology. In C. Shore & S. Wright (Eds.), *Anthropology of policy* (pp. 3–42). New York: Routledge.

Smith, D. E. (1990). *Texts, facts, and femininity: Exploring the relations of ruling.* London: Routledge.

St. Pierre, E. A. (2000a). Poststructural feminism in education: An overview. *International Journal of Qualitative Studies in Education,* 13(5), 477–515.

St. Pierre, E. A. (2000b). The call for intelligibility in postmodern educational research. *Educational Researcher,* 29(5), 25–28.

St. Pierre, E. A. & Pillow, W.S. (Eds.). (2000). *Working the ruins: Feminist poststructural theory and methods in education.* New York: Routledge.

Stivers, C. (1993). *Gender images in public administration: Legitimacy and the administrative state.* Newbury Park, CA: Sage.

Stone, D. (1988). *Political paradox and political reason.* Boston, MA: Scott, Foresman and Company.

Stone, D. (2002). *Political paradox: The art of political decision making,* rev. ed. New York: Norton & Company.

Tyack, D. & Hansot, E. (1988). Silence and policy talk: Historical puzzles about gender and education. *Educational Researcher,* April, 33–41.

Van Dijk, T. (Ed.). (1997). *Discourse as structure and process.* Thousand Oaks, CA: Sage.

Walker, M. (1997). Simply not good chaps: Unraveling gender equity in a South African university. In C. Marshall (Ed.), *Feminist critical policy analysis: A perspective from post-secondary education* (pp. 41–59). Washington, DC: The Falmer Press.

Weedon, C. (1997). *Feminist practice and poststructuralist theory,* 3rd ed. Cambridge, MA: Blackwell Publishers.

Weedon, C. (1999). *Feminism, theory and the politics of difference.* Malden, MA: Blackwell Publishers.

Williams, P. J. (1991). *The alchemy of race and rights: Diary of a law professor.* Cambridge, MA: Harvard University Press.

Williams, P. J. (1997). Spirit-murdering the messenger: The discourse of fingerpointing as the law's response to racism. In A. K. Wing (Ed.), *Critical race feminism: A reader* (pp. 229–236). New York: New York University Press.

Winston, K. & Bane, M. J. (Eds.). (1993). *Gender and public policy: Cases and comments.* Boulder, CO: Westview Press.

Part 1
Productions of Power
through Presence within Absence

A key aspect of feminist poststructuralism (FPS) concerns the ways in which power is understood, conceptualized, and enacted through discursive practices. Power is not something that is hierarchically positioned, never to be disrupted or resisted. Instead, power constructs relationships and opportunities, as well as the very terms through which policy and resistance can be understood and engaged. In *Reconstructing policy in higher education*, several chapters provide outstanding examples of the potential of FPS policy analysis to help educators, scholars, and policy-makers better understand how social policy both represents and produces particular power relations. In this section, we focus on three chapters. First, we consider Jana Nidiffer's chapter on representations of women's involvement in suffrage. We then turn to Tatiana Suspitsyna's chapter on the Department of Education's policy rhetoric under the Bush administration. Finally, Suzanne Gordon, Susan Iverson, and Elizabeth Allan's chapter on how women leaders are portrayed in *The Chronicle of Higher Education* is presented.

Disparities in educational experience and representations have been present throughout history. History tells a story of events that are constructed as meaningful by the storytellers. Yet, which stories are left out or deemed as meaningless by mainstream histories? Which stories are constructed as central and, therefore, powerfully assume the "front page" of the history of a given topic? Jana Nidiffer's chapter poignantly points out how women's involvement in suffrage took shape in higher education contexts and was influenced by local circumstances and the political climate of the time. Yet, Nidiffer also challenges the silences assumed by university leaders and faculty members about women's involvement in suffrage activities. We know from this chapter that women who were affiliated with postsecondary education were actively involved in social change. We also know that such involvement intersected with higher education in multiple ways. Yet, university leaders' and historians' silences about women educators' and students' leadership related to suffrage constructed women as lacking power at that time. This absence has shaped the historical texts available to us today, constructed the historical memory that we rely upon today, and minimized our knowledge of women's involvement in significant historical events. Power (or the lack thereof) can be represented both by what is not present, as well as by what is present.

Tatiana Suspitsyna's chapter on the policy discourses associated with Secretary of Education Margaret Spellings during the Bush administration uses Foucault's construction of power-knowledge to examine how speeches and documents produced or disseminated by Spellings constructed particular kinds of policy knowledge and, in doing so, shaped both power and opportunities for resistance. In her analysis, Suspitsyna critically interrogates how knowledge is reified in policy to consider how "historically structured sets of norms, categories, and truths . . . serve to endorse certain voices and silence others" (p. 66). Powerful terms and concepts – such as "accountability," "transparency," "efficiency," and "measurement and testing" – relate to a neoliberal agenda and highlight the role of education in facilitating individual social mobility and contributing to the United States economy. While democracy and citizenship were present in the Spellings documents, they were subsumed under a neoliberal discourse that powerfully positioned the individual and the economy as predominant. Also important in Suspitsyna's analysis is the consideration of who has access to dominant narratives of the time and in what ways. Her chapter raises a difficult dilemma: Dominant discourses associated with educational policy are "logical" to some, but not to others. By this, we mean to say that, for some people, the terms through which policy is created, the value assigned to those terms, as well as the stated intentions of policy "make sense" in the discourses that structure their lives. But this is not uniformly true. What are the forms of resistance that are enacted when policies fail to make sense? What are the costs of those resistances? Or, put differently, what is the cost of policies that are not comprehensible to those they supposedly serve? High school dropout rates clearly indicate certain students' and communities' disenfranchisement with our educational systems. For example, in 2006, 5.8 percent of White students, 10.7 percent of Black students, and 22.1 percent of Hispanic students dropped out of high school prior to graduation and, therefore, were shut out of most postsecondary education opportunities. While more Hispanic men leave school than Hispanic women, and more White men leave school than White women, Black women leave at a rate of 11.7 percent as compared to 9.7 percent of Black men. 16.5 percent of students in the lowest income quartile drop out, whereas only 3.8 percent in the upper quartile do (NCES, 2008). How does the "logic" of the discourses undergirding educational policy contribute to this disparity? How does this logic structure both what (and who) is absent and present in our educational systems?

Gordon, Iverson, and Allan consider contemporary representations of women in leadership and determine that "assumptions about masculinity and femininity are embedded within the descriptions about leadership and produce gendered images of leaders" (p. 82). The researchers examined images of leaders described in *The Chronicle of Higher Education*. Discourses of gender, professionalism, social justice, and Liberal Humanism were identified as contributing to what the nearly half-million readers of *The Chronicle* view as "appropriate" or, at least, "typical" behaviors and viewpoints of women leaders. Gordon, Iverson, and Allan illustrate how, within the intersections of competing discourses, women leaders are challenged in their ability to find a path to legitimacy that is supported within all discourses. Through this analysis, the authors clearly establish the power of discursive constructions, and the ways in which they shape people's lives and experiences differently. In this case, the power associated with leadership is both discursively constrained and produced.

Policy analysis using an FPS framing of power poses many questions and challenges. Finding information is difficult when the dominant narrative has documented one perspective in accessible ways, but not others. Feminist poststructuralism urges attention to silences, but what are the strategies we can use to find and document silences historically? How can we make sense of what was not recorded or articulated, and the values inherent in those constructed absences? Additionally, when dominant discourses are so pervasive, how can one see their underlying values? Conversely, how can one make sense of the resistances and counter-narratives to those dominant discourses? Further, once that task is complete, what can one do with that information? If we know that depictions of leadership and student involvement are shaped by contradictory and gendered discourses, how are we to make sense of that information and interject other discursive framings? These are not merely academic questions. Instead, at a time when there is no lack of rhetoric around inclusion, but many are stymied by ineffective practices, this kind of deep analysis provides a potential opening for change.

Reference

National Center for Education Statistics (2008). Fast facts. Retrieved November 15, 2008 from http://nces.ed.gov/FastFacts/display.asp?id=16.

3
Corrective Lenses

Suffrage, Feminist Poststructural Analysis,
and the History of Higher Education

JANA NIDIFFER

The Larger Story

The history of American higher education, like most story arcs provided in historical texts, has a dominant narrative. This narrative, and the several episodes subsumed under it, is occasionally refined and nuanced as historians tweak various points, but there is remarkable agreement on major turning points and the general trajectory of the story. It will surprise no one that the dominant story in the history of higher education is largely told from a white, male, Protestant, and middle/upper-class point of view.

This much-abbreviated story begins with the founding of Harvard in 1636.[1] From that time until the American Revolution there were nine Colonial Colleges, largely controlled by Protestant denominations. They employed a classically inspired curriculum taught in Latin, adapted primarily from Oxford and Cambridge Universities in England. The Colonial Colleges were joined by numerous other denominationally inspired institutions that were created in the "West" (what is now the Midwest) as the nation expanded; so many that they were described by contemporaries as "springing up like weeds." In the first half of the century, modern subjects were added such as English language and literature and what would become engineering. The American Civil War (1861–1865) is deemed an important turning point, after which the states increased their support of colleges and the U.S. maintained both public and private institutions of higher education.

In the latter decades of the century, scholars – inspired by the Enlightenment and developments in Europe, especially Germany – began to incorporate ideas now recognizable as the *sine qua non* of universities: graduate study, professional schools, and professors who were expected to be researchers. Thus, the University Movement, as this transformation was called, produced two distinct types of institutions: the liberal arts college and the research university. The birth of the university catapulted modernism, empiricism, secularism, and science to the top of the prestige hierarchy, but did not exclude other institutional types or forms of education. This set the U.S. on a path that differs from much of the world by incorporating an array of institutional types.

The university became viewed as an institution fully integral and important to the larger society, not the ivy-covered, insulated, college-on-the-hill of days past. The twentieth century saw the first community college (1901), adding a third distinct type of institution that could be either public or private, and witnessed the basic ideas of the research university expand and develop into what exists today. Another remarkable and unique aspect of American higher education is a post-World War II phenomenon referred to as "massification." The expansion of the post-war economy, the baby boom, and the enhanced mission of the community colleges, all contributed to a society where a greater percentage of adults had some form of post-secondary training than in any other nation. The resulting wide variety of institutions – public and private; religious and secular; graduate and undergraduate – are so loosely connected it is difficult to refer to the U.S. as having one "system" of higher education. Yet, our "system" educates a significant percentage of the adult population, accounts for billions of dollars within the economy, and is recognized as an institution essential to the larger society.

Feminist Poststructural Analysis as a Correcting Lens

One of the key tenets of post-modernist or poststructural thinking is that all knowledge is constructed and therefore subject to interrogation. Perhaps this is especially so in the field of history. In the past, gatekeepers such as journal editors, book publishers, and conference program committees tightly controlled how historical knowledge was disseminated by publishing or refusing to publish particular manuscripts or by rebuffing some authors, and not allowing them to present their work at conferences.[2] In addition, the "stuff of history" – the material used by current historians as data, such as artifacts, written records, the printed word, etc. – was quite likely to have belonged to the privileged of the past. However, in the last two or three decades, there has been more room for scholars interested in people and topics outside of the experiences of white men and matters concerning politics, the economy, and warfare. These new social historians not only extended the *who* of historical study, they also expanded the *what* – by using new types of artifacts (e.g., women's diaries) as historical data.

The history of higher education, as a field of study, also benefited from this trend toward new social history. Writing from different perspectives – using different lenses such as religion, class, race, gender, or prestige – historians have questioned the dominant narrative. One interesting example is the challenge to the "secularization thesis." This widely held notion suggested that universities became secular because being a person of faith was incompatible with being an objective, modernist, scientific researcher – the personification of the professor hero of the University Movement. A cadre of scholars has demonstrated more recently that, in fact, many universities remained very Christian in their character and mission during this period, that science and religion were not as antithetical as depicted, and that perhaps "multi-sectarian" is a more apt descriptor than "secular" (Marsden, 1994; Marsden & Longfield, 1992).

While the challenge to the "secularization thesis" may be considered an example of addressing the "sins of commission" in the foundational work, other scholars have confronted the "sins of omission." These scholars have been, for example, critical of the lack of attention paid to institutional models other than universities or elite colleges. They have argued that too much history has been written, as Linda Eisenmann (1996) noted, from a "prestige-centric" perspective from which historians have studied only elite institutions and then based generalizations for all of higher education on those narrow experiences. Such scholars are reconstructing the histories of women's colleges, community colleges, normal schools, historically Black institutions, and smaller, less prestigious universities (Brint & Karabel, 1989; Drewry & Doermann, 2001; Horowitz, 1984; Ogren, 2005). In another example, historian Clyde Barrow (1990) challenged the "democracy myth" – that the system was truly open to anyone with the determination to gain a degree. He argued convincingly that higher education played a formidable role in constructing the middle class and excluding the lower classes. Further, universities created labor-force competition that – when combined with racism (he discussed sexism to a lesser extent) – explains the concerted effort by university leaders to exclude people of color (and women) from the prestigious echelons of higher education. My own work on the history of the University of Michigan demonstrates how the middle-class culture of emerging universities did as much to discourage attendance by students from the lowest income quartile as insufficient financial aid policies (Nidiffer & Bouman, 2004). University leaders honored their articulated commitment to the ideal of a classless society not by continuing to admit poor students, but by conducting research on poverty instead.

Other scholars are uncovering the history of those who worked and studied in higher education, but whose lives and contributions were neither documented nor appreciated. Recovering the educational experiences of African American students and leaders is one example. Another example is the literature on women's educational history. In the past 25 years, women historians have produced a substantial quantity of scholarship that examines the topic of women in higher education from various perspectives, including explorations of regional differences (especially Northern versus Southern) or status differences (whether the subject was students, faculty or administrators). A very recent work deftly examines the intersection of race *and* gender. Stephanie Evans (2007) explores higher education's role in constructing "whiteness" in addition to what other feminist scholars have demonstrated about higher education's role in constructing "maleness" (Rosenberg, 1982; Rossiter, 1982; Townsend, 1996). Evans (2007) demonstrates how such a construction functioned to exclude African Americans, especially women, because "whiteness" and "maleness" were the hegemonic norms. Other types of work on women include institutional histories of women's colleges, histories of women-dominated professions, biographies of women educators, explorations of the social, cultural, religious, and political attitudes about women and their pursuit of higher education, as well as studies of the lives and conditions of women as undergraduate and graduate students, faculty, and administrators.[3] Much of this scholarship adds significant and rich detail to what is known about women. Unfortunately, little of the work challenges the gendered nature of higher education as an institution. Feminist poststructural analysis (FPS), applied to historical interpretation, provides a means for such scholarship.

Employing FPS analysis in my own work begins with a set of questions I ask of the extant literature before I do the primary source research:

- Who wrote the current story and what sources were used?
- Who benefits from the story being told in this particular way and what are the consequences of having knowledge framed in this manner?
- What was the lens of analysis used? Was class, race, gender, or some combination, used as a lens?
- Where were the women of different races and classes in this story? What were their experiences?

To self-interrogate when my research is complete, I ask the above questions of my own work. Turning from my scholarship back to the extant literature, I then inquire:

- How do the experiences of the women in my research compare to those of the actors in the dominant narrative? If this history were written with women as the center of analysis, how would the story be different?
- Do my results challenge any of the assumptions of the dominant narrative? How can the dominant narrative be modified to incorporate my findings?

College Women as Suffrage Activists

The history of the suffrage movement is typically divided into two eras, often referred to as the first and second waves (see especially Baker, 2002; Flexner, 1959; Kraditor, 1981; Scott & Scott, 1982). Briefly, the first wave was dominated by the ante-bellum activities of Susan B. Anthony and Elizabeth Cady Stanton and is best known for the 1848 convention in Seneca Falls, New York. At that gathering, Anthony and Stanton presented the "Declaration of Sentiments," modeled after the Declaration of Independence, outlining the rationale and philosophy of women's suffrage. At this time in American history, reform-oriented individuals were likely to be both pro-woman's suffrage and anti-slavery. With the impending Civil War, most abolitionists persuaded suffrage supporters to suspend their demands so that the country could attend to the larger injustice of slavery – a strategy that delayed granting suffrage to women for over half a century. After the war, there was no real momentum in Congress to give women the vote, even though the Fifteenth Amendment to the Constitution granted suffrage to African American men. Most suffragists were angered by the neglect and some felt it was a complete betrayal. Sadly, this juxta-position of race- and gender-based struggles for enfranchisement contributed to tensions between white and African American suffragists during the early twentieth century (Gordon, 1997; Knupfer, 1996; Terborg-Penn, 1998). Toward the end of the nineteenth century, the cause of woman's suffrage was re-invigorated. Spurred by Wyoming granting women the vote in 1890, there was a resurgence of activity. After 1900, the cause gained further momentum and eventually succeeded when the Nineteenth Amendment became law in 1920. With many of Anthony's original cohort of supporters deceased or retired from political work, leadership of the second wave was assumed by younger, mostly college-educated women.

In 1900, two Radcliffe alumnae began what became the College Equal Suffrage League (CESL), an organization dedicated to informing and enlisting the help of college students. With the help of CESL, students – first at Eastern women's colleges and later at single-sex and coeducational institutions nationally – strove to inform and persuade their classmates of the need for involvement in the suffrage cause. Although a separate entity, CESL formally affiliated with the National American Woman Suffrage Association (NAWSA). This was the first time that college students were explicitly recruited by an adult political organization, initiating a form of student activism heretofore unseen. Not only did CESL create a new strategy of political activism for students, it linked alumnae with students and faculty from their alma maters in collective activity. For some students, it spurred life-long democratic participation as several former CESL members continued their political involvement through the League of Women Voters as adults. In addition, CESL enabled a small number of female educational leaders to have a national voice discussing a contemporary issue, an opportunity many of their male counterparts had already experienced. Yet, unfortunately, the political activism of the women students and faculty allies and short-lived CESL has received only scant attention.[4] This groundbreaking, albeit small, organization is missing from the history of women's education, the history of woman's suffrage, and the history of student activism.

The origin of CESL can be traced to a student in Radcliffe's class of 1898, Maud Wood Park. She and classmate Inez Haynes (soon to be Gilmore) invited Alice Stone Blackwell to speak on campus toward the end of their college careers. Park and Haynes became interested in the "woman question" as college students and were dismayed when woman's suffrage was defeated in an 1895 mock vote in Massachusetts (Marzzacco, 2004). Concerned that their classmates were apathetic or even antagonistic, the young women worried about student reaction to Blackwell's talk. They needn't have – the event was a resounding success. Convinced that college women should not only be educated about suffrage, but that they could and should become important members of the suffrage movement – adding youthful energy and enthusiasm to established suffrage organizations that were "in the doldrums" (Marzzacco, 2004, p. 7) – Park and Haynes decided to organize students.

In 1900, shortly before the upcoming National American Woman's Suffrage Association (NAWSA) convention, a group of college-educated women met in downtown Boston. They decided, at Maud Wood Park's urging, that they should organize, not just as women in favor of suffrage, but as *College Women* per se. After the NAWSA conference, Park and 25 of her college-educated friends formed the CESL and drew up a constitution.[5] The stated purpose of the League was to "promote equal suffrage sentiment among college women, both before and after graduation, and to stimulate interest in the movement for equal rights."[6]

Throughout the 17-year history of the CESL, a significant distinction was made between the women who were college-educated alumnae and the women college students. The term "college women" almost always meant alumnae while undergraduates were often referred to as students, or occasionally, "college girls." Thus, the original intent was to organize alumnae to educate students so that when the students graduated, they would be knowledgable about suffrage and work with their local or state pro-suffrage organization. However, the CESL eventually became an organization through which students became activists while still in college.

Park remembered that she often *thought* about suffrage while at Radcliffe, but that it never occurred to her that there was something to *do*.[7] She wanted the students who came after her to understand that there was plenty to be done. In addition to preparing students to be suffrage workers after graduation, she wanted some societal acknowledgment that educated women were pro-suffrage. She also wanted to see educated women connect to the faculty of their alma maters and unite on-campus and off-campus women around the suffrage issue. It was important to Park that this connection was made obvious to the public and, in future suffrage parades, the college women marched as a unit – much like groups of nurses or teachers did – under a banner with the alma mater's name, wearing brightly colored sashes identifying each woman with her institution, or a CESL ribbon.

Members of the new organization began fund raising. CESL's first effort was a common suffrage educational and money-making tool – they put on a play. They also held teas, membership drives, and mailed pledge cards to potential donors. A particularly clever idea was the creation of the Lucy Stone Fund. Stone was the first Massachusetts woman to earn a full college degree and an iconic figure in the early suffrage movement. The CESL solicitation cards told donors that their money would be used especially to organize chapters of CESL in colleges admitting women; publish suffrage articles, if possible, in college publications; and finance lecturers on suffrage at colleges that admitted women.[8]

Armed with their educational materials, money for speakers and meetings, and tremendous energy, the CESL members of Boston went about getting their message to college students. They first focused on institutions in the immediate vicinity, including Radcliffe, Wellesley, Boston University, and Jackson – the women's college of Tufts University. They encouraged women students to form branches, some of which took names such as the College Equal Suffrage League of Boston University, for example, or the Collegiate League, or simply the Suffrage Club. As the students organized themselves, they could ask the CESL of Boston for assistance and resources.

After helping students organize on campuses in Massachusetts, news of the League's activities spread, especially in New York and then along the East coast. At some point, probably around 1906, M. Carey Thomas, the president of Bryn Mawr College, encouraged Park to establish a *National* College Equal Suffrage League that would help organize local and regional leagues and campus chapters all across the country. Thomas herself organized the first "College Evening" at the NAWSA convention in Baltimore, Maryland in February of 1906. Her purpose was to gather all the college women of NAWSA together to talk about their particular concerns, both as intellectual women and as educators of women students.[9]

Park spent long hours speaking and organizing, enduring all the vagaries of early twentieth-century travel. At various times her plans were altered by heavy storms, train delays, and an epidemic of smallpox that closed one of the colleges where she was scheduled to speak. Whatever the obstacle, Park got her message to campuses. In one trip she visited Northwestern University, University of Chicago, Illinois Normal University, Wesleyan University (of Bloomington, Illinois), Eureka College, Knox College and Lombard College; CESL activities were planned in response to Park's talks at each location.[10]

In December of 1907, Bryn Mawr President M. Carey Thomas wrote to Park urging her to institutionalize "College Evenings" at each annual NAWSA convention.[11] President Thomas wanted "unity" among all the leagues and thought they should adopt a formal constitution at the convention. The expressed goal of the new constitution was like the earlier one: to educate college girls and women before and after graduation on the issue of suffrage. The new constitution also specified, in almost agonizing detail, precisely what a campus chapter should do:

> . . . hold at least two public meetings, and if possible, a general address on the subject of women's suffrage, and for one annual meeting of the Chapter to be held in April or May (the period between April 15th and May 15th is suggested) which a member of the Council of the National League shall be invited to attend. In addition to these two regular meetings a third public meeting should, whenever possible, be arranged for to be

devoted to a debate on the topic of woman suffrage, a play on the subject, or another address. An important part of the work of College Chapters is to bring to the attention of every member of the student body accurate information and strong arguments on the subject of equal suffrage. . . . Statistical information, suffrage literature of all kinds and traveling suffrage libraries may be obtained.[12]

Evidence suggests that on college campuses with CESL chapters or other types of suffrage clubs, students made suffrage an issue harder to ignore and provided an avenue for students to *do* something.

The amount of suffrage activity on campus was related to a variety of factors. First, the presence of male students was often a deterrent. There is no evidence that all-male institutions had suffrage clubs, although I found a rather vague reference in a Bryn Mawr publication to an anti-suffrage club at nearby Haverford College. At institutions with coordinate colleges, such as Radcliffe at Harvard, Jackson at Tufts, Pembroke at Brown, and Barnard at Columbia, the suffrage activity was contained within the women's college. CESL chapters did exist at coeducational institutions, and an early visit by Maud Wood Park to Ann Arbor was revealing. In 1908, Park visited the University of Michigan, often regarded as one of the more supportive coeducational universities for women, especially under president James Angell who publicly supported women attending the university. Park met with the dean of women, Myra Jordan, who was personally supportive of suffrage, but Jordan indicated that the "self-consciousness of women students because of co-educational criticism, would make separate suffrage organization difficult" (Gerda, 2004). Park talked with several others on campus, including President Angell and summed up her visit in her 1908 CESL report: "All felt that the situation is very difficult because of co-educational conditions, and of ridicule aroused by reports of suffragette movement in England; they say that it is necessary to have some well-known speaker present our subject before a Chapter can be formed. . . . They want Florence Kelly who is already known and well liked in Ann Arbor."[13]

The level and prominence of suffrage activity was also influenced by institutional type. For example, a recent history of normal schools in the U.S. revealed that although the students believed in women's capacity to earn a living and be accomplished, professional teachers, the majority of students were not "Bloomer women" as they called the more outspoken or "radical" women of their day who wore the billowing costume introduced by Amelia Bloomer in lieu of conventional dress. Despite the large number of women students enrolled, and even the smattering of faculty who were vocally pro-suffrage, normal-school students generally did not agitate for equal rights or suffrage (Ogren, 2005). This trend was corroborated by a 1917–1918 annual report of the Boston CESL in which the secretary noted that it was difficult to establish chapters at normal schools even in Massachusetts – the birthplace of both normal school education and the CESL.[14] In addition, there is no evidence to suggest that anyone reached out to any of the fledgling community colleges. Although women's colleges were an obvious choice, the CESL list of possible campus visits did not include the new Catholic women's colleges and the young Spelman and Bethune Colleges that educated primarily African American women.[15]

In addition to the presence of male students and institutional type, the amount of suffrage activity on campus was influenced by local circumstances including the local political climate and the level of administrative, especially presidential, support. A comparison of the suffrage activities at the "Seven Sisters" (Barnard, Bryn Mawr, Mount Holyoke, Smith, Radcliffe, Vassar, and Wellesley Colleges) provides a glimpse at the impact of local conditions. Alumnae of these institutions were quite over-represented in East Coast suffrage activity, but what transpired on campus was shaped by the local situation and level of support. For example, Barnard (New York, NY) and Radcliffe (Cambridge, MA) both had male presidents who were rather indifferent to suffrage, but not openly hostile. However, they were located in urban settings rife with suffrage activity. At these colleges the women students were not limited to on-campus activities and participated in both campus and state suffrage organizations.[16]

Wellesley's leaders, Caroline Hazard and later, Ellen Pendleton, were active in NAWSA. Smith College president Laurenus Clark Seelye was generally supportive of suffrage – he allowed an organization and visiting speakers such as Jane Addams – but was not involved in national organizations.[17] On both campuses, the student bodies were generally pro-suffrage, although not by large margins, and students were less likely than Radcliffe and Barnard students to be involved in state or regional organizations. However, both colleges sent representative students to march in the famous 1913 suffrage parade. Held in Washington, DC on the day of Woodrow Wilson's inauguration, the parade had been organized by Alice Paul and the National Woman's Party.

The presidents of Mount Holyoke and Bryn Mawr Colleges, Mary E. Woolley and M. Carey Thomas, respectively, were active, national leaders in NAWSA. The more conservative political leanings of Mount Holyoke students made the amount of activity on that campus pale in comparison to the swirl of events at Bryn Mawr.[18] Students' experience at Vassar under the presidency of James Monroe Taylor (1886–1914) demonstrated the constraints under which students worked when the administration was openly hostile to suffrage. Taylor refused to allow the students to form a suffrage club, and did not allow pro-suffrage speakers such as Jane Addams on campus.[19] The 1877 Vassar graduate Harriot Stanton Blatch, daughter of Elizabeth Cady Stanton, recalled trying to "speak to the girls" on campus. Blatch had been invited in 1908 by Vassar student Inez Milholland who went on to become an important member of the National Woman's Party and a "martyr for the movement" because her constant traveling and speaking so taxed her that she died of pernicious anemia in 1916 (Gilmore, 1977; Lumsden, 2004). Milholland wanted Blatch's talk to be delivered on campus, but President Taylor refused permission, and Blatch ended up speaking at a cemetery near the campus. Blatch was very distressed by her experience at her alma mater: ". . . and what indeed was more important. Here was an educational institution for young women of maturity, only a little under or just over the very age when citizens reach their majority, the age when the State regards its citizens as fit to exercise their right to vote. What [could be] more proper than for this body of young women to gather together and discuss woman suffrage with older women?" (Blatch & Lutz, 1940, p. 108). In 1914, the situation on the Vassar campus was reversed when President Taylor was replaced by Henry Noble McCraken who welcomed considerable suffrage activity.[20]

On every campus, the primary activity of student activists was to raise awareness of the suffrage issue among other students. They used numerous methods to accomplish this task. They made great use of college publications, especially at the women's colleges, with essays, editorials, short stories, and poems dedicated to suffrage. The students held public debates, put on plays, and brought in speakers of national or local renown. Some of these speakers had a powerful impact on the students as evidenced by their diary entries. For example, one Bryn Mawr student (class of 1910) wrote, "The greatest result her speech had on the college was the realization of the necessity for people to take more interest in politics."[21]

Students also responded to what they heard in campus debates. A Mount Holyoke student wrote her mother in April of her senior year, "At debating society last evening we had an informal debate on Woman Suffrage, and then took a vote as to those who favored it and who did not and it came out a tie until the president voted which gave it to the affirmative. Dinner bell . . . lots of love as ever, Helen."[22]

The majority of the students' activist efforts on campus were aimed primarily at their fellow students. The most obvious activity was marching in parades. This made their support of suffrage public, but their related activity exposed the young women to ridicule, and upon a couple of occasions, harassment and even attack. Marching could also lead to finding one's name or photograph in the local newspaper and arousing parental disapproval (Gilmore, 1977; Paul, 1976; Stevens, 1976).

By 1917, the politics of suffrage had changed considerably. The primary strategy of NAWSA had been to win suffrage state-by-state until it was obvious to the federal Congress that suffrage was needed for the entire country. A younger group of women led by Alice Paul, a brilliant, determined, and savvy Bryn Mawr graduate, believed that a more effective strategy was to pressure Congress for an amendment to the U.S. Constitution. Initially, Paul worked under the auspices of NAWSA in their Washington, DC office as part of their Congressional Committee, but she grew fatigued by the "old fashion-ness" of the suffrage pioneers who remained a strong presence in the organization. Concomitantly, NAWSA leaders were put off by Paul's brashness and confrontational techniques.

One of Alice Paul's more flamboyant and controversial tactics was to schedule a suffrage parade on the day of Woodrow Wilson's inauguration in March, 1913. This parade drew a considerable number of marchers and onlookers and was covered in most newspapers and campus publications. Interestingly, it was the parade that acted as the catalyst for African American women students to become activists, rather than the African American press. Many African American leaders and intellectuals were publicly in favor of women suffrage, including W. E. B. DuBois, editor of the NAACP's journal, *The Crisis*. However, news of the parade inspired young women at Howard University to act. A group of students was dissatisfied with the first African American sorority, Alpha Kappa Alpha (AKA), for its lack of political activism. They formed the second sorority, Delta Sigma Theta, for the explicit purpose of marching in the 1913 suffrage parade in Washington, DC. Perhaps it is not surprising that given racist attitudes in the white suffrage movement, I have not found examples of African American and white students who worked together.[23]

In response to tactics such as the Inauguration Day parade, NAWSA's president, Carrie Chapman Catt, increasingly distanced herself from Paul's group. Inevitably, Paul formed a separate suffrage organization later dubbed the National Woman's Party (NWP). Several of the younger, more recent alumnae working for suffrage were attracted to the perceived youth and vitality of the NWP and were less interested in affiliation with NAWSA (Gilmore, 1977; Stevens, 1976). Two years later, and just months before the Nineteenth Amendment was ratified, NAWSA President Carrie Chapman Catt organized a new group, the League of Women Voters, and appointed Maud Wood Park as its first president. Park's primary goal was to encourage women to stay active politically and to do so "responsibly" – in part a response to anti-suffrage complaints that women would not be "intelligent" voters (Gilmore, 1977; Stevens, 1976).

The Impact of this Suffrage Research

An FPS perspective implores scholars to "ask questions that produce different knowledge, and produce knowledge differently" (St. Pierre & Pillow, 2000, p. 1). It is interesting to note that as a discipline, history has been subject to analysis from different perspectives (postcolonial theory, critical race theory, Marxism, feminism, etc.) for a few decades. Yet the dominant narrative, especially as it appears in history textbooks, has remained remarkably resistant to new information and perspectives gleaned from these efforts. More traditional historians have given such work the derisive name of "revisionism," implying that the "real history" was revised to suit the political agenda of the author.

My research on suffrage has implications for two aspects of the dominant narrative: the history of student activism – a more recent addition to the literature; and the history of the University Movement. Before the student unrest of the late 1960s fueled interest in student activism, historians paid little attention to undergraduates' lives. In response to events of the 1960s, numerous books on activism appeared in the 1970s, especially by sociologists. So, historians responded to the public's increased interest with texts that examined student life throughout the entire history of higher education (Horowitz, 1987). While this work added students' experiences to the dominant narrative, it did not change the narrative in any substantial way. In contrast, the University Movement is absolutely key to the dominant narrative and was discussed in much of the extant literature. To discuss the implications of my work for these two elements, I revisit the questions mentioned above that I ask at the conclusion of my research:

- How do the experiences of the women in my research compare to those of the actors in the dominant narrative? If this history were written with women as the center of analysis, how would the story be different?
- Do my results challenge any of the assumptions of the dominant narrative? How can the dominant narrative be modified to incorporate my findings?

Student Activism

The phrase "student activism" often evokes images from the 1960s of students protesting America's involvement in Vietnam or the outrages of racism and the lack of adequate civil rights legislation. The campus unrest of the 1960s splashed across television screens, shocking the nation and creating both popular and scholarly interest in college student protests. Early writing on the subject tended to be either romantic or alarmist, deifying or demonizing the students. However, the passage of time, thoughtful reflection, and careful scholarship have produced a portrait of student activism that is more balanced and nuanced. For example, recent scholarship has demonstrated that protest activity was highly correlated to socio-economic levels. Students from middle-class or wealthier family backgrounds participated in activism to a much greater extent than students from the lower-income families.[24] Historians of activism draw important distinctions among the types and character of student political activity. Based on this body of work, I have identified three dimensions useful in discussing student activism and comparing activism of different eras: *location*, *content*, and *control*.

- Location refers to whether the protests took place on campus or at another site. There is an important difference between students, as citizens, being involved in social issues and students, as students, using the campus as a forum. Thus, students in the 1850s working with local abolitionist groups is a different form of student activism from students forming a Student Abolitionist Society and protesting on campus.

- *Content* pertains to the specific issue about which students were protesting. It is important to distinguish between "campus protests" concerning various on-campus (or in-house) issues and "political activism" linked to larger social or political questions. The historical literature reveals that during both the nineteenth and twentieth centuries, a significant percentage of protest activity was related to on-campus issues (parietal rules, for example) rather than larger social or political issues.
- *Control* refers to the role played by "adults" (non-college students) from social or political organizations, and their relationship to the student organization.
- Historical scholarship on student involvement in national politics reveals that the political activism of the 1960s had important ante-cedents in the 1930s, especially in terms of control. Scholars generally agree that the pivotal difference between the political activism of the 1930s and the 1960s was the role played by "adult" (again, meaning non-college students) political groups (Cohen, 1993; Cornell, 1969; Feuer, 1969; Johnson, 1998). In the 1930s, adults, especially those from the American Socialist Party and other left-wing organizations, recognized the potential of college students as political activists for their cause and were responsible for inspiring, enlisting, and even financing campus activities. In contrast, students of the 1960s were typically self-motivated and less likely to be working for established political organizations or under the direction of adult political operatives.

The historical scholarship of student activism also asserts that the so-called "New Left" activism of the 1930s was the first time college students were enthusiastically recruited by adult political activists and affiliated with adult organizations. Further, unless the central thesis of the scholarship is the women's movement per se, general literature on activism barely mentions – or ignores completely – issues more germane to women, such as entry into the professions, temperance, suffrage, sexual liberation, equal pay, creation of women's studies programs, or reproductive rights.

My research demonstrates that, in fact, it was women students who first affiliated with adult organizations and women political operatives who first recognized the potential of engaging college students in their efforts. Thus, at a minimum, my work offers a correction of fact: suffrage activism, not the leftist activity of students in the 1930s, was the first student activism affiliated with adult political organizations.

A more interesting question to ponder is how the whole student activism story of the twentieth century would be told differently knowing that women set the precedent for activism to come. Perhaps the issue of suffrage and the participation of women students were ignored because political activity was considered a male domain. Thus, male historians – especially those writing before the 1970s who had not yet witnessed the modern women's movement – were uninterested in women's issues, did not study students at women's or coordinate colleges, and failed to acknowledge either the efforts of women students or the successful tactics of adult suffragists.

The University Movement

Unlike student activism, which merited little attention in the dominant narrative, the development of the American university was a fundamental and important theme. The literature on the University Movement is extensive, but I will focus here on two key implications. [25] First, within academia, the birth of the university catapulted modernism, empiricism, secularism, science, and "pure" research to the top of the prestige hierarchy. Yet one aspect was not discussed that had implications for the patriarchal nature of the university – and therefore for the lives of women within the institution: the epistemological developments and the concomitant expansion of scientific disciplines was an incredibly gendered phenomenon. For example, rationality and empiricism were heralded as central to intellectual development and key to finding "truth" under the dictates of modernism and the scientific method; they were gendered male and presented in stark contrast to "female" attributes such as emotion or intuition. Similarly, disciplines that were thought of as more scientific tended to be more prestigious and became progressively more lucrative in the labor market. Some disciplines, desperate for the imprimatur of science, became social *sciences* and cleaved the more feminine aspects into separate efforts. For example, sociology became more empirical while social work – considered feminine – developed separately. In general, anything considered female, feminine, or womanly was deemed less significant.

The second key assertion in the literature describing the University Movement is that the university became increasingly important in social movements and national affairs and developed into a substantial economic actor. The University Movement coincided with the Progressive Era (approximately 1900–1918) when many Americans became entranced with the power and potential of science to solve technological and social problems. The Progressive Era was perhaps best known for its many reform efforts and, nationally, a deferential confidence in (usually male) "expertise" emerged. Thus, occupations that required obtaining such expertise became professions, and their practitioners were professionals. Because universities were the institutions that both created the knowledge base of professions and then conferred status on practitioners by awarding the necessary degrees for entry, universities became the gatekeepers of the professional (middle) classes (Barrow, 1990).

State and national leaders also relied on university expertise. For example, President Woodrow Wilson, former president of Princeton University, tapped the research capacity of universities to aid in U.S. foreign policy and defense at the outbreak of World War I in Europe. Some institutions, especially public universities, modified their missions to state explicitly that it was appropriate, even desirable, for the institution to work on problems affecting a state's economy. In other words, *applied* research was placed on par with *pure* research. Nowhere was this more evident than at the University of Wisconsin that described such efforts as the Wisconsin Idea (Curti & Carstensen, 1949; Steffens, 1909).

My research thus far illustrates that university faculty and leaders paid little attention to suffrage. I have found examples of students at coeducational universities such as Cornell, Berkeley, and Michigan, engaged in the suffrage fight, bringing in speakers, debating, writing editorials, and marching in parades. Yet, public stances taken by university presidents on the issue were infrequent. [26] In the dominant narrative, the presidents of several prominent institutions during the University Movement are considered "giants." Such men as James Angell (Michigan), Charles Eliot (Harvard), Daniel Gilman (Johns Hopkins), William Rainey Harper (Chicago), David Starr Jordon (Stanford), and Andrew White (Cornell) are described as exemplars of the new university leadership, voicing their views about important national social, economic, and political issues. Yet, my research challenges the assertion that universities were only partially involved in to the national political scene: university leaders paid scant attention to an issue that not only modified the U.S. Constitution, but it gave over 50 per cent of the adult population the right to participate in our democracy! Taken in that light, suffrage was arguably the most important social and political issue of the era, yet the "giants" of emerging universities gave it little heed. This result should prompt a re-evaluation of the claims of the centrality of universities during this era. Such an omission communicates a great deal about the marginalization of women and women's issues within the development of higher education.

Discussion

As a discipline, history particularly lends itself to aspects of FPS. At any point in time, multiple realities existed (as they do in the present), but any work of historical scholarship depicts only a finite number of points of view. For example, within the history of higher education, the perspective of senior administrators differed from the world of undergraduates, which was removed from the views of anyone who aspired to, but was denied, entrance to the institutions. However, there was often a prestige hierarchy among the historical actors and those deemed most prestigious – in the case of higher education history that was usually presidents, founders, or faculty members – held the point of view most often told by historians.

Identifying and articulating the perspectives of the "others" is the first essential task for historians; a process often described as "recovery" or "reclaimed history." Social historians of higher education have accumulated almost three decades of scholarship on "others" – women as students, faculty, and administrators; people of color also in multiple roles; religious leaders during the so-called secular revolution; smaller institutions such as normal schools and community colleges; and other groups excluded from higher education such as immigrants or the poor. This recovered history is growing richer and deeper, but I feel much of it is "additive." In other words, the dominant narrative goes largely unchallenged while the additions of recovered history fill in, almost as sidebars to the front-page story.

Challenging the dominant narrative is difficult intellectually and culturally. Intellectually, the work is demanding because it requires more work to uncover sources that have not yet been mined and fully archived. It can also be difficult to find material on historical actors who were not considered important in the past. For example, I have visited the archives of coeducational institutions where there was no effort expended in keeping track of women students' name changes. So, when I came across the name of an adult woman using her *married* name while working for suffrage who mentioned that she was interested in the cause while in college, I was often frustrated in trying to find her college records which were likely under her *maiden* name. In contrast, most of the archives in which I have worked at women's colleges keep multiple, cross-referenced lists of women students' name changes throughout a lifetime. Women students were not valued in the past by the coeducational institution in the same way they were at the women's college, and that makes the work of the historian that much harder. There are countless other examples.

Interrogating the dominant narrative may also be intellectually challenging because it may require the historian to "prove the negative" or to write speculatively. For example, my assertion that university presidents did not use their bully pulpit to speak on suffrage in ways analogous to their pontifications on other issues, I am trying to prove a negative or find records that demonstrate that they did *not* speak on the issue. Further, asking how the story of the University Movement might have been told differently if the original scholars who constructed the narrative considered the experience of women or gender as a category of analysis is important, but it involves some intellectual speculation.

The above limitations are why such work may also be culturally difficult. Scholarship that seeks to prove the negative and engage in intelligent speculation is vulnerable to criticisms from other scholars in the field who do not place the same value on recovered or poststructural analysis. Within the academy, such views may be held by more senior colleagues who act as gatekeepers to journals, presses, and career advancement for younger scholars. This can be a very threatening situation, especially to women and scholars of color. However, the work is worthwhile. These intriguing findings were only brought to light because I and many of my like-minded colleagues are asking questions that produce different knowledge and produce knowledge differently.

Notes

1   Each element of the history of higher education depicted in this section has a corresponding literature; a complete bibliography of such would be extensive. However, the most widely read single-volume history is Rudolph (1962), but it is now quite dated. A worthy replacement to Rudolph is Thelin (2004). Both of these volumes cover all elements of this history in varying depth. Thelin's bibliographic essay is also quite useful to readers seeking more information.

2   For example, one of the premier professional organizations, the American Historical Association (AHA), was so reluctant to allow the work of women historians on women's topics to be part of the annual conferences, that 20 women historians began the Berkshire Conference of Women's Historians in 1930. The "Big Berks," as it is known, still meets every three years.

3   This literature is extensive, but what follow are examples of book-length works in each "genre." Institutional histories: Horowitz (1984), Kaufman (1991), and Palmieri (1995). Biographies: Antler (1987a), Farnham (1994), and Horowitz (1994). Social attitudes: Antler (1987b), Bronner (1992), Drachman (1993), Frankfort (1977), Gordon (1990), Glazer & Slater (1987), Ihle (1992), Kelley (1979), Lagemann (1979), Lasser (1987), and Rosenberg (1982). Lives of women as students, faculty, or administrators: Bashaw (1999), Clifford (1989), McCandless (1999), Nidiffer & Bashaw (2001), Nidiffer (2000), and Noble (1956).

4   This history has been reconstructed from scattered primary sources for the most part. I first became aware of and curious about CESL from studying the programs of the NAWSA annual conferences that included "College Night" sponsored by M. Carey Thomas of Bryn Mawr and Maud Wood Park representing CESL. Some of the suffrage literature has brief mentions of it, but the only document I found that focused on CESL was a recent dissertation by Marzzacco (2004) which was helpful in some respects, although I had already seen most of her primary sources.

5   Untitled newspaper clipping. NAWSA Papers, Subject file: College Equal Suffrage League, reel 32, LOC.

6   Untitled newspaper clipping. NAWSA Papers, Correspondence, Box 8, reel 5, LOC.

7   Maud Wood Park Address reprinted in "The College Evening" of the Thirty-Eighth Annual Convention of the National American Women's Suffrage Association, held in Baltimore, February 8, 1906. NAWSA Papers, Correspondence, Box 8, reel 5, LOC.

8   Untitled newspaper clipping. NAWSA Papers, Correspondence, Box 8, reel 5, LOC.

9   NAWSA Papers, Correspondence, Box 8, reel 5, LOC.

10   Ibid.

11   M. Carey Thomas to Maud Wood Park, December 11, 1907. Maud Wood Park Papers, Subject file, Container 7: Boston Equal Suffrage League. NAWSA Papers, Correspondence, Box 8, reel 5, LOC.

12   "Constitution of the NCESL." NAWSA Papers, Correspondence, Box 8, reel 5, LOC.

13   "Report, Dec. 7–13, (Inclusive) 1908." Maud Wood Park Papers, Subject file, Container 9: National College Equal Suffrage League, Reports – 1908, 1912. NAWSA Papers, Correspondence, Box 8, reel 5, LOC.

14   In a 1918 report for the Boston CESL, the secretary noted, "This past year they have tried to keep up with their main objective as well as take on War Work. They kept up with the NCESL chapters of Radcliffe, Wellesley, Jackson, and Boston University, but were not able to start chapters in Normal schools." CESL of Boston, 1917–1918 – Report of the Secretary. NAWSA Papers, Correspondence, Box 8, reel 5, LOC.

15   Appended to the official constitution of the NCESL is a list of approximately 100 college and universities that were deemed eligible to house a chapter. No obvious normal, two-year, or historically African American colleges are on the list. "Constitution of the NCESL." NAWSA Papers, Correspondence, Box 8, reel 5, LOC.

16 At Radcliffe, for example, the class reunion notes and alumni survey data of members of the campus CESL were examined for comments on their suffrage activity during and after college. Several mentioned belonging to Massachusetts organizations as well as the Radcliffe chapter. In her book, Harriot Stanton Blatch made occasional comments about Barnard women in the New York organizations. (See Blatch & Lutz, 1940.)

17 The desired membership and who actually agreed to serve on the advisory board was discussed in correspondence between Park and Thomas. See Letter from M. Carey Thomas to MWP, December 11, 1907. Maud Wood Park Papers, Subject file, Container 7: Boston Equal Suffrage League. NAWSA Papers, Correspondence, Box 8, reel 5, LOC.

18 Student publications *Tipyn o'Bob*, *The Lantern*, and the *Bryn Mawr Alumnae Quarterly* and the student newspaper gave evidence of numerous, sometimes almost weekly, events beginning as early as 1908. Bryn Mawr College Library, Special Collections.

19 Letter from M. Carey Thomas to MWP, December 11, 1907. Maud Wood Park Papers, Subject file, Container 7: Boston Equal Suffrage League.

20 For example, the campus suffrage club began in 1915, having been forbidden under President Taylor. In addition, various student publications mention suffrage activity on campus after 1915 and note that earlier, students had to participate in local Poughkeepsie organizations because of the non-existent on-campus options.

21 Private Diaries and Scrapbook of Mary Worthington, Volume X; December 7, 1907. Worthington, Mary Whitall, 1910; 12-H Small Collections, BMC Archives, Bryn Mawr, PA.

22 From a letter dated April 18, 1909. Helen W. King, 1909, MS 0068, Box 1, Folder 2. MHC Alumnae Files, MHC Archives, South Hadley, MA.

23 One objectionable strategy, for example, was for white pro-suffrage speakers to argue that educated white women were surely superior to African American men who already had (at least theoretically) the vote.

24 There is a substantial literature on student activism. For this research, I considered only the analytical works, ignoring first-hand accounts of the era and nostalgic reminiscences. Further, I did not rely on work that focused exclusively on one event (e.g. a retelling of the deaths at Kent State in 1970 or strikes against the Spanish Civil War in the 1930s). Instead I looked for examples of scholarship that took a larger, national or even international view of the whole campus unrest phenomenon. Three extensively researched and referenced book-length texts were particularly helpful: Horowitz (1987); DeGroot (1998); and Boren (2001). Scholarly interest was exemplified especially by two sociologists, Seymour Martin Lipset and David Riesman, who wrote on the issue of student unrest, and to a lesser degree, the problems of higher education that catalyzed the students' protests. Their work on higher education of the 1960s includes: Lipset & Altbach (1967) (including chapters on student unrest in several countries of Europe, Asia, and Africa); Lipset (1967); Lipset (1969); Lipset & Schaflander (1971) (Part I of this work was republished by Transaction Publishers in 1993 with the title, *Rebellion in the University*); Lipset & Ladd (1972); Jencks & Riesman (1968); and Lipset & Riesman (1975). Some of these works discuss the nature of the protests of the 1930s, but the most complete work on this topic is Robert Cohen (1993), *When the old Left was young*, which describes the protests of the 1930s as a mass movement. A breakdown of the nature of issues protested, the percentages of students involved, and the demographic characteristics of the protesters is found in Van Dyke (1998).

25 See notes 1 and 2 in this chapter for a listing of the literature consulted.

26 Proving the "negative" as is the case here is quite difficult. However, institutional histories and biographies of several university leaders of the era hardly mention suffrage. Even presidents known to have spoken on a wide variety of national topics left little on suffrage. Harvard University President, Charles Eliot, was a popular and sought-after speaker and his voluminous records include one letter indicating that he was generally opposed to suffrage, but did not care to speak on it. University of Wisconsin President, Charles Van Hise, was not antagonistic to suffrage, but was known to think that the chief beneficiaries were the women themselves, and not the country as a whole, and spoke little in public on the topic. Even the few who did speak on suffrage, a quick glance at their papers in their respective archives reveals that suffrage merited much less attention than other social and political issues of the day.

References

Antler, J. (1987a). *Lucy Sprague Mitchell: The making of a modern woman.* New Haven, CT: Yale University Press.

Antler, J. (1987b). *The educated woman and professionalization.* New York: Garland Publishing.

Baker, J. H. (Ed.) (2002). *Votes for women: The struggle for suffrage revisited.* New York: Oxford University Press.

Barrow, C. W. (1990). *Universities and the capitalist state: Corporate liberalism and the reconstruction of American higher education, 1894–1928.* Madison, WI: University of Wisconsin Press.

Bashaw, C. T. (1999). *"Stalwart Women": A historical analysis of deans of women in the South.* New York: Teachers College Press.

Blatch, H. S. & Lutz, A. (1940). *Challenging years: The memoirs of Harriot Stanton Blatch.* New York: G.P. Putnam's Sons.

Boren, M. E. (2001). *Student resistance: A history of the unruly subject.* New York: Routledge.

Brint, S. & Karabel, J. (1989). *The diverted dream: Community colleges and the promise of educational opportunity in America, 1900–1985.* New York: Oxford University Press.

Bronner, T. N. (1992). *To the ends of the Earth: Women's search for education in medicine.* Cambridge, MA: Harvard University Press.

Clifford, G. J. (Ed.) (1989). *Lone voyagers: Academic women in coeducational institutions, 1870–1937.* New York: The Feminist Press.

Cohen, R. (1993). *When the old left was young: Student radicals and America's first mass student movement, 1929–1941.* New York: Oxford University Press.

Cornell, R. E. (1969). Youthful radicalism and the formation of Communist youth organizations: A historical precedent. In S. M. Lipset & P. G. Altbach (Eds.), *Students in Revolt* (pp. 475–494). Boston, MA: Houghton Mifflin Company.

Curti, M. & Carstensen, V. (1949). *The University of Wisconsin: A history, 1848–1925* (Vols. 1–2). Madison, WI: University of Wisconsin Press.

DeGroot, G. J. (Ed.) (1998). *Student protest: The sixties and after.* London: Longman.

Drachman, V. G. (1993). *Women lawyers and the origins of professional identity in America.* Ann Arbor, MI: University of Michigan Press.

Drewry, H. N. & Doermann, H. (2001). *Stand and prosper: Private Black colleges and their students.* Princeton, NJ: Princeton University Press.

Eisenmann, L. (1996). Women, higher education, and professionalism: Clarifying the view. *Harvard Educational Review, 66*(4), 858.

Evans, S. Y. (2007). *Black women in the ivory tower, 1850–1954: An intellectual history.* Gainesville, FL: University of Florida Press.

Farnham, C. A. (1994). *The education of the Southern belle.* New York: New York University Press.

Feuer, L. S. (1969). *The conflict of generations: The character and significance of student movements.* New York: Basic Books.

Flexner, E. (1959). *Century of struggle: The woman's rights movement in the United States.* Cambridge, MA: Harvard University Press.

Frankfort, R. (1977). *Collegiate women: Domesticity and career in turn-of-the-century America.* New York: New York University Press.

Gerda, J. J. (2004). *A history of the conferences of deans of women, 1903–1922.* Unpublished doctoral dissertation, Bowling Green State University, Ohio.

Gillmore, I. H. (1977). *The story of Alice Paul and the National Woman's Party.* Fairfax, VA: Denlinger's Publishers.

Glazer, P. M. & Slater, M. (1987). *Unequal colleagues: The entrance of women into the professions, 1890–1940.* New Brunswick, NJ: Rutgers University Press.

Gordon, A. D. (Ed.). (1997). *African American women and the vote, 1837–1965.* Amherst, MA: University of Massachusetts Press.

Gordon, L. D. (1990). *Gender and higher education in the progressive era.* New Haven, CT: Yale University Press.

Horowitz, H. L. (1984). *Alma Mater: Design and experience in the women's colleges from their nineteenth-century beginnings to the 1930s.* New York: Knopf.

Horowitz, H. L. (1987). *Campus life: Undergraduate cultures from the end of the eighteenth century to the present.* Chicago, IL: University of Chicago Press.

Horowitz, H. L. (1994). *The power and passion of M. Carey Thomas.* New York: Alfred A. Knopf.

Ihle, E. L. (Ed.). (1992). *Black women in higher education: An anthology of essays, studies and documents.* New York: Garland Publishing.

Jencks, C. & Riesman, D. (1968). *The academic revolution.* Garden City, NY: Doubleday.

Johnson, J. A. (1998). Student activism in the United States before 1960: An overview. In G J. DeGroot (Ed.), *Student protest: The sixties and after* (pp. 12–26). London: Longman.

Kaufman, P. W. (Ed.). (1991). *The search for equity: Women at Brown University, 1891–1991.* Hanover: Brown University Press.

Kelley, M. (Ed.). (1979). *Woman's being, woman's place: Female identity and vocation in American history.* Boston, MA: Hall.

Knupfer, A. M. (1996). *Toward a tenderer humanity and nobler womanhood: African American women's clubs in turn-of-the-century Chicago.* New York: New York University Press.

Kraditor, A. S. (1981). *The ideas of the woman suffrage movement, 1890–1920.* New York: W. W. Norton & Co.

Lagemann, E. C. (1979). *A generation of women: Education in the lives of progressive reformers.* Cambridge, MA: Harvard University Press.

Lasser, C. (Ed.). (1987). *Educating men and women together: Coeducation in a changing world.* Urbana, IL: University of Illinois Press.

Lipset, S. M. (1969). *American student activism in comparative perspective.* Washington, DC: U.S. Department of Labor, Manpower Administration.

Lipset, S. M. (Ed.). (1967). *Student politics.* New York: Basic Books.

Lipset, S. M. & Altbach, P. G. (Eds.). (1967). *Students in revolt.* Boston, MA: Houghton Mifflin Company.

Lipset, S. M. & Ladd, E. C. Jr. (1972). *Contours of academic politics.* Washington, DC: American Enterprise Institute.

Lipset, S. M. & Riesman, D. (1975). *Education and politics at Harvard: Two essays prepared for the Carnegie Commission on Higher Education.* New York: McGraw-Hill.

Lipset, S. M. & Schaflander, G. M. (1971). *Passion and politics: Student activism in America.* Boston, MA: Little Brown.

Lumsden, L. J. (2004). *Inez: The life and times of Inez Milholland.* Bloomington, IN: Indiana University Press.

Marsden, G. M. (1994). *The soul of the American university: From Protestant establishment to established nonbelief.* New York: Oxford University Press.

Marsden, G. M. & Longfield, B. J. (Eds.). (1992). *The secularization of the academy.* New York: Oxford University Press.

Marzzacco, P. (2004). *"The Obligation of Opportunity": Maud Wood Park, the College Equal Suffrage League and the response of women students in Massachusetts colleges, 1900–1920.* Unpublished doctoral dissertation, Harvard University.

McCandless, A. T. (1999). *The past in the present: Women's higher education in the twentieth-century South.* Tuscaloosa, AL: University of Alabama Press.

Nidiffer, J. (2000). *Pioneering deans of women: More than wise and pious matrons.* New York: Teachers College Press.

Nidiffer, J. & Bashaw, C. T. (Eds.). (2001). *Women administrators in higher education: Historical and contemporary perspectives.* Albany, NY: SUNY Press,

Nidiffer, J. & Bouman, J. P. (2004). "The University of the Poor": The University of Michigan's transition from admitting impoverished students to studying poverty, 1870–1910. *American Educational Research Journal,* 41(1), Spring, 35–67.

Noble, J. L. (1956). *The Negro woman's college education.* New York: Bureau of Publications, Teachers College, Columbia University.

Ogren, C. A. (2005). *The American state normal school: "An Instrument of Great Good."* New York: Palgrave.

Palmieri, P. A. (1995). *In Adamless Eden: The community of women faculty at Wellesley.* New Haven, CT: Yale University Press.

Paul, A. (1976). *Conversations with Alice Paul: Woman suffrage and the equal rights amendment.* An interview conducted by Amelia R. Fry. Berkeley, CA: Regional Oral History Office, The Bancroft Library.

Rosenberg, R. (1982). *Beyond separate spheres: The intellectual roots of modern feminism.* New Haven, CT: Yale University Press,

Rossiter, M. W. (1982). *Women scientists in America: Struggles and strategies to 1940.* Baltimore, MD: The Johns Hopkins University Press.

Rudolph, F. (1962). *The American college and university: A history*. New York: Vintage Books.

Scott, A. F. & Scott, A. M. (1982). *One half the people: The fight for woman suffrage*. Urbana, IL: University of Illinois Press.

St. Pierre, E. A. & Pillow, W. A. (2000). *Working the ruins: Feminist poststructural theory and methods in education*. New York: Routledge.

Steffens, L. (1909). Sending a state to college. *American Magazine*, 67 (February), 362.

Stevens, D. (1976). *Jailed for freedom: The story of the militant American suffragist movement*. New York: Schocken Books.

Terborg-Penn, R. (1998). *African American women in the struggle for the vote, 1850–1920*. Bloomington, IN: Indiana University Press.

Thelin, J. R. (2004). *A history of American higher education*. Baltimore, MD: Johns Hopkins Press.

Townsend, K. (1996). *Manhood at Harvard: William James and others*. New York: W.W. Norton.

Van Dyke, N. (1998). The location of student protest: Patterns of activism in American universities in the 1960s. In G J. DeGroot (Ed.), *Student protest: The sixties and after* (pp. 27–36). London: Longman.

4

Purposes of Higher Education and Visions of the Nation in the Writings of the Department of Education

TATIANA SUSPITSYNA

The recent trends of politicization of university governance, privatization, and restructuring, along with the increasing tension between institutional autonomy and public calls for accountability, have led scholars to question the nascent purposes of higher education (Tierney, 2006).[1] Indeed, to what extent are universities capable of producing public goods such as preparing citizens for democracy and educating the workforce for a robust economy? How strong should universities' emphasis be on higher education as a private good, namely, as a personal advantage in the competition for better employment opportunities and upward social mobility? Far from trivial, the teleological question of higher education strikes at the core of universities' *raison d'être* and exposes multiple philosophies that underlie that enterprise. More importantly, when endorsed by authorities, the purposes of higher education create scripts of what post-secondary institutions and an educated nation should be. In other words, they *prescribe certain higher education policy and certain visions of college-educated nationhood. To analyze these scripts is therefore to uncover what Foucault (1972) called "regimes of truth" and their operation in the construction of American higher education and citizenship.

To uncover silenced narratives and examine endorsed visions of higher education goals and college-educated America is the central intent of this chapter, which is based on a discourse analysis of speeches penned by arguably the highest official authority on education policy making in the U.S., the Department of Education. While much has been written about the impact of governmental policies on colleges and universities (e.g., Bastedo & Gumport, 2003; Heller, 2003; McLendon, 2003; Slaughter & Rhoades, 2004) and changes in higher education goals and mission (e.g., Allen, 1988; Checkoway, 2001; Gumport, 2000; Scott, 2006; Zemsky et al., 2005), critical evaluations of the official rhetoric and its implications for practice and policy in higher education are still few (e.g., Shaw & Rab, 2003) and often based on the non-U.S. context (e.g., Davies & Bansel, 2007; Grundy, 1994; Nairn & Higgins, 2007). This study begins to fill this gap by interrogating the federally sanctioned and propagated discourses and exploring their philosophical and political implications for education policy makers in general, and women in particular. With an eye on gendered aspects of the official rhetoric, I seek to answer three interrelated questions: What is the purpose of higher education? Who are the stakeholders in higher education? And, what is the desired and desirable vision of the United States as an educated nation? Conceptually and methodologically, my investigation continues the poststructuralist tradition of discourse analysis in education exemplified by the works of Cherryholmes (1993), Lather (1991), Popkewitz (2000), and others, and draws on feminist critical policy analysis in higher education developed, among others, by Bensimon and Marshall (1997, 2003), Glazer-Raymo (1999), Shaw (1997, 2004), Shaw and Rab (2003), and Stromquist (1993, 1998).

The chapter is presented in three parts. It begins with an outline of the poststructuralist theoretical framework of the study. It then offers an overview of the analytical methods and present findings. It concludes with a broader discussion of the findings in the philosophical and political context of higher education and examines the gendered implications of the officially endorsed visions of higher education and the nation.

Discourse, Power, and the Neoliberal Subject

The theoretical framework of this study is based largely on the works of Michel Foucault and his feminist followers and critics (e.g., Davies et al., 2006; St. Pierre, 2000; Weedon, 1997). Central to my method and discussion are Foucauldian interpretations of discourse, power, and the subject, which I outline in some detail below. I also draw on more recent poststructuralist analyses of neo-liberalism in general and the neoliberal subject in particular.

Foucault saw discourse as a particular way of structuring areas of knowledge, which is embedded in and contributes to relations of power. His famous analysis of madness (Foucault, 1988), for example, showed how medical discourse took over other kinds of knowledge about madness, came to dominate the modern definition of it, and now serves an array of institutions (e.g., health insurance companies, hospitals, criminal courts, etc.) by establishing the standard of normalcy and measuring individuals against it. Thus, to Foucault, discourse is social practice that creates both objects of knowledge (e.g., the concept of madness) and social subjects (e.g., mentally ill people).

To say that in this case discourse is vested with power is not enough, because discourse is also a vehicle through which power is exercised. Conceptualized as management and control of populations, power is intimately connected with knowledge (Foucault, 1990). Institutions of power such as the state, the penal system, and the legislature rely on sciences to examine, measure, explain, and predict populations in order to create knowledge that would make the practice of power more efficient. Examining and measuring someone in the process of generating this knowledge is in itself a way of exercising force over the subject and it constitutes what Foucault (1995) termed 'disciplining' technology of power. Insidious and pervasive of all aspects of life, power to Foucault (1990) is productive rather than domineering, in the sense that it turns individuals into subjects of various discourses by prescribing norms, dispositions, positions, and behaviors that will enable them to function in different areas of society and maintain the existing power structures.

Foucault's analysis of the relationship between power and discursive practices—practices of production and dissemination of discourses—is of grave relevance to this study because of the role that education systems play in producing, inculcating, and disseminating knowledge and with it, power. As Foucault himself put it, "any system of education is a political way of maintaining or modifying the appropriation of discourses, along with the knowledges and powers which they carry" (cited in Fairclough, 2006, p. 51). From a narrower viewpoint, appropriation of discourses on education is also a political practice aimed at claiming power, for discourse "is not simply that which translates struggles or systems of domination, but is the thing for which and by which there is struggle, discourse is the power which is to be seized" (cited in Fairclough, 2006, p. 51).

The issue of power in poststructuralist theory is inextricably linked to the problem of the subject. Since the Foucauldian subject is constructed by discourses and power, it can no longer be viewed as self-sufficient and independent in thought and action as a humanist notion of the subject would have it. As discussed in Chapter 2 of this volume, destabilization and opening of the subject by poststructuralists elicited mixed reactions on the part of feminists and scholars of race. Some (e.g., Christian, 1988; Joyce, 1987) justly pointed at the politically harmful effect of analytical indifference to the voice of the subject (Foucault [1984] famously asked, "What difference does it make who's speaking?") that occurred with the collapse of grand narratives and the death of the author at the time when women and minorities had just begun to get their voices heard. Others were concerned that defining subjects as products of discourses strips away their subjectivity and their moral and political will to act (e.g., Alcoff, 1988; Hartsock, 1989, 1990).

Yet, other scholars (e.g., Allen, 2000; Davies et al., 2006; St. Pierre, 2000; Weedon, 1997) saw the opening of the subject ripe with possibilities of discursive change. As St. Pierre (2000) observes, the poststructuralist notion of subjectivity implies both agency and subjugation because it consists of "a subject that exhibits agency as it constructs itself by taking up available discourses and cultural practices and a subject that, at the same time, is subjected, forced into subjectivity by those same very discourses and practices" (p. 502). This reading of subjectivity is consistent with Foucault's view of power relations as unstable and reversible and with his conceptualization of resistance as constitutive of power; for, as he explained, "in power relations there is necessarily the possibility of resistance because if there were no possibility of resistance (of violent resistance, flight, deception, strategies capable of reversing the situation), there would be no power relations at all" (cited in St. Pierre, 2000, p. 490).

It is with this position that I align myself in this chapter, assuming the possibility of resistance and agency on the part of the subject. The discursive nature of the subject and agency has profound consequences for the project of social change for which I ultimately wish to make an argument. Instead of a global program of transformation that is universally true and just for all, as a humanist vision would intend it, there are multiple struggles specific to different discourses, and areas of life (Sawicki, 1991) and education is one of them. These struggles against dominating discourses on education have to involve a critical interrogation of historically structured sets of norms, categories, and truths that serve to endorse certain voices and silence others: the interrogation that Foucault (1995) developed into a method and termed "genealogy." Following Foucault, I attempt a small-scale genealogical analysis of certain truth claims and strategies that serve to legitimize the position of the speaker. Such an analysis involves an examination of the taken-for-granted value of education to demonstrate how interpretations of that value, far from being politically neutral, are tied to specific interests and economic philosophies, and how those in power (in this case the U.S. Department of Education) promote their particular, neoliberal interpretation as a most rational and commonsense meaning of education. I am specifically interested in the speakers' use of rationality and scientific discourses to justify their political agendas and construct the neoliberal subject. Thus, the goal of this genealogical analysis is not to uncover the origins of the contemporary meanings of education, but to implicate these meanings in past and present relations of power.

The rise of the neoliberal subject is associated with neoliberal market discourses promoted by the economic policies of Reagan and Thatcher in the 1970s. Scholars point at the hybrid nature of the neoliberal subject: it shares flexibility with its poststructuralist counterpart and at the same time owes its emphasis on rationality, autonomy, freedom, and choice to the humanist tradition in social and political theory (Davies et al., 2006). Unlike its humanist predecessor, however, the neoliberal subject redefines the fundamental concepts of freedom, choice, autonomy, and rationality in market terms. While in contemporary discourses choice is seen as an exercise in freedom and participation in democracy, freedom of choice is an exercise in economic rationality that the subject must possess in order to select best-value goods and services at the optimal price (Bansel, 2007). Autonomy is recast as heightened individualism aimed at survival and success in the economy; the survival and success of the subject are themselves linked to larger discourses of national economic competitiveness (Davies et al., 2006; Davies & Bansel, 2005). Rationality is redefined by discourses of knowledge and cultural economy as achieving economic success through education or achieving economic success through cultivating and applying entrepreneurial qualities (Nairn & Higgins, 2007). Thus, freedom is achieved through choice in consumption, rationality is a way to acquire labor market power, and autonomy is a prerequisite of competitiveness.

This conceptualization of the neoliberal subject poses questions about the nature of society, democracy, and education where this subject exercises its agency. As scholars have pointed out, the more natural and inevitable neo-liberalism seems, the more difficult these questions become to answer (Davies & Bansel, 2007). One way to make neoliberal discourses problematic is to excavate the social in the neoliberal subject defined exclusively through the economic. In this study, I examine the tension between the social and the economic as the struggle between two discourses: the silenced discourse of social justice and the dominant discourse of national economic competitiveness.

Data Analysis and Findings

Fairclough (2006) observes that methodologically, Foucault's approach to discourse analysis is not particularly useful, in that it requires large-scale histori-cal investigations in the political, economic, and social contexts surrounding discursive practices. Fairclough offers his own version of Foucauldian analysis, which he calls "textually oriented discourse analysis" (TODA), which, in broad terms, consists of an analysis of linguistic means of expressing power relations embedded in the spoken or written text. Developed outside of feminism, TODA was not designed with a specific aim of studying women. As a poststructuralist analytical method, however, it shares fundamental views on discourse and power with feminist poststructuralism and can be easily adapted to feminist agendas by placing women at the forefront of inquiry. In this study I follow Fairclough's (2006) method and examine how lexical and stylistic means are used to promote particular discourses and ideas. Procedurally, as suggested by Fairclough, and by Gill (2006), my data analysis consists of several operations: namely, coding of the text, identification of critical samples for discourse analysis, and the textually oriented discourse analysis of the chosen samples, which I discuss below.

The selection of the documents preserved the rhetorical continuity of the speeches: they cover the entire period from January 2005 when Margaret Spellings assumed the position of the Secretary of the U.S. Department of Education until September 2007 when I started data analysis. Most of the speeches (144 in total) posted on the Department of Education website during this time were delivered, if not authored, by Spellings. The remaining docu-ments (16) posted under the same Speeches tab represent congressional testimonies of her Assistant Secretaries, Deputy Secretary, and Deputy Chief of Staff. Included in this number is one speech delivered by Spellings's predecessor Secretary Paige, and one delivered by President George W. Bush.

The total of 160 documents was downloaded from the U.S. Department of Education website and imported in the NVivo qualitative analysis software. The narratives were examined for themes and coded. The first round of open coding revealed that the most frequently occurring themes in the speeches were accountability and transparency (68) and efficiency of K-12 education (63), measurement and testing (52), and high school graduates' lack of competitiveness and preparation for the workforce and college (52). Not surprisingly, these themes arose mostly in the context of the No Child Left Behind (NCLB) legislature that Secretary Spellings promoted in her official capacity. In the narratives, they served to provide rationale for NCLB (schools need to be held accountable and efficient), set new goals for schools (to prepare high school graduates for a competitive workforce), and describe methods for reaching them (by measuring and testing student achievement). The theme of accountability and transparency also surfaced in the discussions of higher education, where it was rhetorically linked with access (24) and affordability (23) of college education. Another theme that was featured prominently in the speeches was that of the American Dream (34), which was defined as quality education in general (11), college education in particular (18), or economic success gained through education (5).

The second round of coding focused specifically on themes pertinent to the research questions of the study: the U.S. as an educated nation and the purposes of higher education. The codes were refined and examined for logical relationships and interconnections. Six broad themes were identified as a result: U.S. economic prosperity and global competitiveness as a function of a strong education system (39), the colleges' and universities' responsiveness to the market (19), college graduates' competitiveness in the global market (14), higher education as commodity and investment (21), colleges and universities as testing grounds (7), higher education as pathways to democracy (7), and higher education as pathways to civic engagement in the community (4). The themes of accountability, access, affordability, higher education as a commodity and the codes related to the U.S. and student competitiveness were most interconnected: they overlapped and most often followed one another, assembled by the speakers in rationalized models such as the one used to explain the need for NCLB shown above.

I then proceeded to analyze the coded excerpts in an attempt to trace the genealogy of their themes and describe their power valence within discourses present in the texts. Some themes were evidently subordinated to others. The high frequency of the occurrence of the codes and words "accountability," "transparency," "efficiency," and "measurement and testing" resulted in what Fairclough (2006) calls "overwording." Far from being a stylistic shortcoming, overwording signals intense preoccupation and refers to a particular ideology (Fairclough, 2006, p. 193). In the case of the Department of Education speeches, overwording invoked the ideology of rationality and revealed a preoccupation with the idea of education as a business enterprise that should be governed by the norms of efficiency and accountability. Permeating the texts, the ideology of rationality and rational choice established the primacy of the market discourse over civic, familial, and other discourses on which the speakers drew in their speeches.

Although rationality has been a key feature of administrative bureaucracy in modern times (Weber, 1996/1922), it carries new meanings in postmodern neoliberal contexts. Weber saw rationalization as a key sociocultural process of capitalism and differentiated between four types of rationality: formal, based on calculability, efficiency, and predictability of organizational action; substantive, involving systematic use of values in the actions of the participants and organizations; practical, reflecting individual self-interests; and theoretical, grounded in abstract observation of reality (Kalberg, 1980). It is the first, formal rationality that Weber believed dominated capitalist organizations and stifled other forms of rationality. With its strict hierarchy, discipline, and well-defined rules of conduct, a modern office or a bureaucracy was the epitome of formal rationality oriented toward achieving maximum outputs and reducing organizational uncertainty. With time, however, bureaucracy and its norms of conformity and obedience to authority grew antithetical to free enterprise and innovation, and by the 1970s, rationality got infused with an independent individualist spirit (Nairn & Higgins, 2007). Thus, in contrast to Weber's formal rationality and with some semblance of his practical rationality, neoliberal rationality in the postmodern era describes and legitimizes the entrepreneurial individual who is governed by his/her own economic interest and who actively seeks to maximize his/her profit. This figure of the rational stakeholder occupies a prominent place in the Department of Education speeches and is illustrated in Sample 2 in this chapter.

The following speech samples illustrate the operation of the dominant market discourse in constructing the ideas of higher education purposes, stakeholders, and the American nation. They were selected from other coded excerpts on the basis of three criteria. First, they address the three research questions posed at the beginning of the chapter. Second, each excerpt contains several themes, rather than only one, in order to demonstrate the work of interrelated themes in reinforcing the dominant discourse. Finally, each selected fragment exemplifies a clash or tension between multiple discourses used by the speaker and demonstrates how they are subjugated and subverted by the dominant discourse. This last criterion—combination of discourses and their interaction—describes interdiscursivity. In short, the criteria ensure that the samples can elucidate the process and results of the federally endorsed discursive construction of higher education and the nation.

The first sample is a fragment of Secretary Spellings's speech delivered at the National Postsecondary Education Cooperative Symposium on Student Success in November 2006. In the excerpt, she addresses the audience to offer her vision of goals and purposes of higher education in the current fast-paced and changing environment.

Sample 1

[1] Thanks to people like you, higher education has long been one of the undeniable strengths of our nation. In quality, diversity, and character, it's the envy of the world. American universities have been the incubators of great ideas, the birthplaces of great inventions, and the testing grounds of great individuals—all thanks to their great tradition of questioning long-held assumptions, testing new theories, and refining newer and better ways of getting the job done.

[2] The rigorous inquiry and analysis that have defined the academy for generations are now more important than ever. As Harvard's Interim President Derek Bok told you yesterday, "College students are . . . competing for the first time with very bright, ambitious people all over the world who are . . . anxious to get their share of the largest and most successful economy in the world."

[3] To succeed in our ever-changing, ever-flattening world, students need critical thinking and problem-solving skills—the kind that our higher education system has always excelled at providing. At the same time, we're counting on institutions like yours to adapt and grow to serve more students of every age and background . . . because it's not just the world that's changing; our nation is changing, too. And we must ensure that higher education is keeping pace.

[4] Nearly two-thirds of all high-growth, high-wage jobs created in the next decade will require a college degree; a degree only one-third of Americans have. Unlike when I was growing up, you now need a high school diploma and a couple of years of college to succeed as a mechanic or plumber or electrician. (November 2, 2006)

The excerpt contains several themes: colleges and universities as testing grounds, college graduates' competitiveness in the global market, and colleges' and universities' responsiveness to the market. It draws on several discourses. With its vocabulary suggesting creative ideation and experimentation, the first paragraph (marked 1 in the sample) appears to owe its origin to discourses on civic education and democracy. The speaker, however, never states that innovation and testing relate to the political public sphere, which would be consistent with the meaning of democracy as a public space for contesting ideas (see, for example, Pusser's (2006) discussion on universities as public spheres). The ending of the paragraph neither negates nor confirms this presumption: the word "job" in "getting the job done" may mean both work and task, and as such belongs to a variety of both economic and non-economic discourses.

The second paragraph opens with a piece of academic discourse ("rigorous inquiry and analysis") followed by a quote by Derek Bok, the former president of Harvard University and an authority on higher education. The quote, however, immediately draws on the market discourse of economic competition. The beginning of the third paragraph parallels the opening of the second: the speaker again invokes the academic discourse ("critical thinking and problem-solving skills") and then asks colleges and universities to adapt to the changing environment. Although the academic discourse and the market discourse compete for domination of meaning making in these paragraphs, it is not yet clear whether the speech should be interpreted through the academic or economic prism. Broadly defined as "the world" and "our nation," the environment is not yet defined in market terms. Similarly, adapting "to serve more students of every age and background" is not formulated as a problem of economy either, and may even suggest a social justice issue.

The fourth paragraph resolves the ambiguity in favor of market connotations. What was vaguely described earlier as an "ever-changing, ever-flattening world" and "our nation" now becomes "global market" and "national economy." The testing grounds of higher education leave their tentative place in the political public sphere suggested by the first paragraph and get situated in the industrial and entrepreneurial private sector. The multiple meanings of education as a public sphere for testing ideas, learning democracy, and promoting social justice, which were invoked in paragraphs 1 and 3, get foreclosed and the economic interpretations of higher education take center stage. The purposes of higher education are then unequivocally understood as adapting to the market, producing competitive economic actors, and creating innovations for business and industry.

The domination of the market discourse as the main (re)source of meaning making in the sample is reinforced through the speaker's imparting rationality to her statements. Throughout the fragment she uses objective modality, i.e., assertions without hedges, adverbs and adjectives suggesting degrees of possibility, or references to her own opinion (e.g., I think, I believe, in my opinion, etc.). Objective modality, as Fairclough (2006) points out, has the ability to universalize partial perspectives. Until the very last sentence where Secretary Spellings remembers her adolescence, her pronouncements appear to be facts rather than her own, albeit federally sanctioned, conjectures. The effect of objectivity is multiplied by her citing statistics, an ultimate source of scientific knowledge, and quoting the well-known authority on education, Derek Bok.

Whereas Sample 1 shows how higher education is discursively constructed as a market entity at the expense of its political and social functions, Sample 2 demonstrates how a chief stakeholder in higher education, the parent, is also defined in economic terms. Sample 2 is a fragment of the speech with which Secretary Spellings addressed business and higher education leaders at a meeting in New York in February 2007. The excerpt illustrates the interconnections between two themes: accountability and higher education as commodity and investment. The excerpt also contains one of the most frequently used similes in the speeches: the comparison between shopping for a car and choosing a college appears at least seven more times between 2006 and 2007. Before making it into Spellings's text, the simile must have been familiar to the public for some time. The *U.S. News & World Report* was known to make parallels between the university and car industry as early as 1994 (Readings, 1996, p. 28).[2]

Sample 2

[1] That brings me to accountability.

[2] In almost every area of our government—and certainly in the corporate world—we expect transparency and accountability in return for our investments. But over the years, we've invested tens of billions of dollars in taxpayer money in higher education and basically just hoped for the best. As a result, we don't have a very good picture of how the system works today and how it could be improved.

[3] We live in the "Information Age." If you want to buy a new car, you go online and compare a full range of models, makes, and pricing options. And when you're done, you'll know everything from how well each car holds its value down to wheel size and number of cup-holders.

[4] The same transparency and ease should be the case when students and families shop for colleges—especially when one year of college can cost more than a car! (February 15, 2007)

The first one-sentence paragraph signals that the utterances that follow will define accountability. The second paragraph indeed explains accountability by defining it exclusively in capitalist terms as financial responsibility to the investor. If in the previous sample the U.S. as a nation is designated as market, here it is the government that behaves as an economic macro-actor that invests large sums of money and expects good returns. The following paragraph introduces the car simile and changes the genre from the official public speech to a colloquial talk and the speaker's subject positions from a government official to an average consumer. This paragraph is rather effective at inducing the listeners to accept the speaker and her message, for once the topic of car shopping is introduced, they are transformed from a passive audience of the official speech into active, though silent, interlocutors who share the speaker's experiences in consuming. This shift is accomplished when the governmental "we" of the first paragraph is extended rhetorically to include the "you" of the listeners via the mediation of the speaker who is both part of the "we" as Secretary of Education and part of the "you" as a consumer. The final fourth paragraph continues to blend the official public and colloquial genres. The exclamatory ending stresses the significance of her previous statements and rhetorically emphasizes their taken-for-granted truthfulness: when both

Secretary Spellings and an average consumer Spellings promote the same message, the message makes good sense.

Presented to various audiences of parents, students, educators, business leaders, and politicians in 2005–2007, the car-shopping simile contains a particular gendered and classed construction of the parent as a stakeholder in education. The parent here is noticeably defined as a consumer and a rational economic subject who seeks the best price for the required car specifications. This parent has also a particular gender and class. Technical knowledge of "full range of models, makes, and pricing options" and details of the wheel size has traditionally been associated with masculinity (Mellstrom, 2002). In this case, it does not matter that women and men are consumers of cars equally. In dominant discourses on technology and gender, it is men who are defined through technology, while women represent nature (Cockburn, 1985; Faulkner, 2000). To appeal in the speech to the listeners' technical knowledge is therefore to invoke the dominant construction of the bearers of that knowledge—men. Furthermore, these men in Secretary Spellings's vision are decidedly middle to upper class: a home computer, home Internet connection, and the fiscal ability to purchase a car are markers of middle socio-economic status.

Although on different occasions, Secretary Spellings refers to other stakeholders in higher education in addition to parents such as legislators, policy makers, academics, and business investors, none of these stakeholders except for parents represent the familial private sphere. As Sample 2 shows, however, the private sphere is not impervious to the influence of dominant market discourses. Good parenthood is defined as good consumerism. Good parents are rational economic actors who do a cost and benefit analysis before purchasing their child's education. Rationality then crosses the boundary of the public sphere and pervades behavioral norms of familial relationship. Thus, higher education stakeholders are first and foremost consumers, irrespective of their location in the public or private sphere of society.

Whereas Samples 1 and 2 contained references to the American nation as a market space and an economic macro-actor, Sample 3 illustrates how the political and social identity of the nation is subsumed under its economic power. The political and social are effectively cancelled and reinterpreted as a facet of the economic life. Sample 3 represents the opening remarks of Secretary Spellings's speech delivered in June, 2007 at a regional higher education summit.

Sample 3

[1] Our country's investment in higher education has yielded a tremendous return. Our colleges and universities have given generations of citizens the ability to pursue the American Dream and have long been the envy of the world.

[2] But recent data shows we're in danger of losing that position.

[3] By 2012, we will have 3 million more jobs requiring a bachelor's degree within ten years—and when we disaggregate the data, it's much worse.

[4] By age 24, 75 percent of students from the top-income bracket have earned a degree.

[5] At the same age, less than 9 percent of low-income students have earned one. Nine percent!

[6] Our competitive economy is making new and greater demands. Ninety percent of the fastest-growing jobs require post-secondary education or training. Sixty percent of Americans have no post-secondary credentials at all.

[7] At a time when more Americans need a degree, it's becoming more difficult to get one—particularly for low-income and minority students.

[8] That's why I've made higher education reform a priority. We're all engaged in a robust dialogue. Many stakeholders—states, institutions, Congress—are working pro-actively to address the challenges around access, affordability, and accountability and momentum is building. (June 14, 2007)

The first sentence in the opening paragraph firmly places the speech in a neoliberal market discourse: the United States is cast as a successful capitalist macro-actor that invests profitably; higher education is presented as a business sector of the economy. Although the noun "citizens" in the second sentence is emblematic of discourses on citizenship and democracy, it does little to replace the market discourse established in the first sentence. As a result, citizenship is effectively conflated with consumerism. In the light of the market imagery of the opening remark, the meaning of the American Dream is ambiguous and can be understood both as an egalitarian ideal of access to college education and as an individual goal of upward social mobility and economic success.

The following paragraphs unequivocally re-establish the dominance of the market discourse. The audience is presented with statistical data on changing market demands and unsatisfactory college education attainment rates in paragraphs 2 through 6. Remarkably, in Secretary Spellings's narrative, what is typically regarded as a social justice issue—unequal educational opportunities for students of different races, ethnicities, and socio-economic backgrounds—does not warrant any social critique or commentary and is couched exclusively in economic terms. In the logic of this discourse (our competitive economy requires more college degrees, some populations do not have college degrees, therefore, some populations do not meet the needs of our competitive economy), low college admission rates of low-income and minority students are problematic because these students fail to contribute to U.S. competitiveness in the global market. Since the neoliberal capitalist discourse has no space for accounting for historical, social, and political aspects of inequality, they are rendered invisible, and for rhetorical purposes, non-existent. For this reason, the call for greater access in the last sentence is sterile: hijacked from discourses on social justice and democracy, the word "access" becomes an economic designation that forms a seamless triumvirate with affordability and account-ability.

In this discourse, the college-educated nation of the United States is oblivious of its social ills and its legacy of racial and gender inequality. Blind to social justice issues, it also lacks the tools to examine itself critically, as these tools are furnished by the now marginal discourses pushed to the periphery of the neoliberal market discourse.

Discussion

The key findings of this analysis may be summarized in two observations. First, in the official texts, the purposes of higher education are increasingly defined through their enabling of individual social mobility and their contribution to the U.S. economy. Thus, instruction in citizenship and democracy, which has been a central purpose of higher education at least since the American Revolution (Geiger, 1999), is becoming eclipsed by economic considerations. Although genealogically the current narratives of higher education contri-butions to economic advancement in public and private interests are offsprings of several pragmatist, communitarian, and neoliberal philosophical traditions (Kezar, 2004), at present they are absorbed into larger neoliberal market discourses. In the Department of Education writings, state legislators are brokers between post-secondary institutions' goods and the market; students and parents are consumers exercising their power of (rational) choice; colleges and universities are rationalized organizations governed by prescribed rituals of efficiency and rationality in the name of greater outputs.

This vision of higher education is highly problematic from a feminist perspective, for it solidifies institutionalized sexism inherent in the current operation of educational organizations and society at large. Focusing on teach-ing young women autonomy, free choice, and competitiveness, (neo-)liberal education is oblivious to the historic, political, social, and cultural forces that shape women into subjects who will not be able to fully partake of these rights and privileges (Arnot & Dillabough, 1999). Since the social and moral order relies on normative femininity to produce caretakers of children and families, women are constrained by dominant political and economic discourses in their choice of subject positions in the non-familial public sphere (Arnot & Dillabough, 1999). It is the male, then, who is the proper neoliberal subject. The maintenance and perpetuation of neoliberal discourses, however, are dependent on women's uncritical belief in their equal opportunities to exercise that freedom and autonomy. As disseminators and bearers of neoliberal discourses, colleges and universities maintain the illusion that their promise of upward social mobility applies equally to female and male graduates.

The obsessive focus of policy makers on accountability and efficiency has been well documented in the United States (e.g., Tierney, 2006), the United Kingdom (e.g., Morley, 1997), New Zealand (e.g., Nairn & Higgins, 2007), and other post-industrial nations. As the Department of Education speeches demonstrate, the avowed goal of this push toward greater accountability is to make higher education more socially efficient, i.e., to promote the national economy by providing the labor markets with well-trained professionals. Social efficiency, along with citizenship preparation, has been an important public good that higher education has produced for the benefit of all (e.g., see a detailed discussion on the public and private goods of education in Labardee, 1997). Yet, the dominant market discourses allow little room for examining whether this public good is delivered equally to women and men, or to racial/ethnic minorities and whites. When issues of social justice such as unequal access and retention rates are redefined in economic terms as impediments to national competitiveness, and democratic freedom is reinterpreted as the freedom to consume, colleges and universities cease to be public spaces for testing ideas about democratic governance and equality. Indeed, the rationalist epistemology of the drive for efficiency and accountability is deeply suspicious of the "irrational" interference of politics in the management of higher education industry (Morley, 1997).

Second, in the rhetoric of the Department of Education, the nation is discursively constructed as a market space. Endowed with the qualities of competitiveness, robustness, strength, and domination, this construction bears unmistakable markers of heterosexual masculinity. As a masculine macro-actor, the college-educated U.S. seeks to establish global dominance and gain access to other economies—the sexual imagery of penetration here is consistent with larger narratives of global entities conquering local markets (Freeman, 2001).

With their emphasis on economic success and market competition, the officially sanctioned discourses on the purposes of higher education and the nation as a developed global capitalist market create what Sassen (1998) calls "a narrative of eviction" that silences and excludes stories that disrupt their order (p. 82). One of the excluded texts is that of citizenship. Although admittedly, for much of its history, citizenship has been defined by the masculine norm (Coole, 2000; Yuval Davis, 1991), the current centrality of the market and the expulsion of citizenship preparation to the periphery of the official discourse is nevertheless a significant shift. While the gender and racial bias of political citizenship was thoroughly examined by feminist political theorists (e.g., Yuval Davis, 1991), once citizenship was redefined as a right to make the best consumer choice, its bias became less visible behind the ideology of meritocracy and the alleged neutrality of the market. As citizens of this nation market live and succeed in life through economic relations, a fiscal economy pervades their existence and "becomes simultaneously a social and emotional economy" (Bansel, 2007, p. 284). In this model of nationhood, the purpose of post-secondary institutions and higher education policy is to re-enact and reinforce the naturalness of that particular (masculine) version of capitalist subjectivity, which is best exemplified by a middle-class heterosexual paterfamilias shopping for college for his children.

As a source of education policy making legitimized by the chief executive power in the country, the U.S. Department of Education is a producer and transmitter of the dominant discourses on the purposes of higher education and the desired ideal of nationhood that higher education should promote. While feminist poststructuralist (FPS) critique cannot aspire to improve on the existing formulations of higher education policy, which would be an inherently modernist project, it can strategically interrogate the existing discursive relations among college education, market, and citizenship and facilitate a textual opening that would allow new higher education teleology, a different articulation of nationhood, and another vision of the nation. In this possibility to rupture and enable texts lies poststructuralism's analytical and political utility for higher education (Dumont, 1998), since, as a discursive production, policy in higher education does not have ontology of its own and is perpetually a site of contested and negotiated meaning.

It seems to me, therefore, that the current task of poststructuralist feminists is nothing less than ripping holes in the discursive fabric of the propagated visions of higher education and bringing forth new notions of the economic and the political that are inclusive of women and minorities. After all, as Davies and Bansel (2007) point out, the advancement of the neoliberal agenda in education is neither natural, nor inevitable. With its rich repertoire of excavational and deconstructive tools, FPS is well positioned to show why and how market conceptualizations of higher education are injurious to a great number of its participants and the nation as a whole.

Notes

1   I am grateful to Becky Ropers-Huilman, Elizabeth Allan, and Amy Scott Metcalfe for their comments and suggestions on this chapter.
2   I thank Elizabeth Allan for this point.

References

Alcoff, L. (1988). Cultural feminism versus post-structuralism: The identity crisis in feminist theory. *Signs*, 13(3), 405–436.

Allen, A. (2000). The anti-subjective hypothesis: Michel Foucault and the death of the subject. *The Philosophical Forum*, 31(2), 113–130.

Allen, M. (1988). *The goals of universities*. Milton Keynes, UK: Open University Press.

Arnot, M. and Dillabough, J.-A. (1999). Feminist politics and democratic values in education. *Curriculum Inquiry*, 29(2), 159–189.

Bansel, P. (2007). Subjects of choice and lifelong learning. *International Journal of Qualitative Studies in Education*, 20(3), 283–300.

Bastedo, M. and Gumport, P. J. (2003). Access to what? Mission differentiation and academic stratification in U.S. public education. *Higher Education*, 46(3), 341–359.

Bensimon, E. M. and Marshall, C. (1997). Policy analysis for postsecondary education: Feminist and critical perspectives. In C. Marshall (Ed.), *Feminist critical policy analysis: A perspective from postsecondary education* (pp. 1–21). London: Falmer Press.

Bensimon, E. M. and Marshall, C. (2003). Like it or not: Feminist critical policy analysis matters. *The Journal of Higher Education*, 74(3), 337–349.

Checkoway, B. (2001). Renewing the civic mission of American research university. *The Journal of Higher Education*, 72(2), 125–147.

Cherryholmes, C. H. (1993). Reading research. *Journal of Curriculum Studies*, 25(1), 1–32.

Christian, B. (1988). The race for theory. *Feminist Studies*, 14(1), 67–79.

Cockburn, C. (1985). *Machinery of dominance: Women, men, and technical know-how.* London: Pluto.

Coole, D. (2000). Cartographic convulsions: Public and private reconsidered. *Political Theory*, 28(3), 337–354.

Davies, B. and Bansel, P. (2005). The time of their lives? Academic workers in neoliberal time(s). *Health Sociology Review*, 14(1), 47.

Davies, B. and Bansel, P. (2007). Neoliberalism and education. *International Journal of Qualitative Studies in Education*, 20(3), 247–259.

Davies, B., Browne, J., Gannon, S., Hopkins, L., McCann, H., and Wihlborg, M. (2006). Constituting the feminist subject in poststructuralist discourse. *Feminism and Psychology*, 6(1), 87–103.

Dumont, C. (1998). The analytical and political utility of poststructuralism: Considering affirmative action. *Canadian Journal of Sociology*, 23(2/3), 217–237.

Fairclough, N. (2006). *Discourse and social change.* Cambridge, UK: Polity Press.

Faulkner, W. (2000). The power and the pleasure? A research agenda for "making gender stick" to engineers. *Science, Technology, and Human Values*, 25(1), 87–199.

Foucault, M. (1972). *Power/knowledge.* New York: Pantheon.

Foucault, M. (1984). What is an author? In Paul Rabinow (Ed.), *The Foucault reader* (pp. 101–120). New York: Pantheon.

Foucault, M. (1988). *Madness and civilization: A history of insanity in the Age of Reason.* Translated by R. Howard. New York: Vintage Books.

Foucault, M. (1990). *The history of sexuality.* Translated by R. Hurley. New York: Vintage Books.

Foucault, M. (1995). *Discipline and punish: The birth of the prison.* Translated by A. Sheridan. New York: Vintage Books.

Freeman, C. (2001). Is local: Global as feminine: Masculine? Rethinking the gender of globalization. *Signs*, 26(4), 1007–1037.

Geiger, R. (1999). Ten generations of American higher education. In P. G. Altbach, R. O. Berdahl, and P. J. Gumport (Eds.), *American higher education in the twenty first century: Social, political, and economic challenges* (pp. 38–690). Baltimore, MD: Johns Hopkins University Press.

Gill, R. (2006). Discourse analysis. In M. W. Bauer and G. Gaskell (Eds.), *Qualitative researching with text, image and sound: A practical handbook* (pp. 172–190). London: Sage.

Glazer-Raymo, J. (1999). *Shattering the myths: Women in academe.* Baltimore, MD: Johns Hopkins University Press.

Grundy, S. (1994). Which way toward the year 2000? Contrasting policy discourses in two education systems. *Curriculum Inquiry*, 24(3), 327–347.

Gumport, P. J. (2000). Academic restructuring: Organizational change and institutional imperatives. *Higher Education*, 39(1), 67–91.

Hartsock, N. (1989). Postmodernism and political change: Issues for feminist theory. *Cultural Critique*, 14(1), 15–33.

Hartsock, N. (1990). Foucault on power: A theory for women? In L. Nicholson (Ed.), *Feminism/Postmodernism* (pp. 157–176). New York: Routledge.

Heller, D. (Ed.). (2003). *The states and higher education policy: Affordability, access, and accountability.* Baltimore, MD: Johns Hopkins University Press.

Joyce, J. A. (1987). The Black Canon: Reconstructing Black American literary criticism. *New Literary History*, 18, 341–342, 347.

Kalberg, S. (1980). Max Weber's types of rationality: Cornerstones for the analysis of rationalization processes in history. *American Journal of Sociology*, 85, 1145–1179.

Kezar, A. (2004). Obtaining integrity? Reviewing and examining the charter between higher education and society. *The Review of Higher Education*, 27(4), 429–259.

Labaree, D. F. (1997). Public goods, private goods: The American struggle over educational goals. *American Educational Research Journal*, 34(1), 39–81.

Lather, P. (1991). *Getting smart: Feminist research and pedagogy with/in the postmodern.* New York: Routledge.

McLendon, M. K. (2003). Setting the governmental agenda for state decentralization of higher education. *The Journal of Higher Education*, 74(5), 479–515.

Mellstrom, U. (2002). Patriarchal machines and masculine embodiment. *Science, Technology, and Human Values*, 27(4), 460–478.

Morley, L. (1997). Change and equity in higher education. *British Journal of Sociology of Education*, 18(2), 231–242.

Nairn, K. and Higgins, J. (2007). New Zealand's neoliberal generation: Tracing discourses of economic (ir)rationality. *International Journal of Qualitative Studies in Education*, 20(3), 261–281.

Popkewitz, T. S. (2000). The denial of change in educational change: Systems of ideas in the construction of national policy and evaluation. *Educational Researcher*, 29(1), 17–29.

Pusser, B. (2006). Reconsidering higher education and the public good: The role of public spheres. In W. G. Tierney (Ed.), *Governance and the public good* (pp. 1–11). Albany, NY: State University of New York Press.

Readings, B. (1996). *The university in ruins.* Cambridge, MA: Harvard University Press.

Sassen, S. (1998). *Globalization and its discontents.* New York: New Press.

Sawiski, R. (1991). Foucault and feminism: Toward a politics of difference. In M. L. Shanley and C. Pateman (Eds.), *Feminist interpretations and political theory* (pp. 217–231). University Park, PA: The Pennsylvania State University Press.

Scott, J. C. (2006). The mission of the university: Medieval to postmodern transformations. *The Journal of Higher Education*, 77(1), 1–40.

Shaw, K. M. (1997). Remedial education as ideological background: Emerging remedial education policies in the community college. *Educational Evaluation and Policy Analysis*, 19(3), 284–296.

Shaw, K. M. (2004). Using feminist critical policy analysis in the realm of higher education: The case of welfare reform as gendered educational policy. *The Journal of Higher Education*, 75(1), 56–79.

Shaw, K. M. and Rab, S. (2003). Market rhetoric versus reality in policy and practice: The Workforce Investment Act and access to community college education and training. *The Annals of American Academy of Political and Social Sciences*, 586, 172–193.

Slaughter, S. and Rhoades, G. (2004). *Academic capitalism and the new economy: Markets, states, and higher education.* Baltimore, MD: Johns Hopkins University Press.

St. Pierre, E. A. (2000). Poststructuralist feminism in education: An overview. *International Journal of Qualitative Studies in Education*, 13(5), 477–515.

Stromquist, N. P. (1993). Sex-equity legislation in education: The state as promoter of women's rights. *Review of Educational Research*, 63(4), 379–407.

Stromquist, N. (1998). Institutionalization of gender and its impact on educational policy. *Comparative Education*, 34(1), 85–100.

Tierney, W. G. (Ed.). (2006). *Governance and the public good.* Albany, NY: State University of New York Press.

U.S. Department of Education. (November 2, 2006). Secretary Spellings delivered remarks at National Postsecondary Education Cooperative Symposium on Student Success in Washington, D.C. Retrieved April 5, 2009 from http://www.ed.gov/news/pressreleases/2006/11/11022006.html.

U.S. Department of Education. (February 15, 2007). U.S. Secretary of Education Margaret Spellings leads discussion with business and higher education leaders in NYC on importance of engaging businesses in the future of America's students. Retrieved April 5, 2009 from http://www.ed.gov/news/pressreleases/2007/02/02152007.html.

U.S. Department of Education. (June 14, 2007). Secretary Spellings delivers remarks at Boston higher education summit. Retrieved April 5, 2009 from http://www.ed.gov/news/press releases/2007/06/06142007a.html.

Weber, M. (1996/1922). Bureaucracy. In J. M. Shafritz and J. Steven Ott (Eds.), *Classics of organization theory* (4th ed.) (pp. 80–85). Philadelphia, PA: Harcourt Brace.

Weedon, C. (1997). *Feminist practice and poststructuralist theory.* Oxford, UK: Blackwell.

Yuval-Davis, N. (1991). The citizenship debate: Women, ethnic processes and the state. *Feminist Review*, 39(3), 58–68.

Zemsky, R., Wegner, G. R., and Massy, W. F. (2005). *Remaking the American university: Market-smart and mission-centered.* New Brunswick, NJ: Rutgers University Press.

5

The Discursive Framing of Women Leaders in Higher Education

SUZANNE GORDON, SUSAN V. IVERSON,
AND ELIZABETH J. ALLAN

Leadership and institutional policy-making are often linked in the context of higher education; academic leaders are frequently called upon and expected to participate in and/or oversee policy development, implementation, and enforcement at the institutional level. While policy-making is rarely, if ever, a linear and rational process, leaders, both formal and informal, can exert influence in policy processes (Conway, Ahern, & Steuernagel, 2005). It is likely then that the ways in which leadership is commonly understood, and the lenses through which leaders are perceived, may shape policy and its outcomes. This chapter examines discourses constituting prominent images of leadership and considers how these images contribute to shaping perceptions of women leaders in U.S. higher education.

Historically, traditional notions of leadership focused on the "heroic" or "great man" who successfully led regardless of environmental influences through the skilled use of personal attributes, interpersonal abilities, and technical management skills (Birnbaum, 1988; Burns, 1978; Chemers, 1997; Kezar, Carducci, & McGavin-Contreras, 2006). Over the years, these dispositional and behavioral theories and descriptions of the autonomous leader (frequently exhibited in the context of postsecondary education through the positional authority granted the university president) have largely shifted to a social constructivist view of leadership that explains how forces of power, both internal and external to the academy, shape leaders and leadership styles (Baldridge et al., 1977/2000; Bensimon & Neumann, 1993; Berquist, 1992; Birnbaum, 1988; Bolman & Deal, 2003).

The idea of a solo leader directing from atop a hierarchical organization has been challenged by more recent theories of leadership that explore the importance of followers to leadership, leadership as a process, team leadership, variable power influences, culture, and organizational learning, typically framing the leader as a collaborative member of a team with transformative potential (Bensimon & Neumann, 1993; Braga, 2008; Kezar et al., 2006). The communicative, inclusive, relational leader focuses on information-sharing and relationship-building in a decentralized organization (Fullan, 2001; Kezar et al., 2006; Wheatley, 1992).

While contemporary scholarship in higher education tends to advocate for relational (team) models of leadership, and suggests autonomous ("great man") perspectives are no longer dominant (Bensimon, Neumann, & Birnbaum, 1989), images of autonomous approaches to leadership continue to circulate and influence beliefs about leadership (Allan, Gordon, & Iverson, 2006; Eddy & VanDerLinden, 2006; Ford, 2006). The persistence and valorization of these images, despite the critiques of such approaches, raises important questions. For instance, Tierney (1991, p. 20) asks:

> What are the underlying values, forms of discourse, and organizational and social structures that function to preserve the possibility of leadership in some types of leaders (dominant culture males, for instance), and that work to subvert the leadership of others (from marginal cultures)?

With this question as our backdrop, and as an extension of our analysis of leadership discourses (Allan et al., 2006), we sought to identify and analyze discourses taken up to construct images of women and leadership circulating in *The Chronicle of Higher Education*. *The Chronicle*, one of the most widely read U.S. periodicals about higher education, serves as an important vehicle for conveying information and shaping images about postsecondary education. More than 450,000 college and university administrators and faculty members subscribe to *The Chronicle*, and, as such, this weekly publication can be considered a leading source of information for those whose professional lives are invested in higher education.

Drawing on a feminist poststructural (FPS) approach to analyzing discourse, we identified the predominant discourses that shape images of women and leadership in the context of U.S. postsecondary education. The following research questions framed this study: (1) What are the predominant images of women who are described as exhibiting leadership in *The Chronicle of Higher Education*? and (2) What discourses are employed to shape these images?

The Chronicle, like other news media, presents articles and opinion pieces that draw upon many discourses circulating in public and academic arenas. While news is deceptively represented as value-free information, some scholars suggest they are "highly orchestrated ways of understanding social (including gendered) relations that encourage commitment to share a particular interpretation of and ways of seeing the world that are entirely partial and that preserve the male-ordered status quo" (Byerly & Ross, 2006, pp. 39–40). In relation to leadership, we view *The Chronicle* as a medium that carries discourses that contribute to constructing perceptions of leadership; as such, it both reflects particular realities and actively shapes images about women leaders and leadership in higher education.

Findings from our investigation suggest that (taken-for-granted) assumptions about masculinity and femininity are embedded within the descriptions about leadership and produce gendered images of leaders. Men are typically portrayed as autonomous and authoritarian, and in these portrayals, leadership emerged as a set of one-way directive behaviors. This construction is consistent with early social scientists' assertions that leadership qualities were innate, and that certain people were born naturally endowed with leadership greatness traits (Burns, 1978). In contrast, women leaders emerged as more collaborative, relational, and transformational in their approach to leadership (Barton, 2005). Yet, this "woman's approach" was often framed by experts as more risky and atypical; transformational and relational leadership were generally questioned and challenged (Blackmore, 1999; Fletcher, 2002, 2004). The traditional measures of leadership tend to reinforce a culture of sameness, favoring individuals who are socially, intellectually, and ideologically similar (Bensimon, 1995, p. 603). Expectations of leadership combined with assumptions about masculinity and femininity may shape attitudes and behaviors that marginalize women leaders and serve to shape gendered norms for what constitutes a "real" leader (Allan et al., 2006; Ford, 2006).

Theoretical Framework

Discourse

For this research, we draw upon understandings of discourse that align with FPS perspectives largely influenced by the work of French philosopher Michel Foucault (Baxter, 2003; Mills, 1997; Weedon, 1997). Building on this work, we understand discourses in the plural sense to be dynamic constellations of words and images that legitimate and produce a given reality (Allan, 2003). Thus, it is through discourse that we come to interpret the physical and social aspects of the world in which we live and also our sense of self in relation to these realities (Mills, 1997). Since discourses serve as lenses for making sense of the world and ourselves in relation to it, they not only shape thought, but practice as well. Discursive practice, a term that refers to practices produced by/through discourse, is a vital aspect of FPS (Baxter, 2003). In this research, we frame leadership as a type of discursive practice.

Discourses taken up more readily tend to be reaffirmed through their institutionalization, and as a result, other discourses may not appear as obvious or familiar. These dominant discourses can be identified most easily by the way in which they appear to be "natural." The fact that they are just one among many different discourses tends to be overlooked (Coates, 1996). For instance, the dominant discourses of femininity and masculinity provide parameters for acceptable behavior on the part of women and men in a particular context. According to Mills (1997), "these discursive frameworks demarcate the boundaries within which we can negotiate what it means to be gendered" (p. 18). As a result, it comes to be seen as normal or natural for women and men to perform in ways that fall within these discursive boundaries (Allan, 2008).

Importantly, in analyzing the images of women leaders that emerge from writings in *The Chronicle of Higher Education*, we did not accept the language as simply a reflection of the authors' views or the views of those quoted. Rather, when viewed through the conceptual framework of discourse theory, we proceeded from the premise that images in *The Chronicle* are made possible because they draw upon familiar discourses; that is, discourses that are so pervasive they are taken for granted. Thus, whether the leadership image is relayed by the journalist or directly quoted by the academic leader interviewed by the journalist, the images are assembled and drawn from largely the same pool of discursive resources. These seldom-questioned dominant discourses tend to eclipse alternative possibilities for shaping images of women leaders. Shining the spotlight on these images can provide important clues about the discursive shaping of norms and expectations about leadership in higher education. Further, the findings from this study can assist women leaders with understanding and anticipating how their work may be interpreted against the backdrop of dominant discourses.

Feminist Theoretical Perspectives on Gender

A feminist analysis of leadership illuminates how images of leaders may be represented in gendered ways. Since gender norms are so often taken for granted, they are less likely to be scrutinized. Most are not likely to be fully conscious of cultural and social assumptions about gender, since, through socialization, gender norms have been carefully taught and reinforced by family, peers, schools, media, and community (Byerly & Ross, 2006; Carli, 2001; Ridgeway & Correll, 2004). For the purposes of this analysis, a feminist lens exposes how leadership is often defined in masculine terms; how gender stereotypes associate greater status and competence with men than with women; and the leaders who emerge (meaning those who match the prototypical characteristics of leaders) are men (Eagly, 2005; Ridgeway, 2001).

This chapter draws upon feminist perspectives and theories of gender that examine how cultural expectations about femininity and masculinity shape understandings of women and men as gendered selves. Feminist theorists contend that dominant expectations of masculinity and femininity are largely learned and performed, rather than rooted in one's biology (Allan, 2004; Layton, 2004; Lorber, 2004). Thus, gender includes socio-cultural identity markers (e.g., clothing, hairstyles) that signal one's maleness or femaleness. Gender performance is tied to culture and based upon behavioral norms that are somewhat fluid depending on time and place. Thus, even while there are cultural and regional differences in expectations of gendered behavior, dominant discourses and consequent constructions of gender suggest a universality of maleness and femaleness (Lazar, 2005), the framings of which are central to this analysis. At the same time, we align our thinking with scholars who have illuminated the multiplicity of identity and experiences, shaped not only by one's gender, but also by race, sexuality, class, age, and other identity statuses (Crenshaw, 1991; Kimmel, 2000; Reynolds & Pope, 1991; West & Fenstermaker, 1995).

While gender norms shift over time and across cultures, dominant discourses of gender (in the West and many industrialized societies) suggest distinct conceptions of masculinity and femininity that generally operate as two poles of a gender binary (Bem, 1993; Layton, 2004; Ridgeway & Correll, 2004). Men and women, as boys and girls, learn expectations about gender that tend to position masculine and feminine as polar opposites. In such a schema, being a "real man" requires men to stifle feelings, be strong, competitive, and independent. Conversely, "good girls" learn to be relational, nurturing, dependent, submissive, and passive. Acting in gender-appropriate ways is supported through a variety of cultural reinforcements from the earliest days of childhood through adulthood (e.g., media, toys, clothing). Alternatives to these dominant constructions exist, but quite often, pushing the boundaries around gender can yield negative consequences as those who do not conform to the expectations for their gender are frequently labeled in ways perceived negatively or as deviant. For example, boys learn early that behaving in ways perceived to be feminine will render them a "wimp," "sissy," or "girl" (Kimmel, 2000).

Negative reinforcement for violating gender norms exists for adults as well. For instance, if women leaders are perceived as a bit too aggressive, they risk being called a bitch, whereas men leaders would likely be praised as exhibiting strength and resolve for the same behavior. Conversely, if men leaders display tearful emotions, they risk being framed as weak. Yet, women leaders, too, are often subject to the same scrutiny, especially if their behavior is exhibited within the professional sphere that has long been a largely masculine domain (Rudman & Glick, 2001). If women leaders behave in ways that have been constructed as feminine (e.g., displays of emotion), they risk being questioned for their abilities to endure the stresses of the leadership position (Ridgeway, 2001). McArdle (2008), on her *The Atlantic.com* blog, sums up the challenges for a woman: "Act too commanding, and you're a bossy shrew; stay low-key and you're weak" (para 1).[1]

FPS perspectives, including understandings of the discursive constitution of masculinity and femininity, provide the conceptual backdrop for this analysis of the images of women leaders as portrayed by *The Chronicle of Higher Education* from 2005 to 2006. Leadership theories and their application to the context of higher education provide a framework for interpreting the findings and their implications which we will describe after a brief review of our research methods.

Methods

The sample for this study consisted of 268 items – articles and opinion pieces (editorials and letters to the editor) – published in *The Chronicle of Higher Education* between November 1, 2005 and October 31, 2006 (retrieved November 21, 2006 from http://chronicle.com). These articles were selected from a larger pool of 1,225 items that were retrieved through a computer search function provided by *The Chronicle* using the keyword "lead." Articles with only a superficial reference to leadership were eliminated from the sample. For example, in some articles the word "leadership" appeared only in the title of a person or program. We further refined the sample by selecting articles related to women in U.S. postsecondary education.

We read and analyzed the articles in the dataset drawing upon established methods of coding and categorizing to identify broad themes and predominant images of women and leadership. Beginning with an inductive approach to coding the data, we first worked independently to analyze the predominant images of women leaders that emerged from *The Chronicle* dataset. Codes were then compared and determinations were made about emergent categories and themes relative to the central question of "what are the predominant images of women who are described as exhibiting leadership?" We then reread the data deductively with an agreed-upon set of codes developed from our initial inductive process. Working both independently and collaboratively, this iterative process of coding and categorizing led us to identify the predominant images of women described as exhibiting leadership in *The Chronicle*. From there, we worked in the same way to identify the discourses shaping these images. These images and the discourses supporting them are the focus of our findings.

Findings and Interpretations

Dominant gender discourses of femininity and masculinity, and discourses of professionalism and liberal humanism emerged as prominently contributing to shaping leadership images. Two discursive strands of the dominant discourse of femininity, caregiving and distress, construct images of *caretaker leaders* and *vulnerable leaders*, respectively. The discourse of professionalism gives rise to the image of women leaders as *experts*, and, intersecting with the discourse of femininity, produces an image of women as *relational leaders*. A tension between the discourses of femininity and masculinity produces a dichotomy of compliance/noncompliance with gendered norms and expectations, situating women leaders in a "double bind." Finally, a social justice strand of the liberal humanist discourse constructs the image of a *social justice leader*. We now turn to describing each of these in more detail.

Gendered Discourses

DISCOURSE OF FEMININITY

As described earlier, discursive constructions of gender have real consequences. Dominant gender discourses, including a discourse of femininity, shape images of women as caring, nurturing, relational, collaborative, and supportive. Femininity is also characterized by vulnerability and dependence, compassion and belonging, cooperation and communication. In general, gender theory contends that hegemonic femininity is more passive than active – it is about being an object of desire, to be looked at and to be on display, and to have mastered the skills of psychological, domestic, and sexual service that men expect (Mills, 1992; Ridgeway & Correll, 2004) as the following data excerpt depicts. In this *Chronicle* article, book author Mr. Ramo, delineates several "tidbits" on how to conduct a useful meeting, noting that "a good meeting leader is like a chameleon, adapting his or her skill and expertise to the topics at hand." However, he goes on to differentiate how women leaders would conduct meetings.

> Women entering a meeting must "understand that your male coworkers are likely to see you – if only for a subconscious second – as a sexual object, no matter how hard you try to disguise this." And women pay more attention to attire than men do, the author says. Women who lead meetings should beware, Mr. Ramo says, because they will experience more prejudice from attendees. "The truth is," he writes, "a very attractive woman can upset a meeting" (Strout, 2006).

In addition to being depicted as objects of sexual attention, women leaders are described as supportive, motherly, caring, fearful, threatening, and threatened. These characterizations are made visible through a dominant discourse of femininity, and two of its discursive strands, caregiving and distress, that serve to construct images of women leaders as caretakers and vulnerable, respectively.

THE CARETAKER

Prominent in our findings about the discursive construction of women leaders is the foregrounding of women's identities as caretakers including emblematic descriptions of women as mothers and wives. For example, women leaders are characterized as "working full time and raising children with my husband" (Lujan, 2006) or as "a freckled professor with short hair and a voice that makes history sound like a lullaby" (Ashburn, 2006a); a new university president is described as "a petite grandmother of three" (Fain, 2006b). We contend these characterizations are made visible by a caregiving strand of the dominant discourse of femininity.

Women leaders described in our data testify to the "challenges of combining motherhood and a career" (Sanoff, 2006); however, this is framed as a taken-for-granted reality: if women choose to have husbands and children and a career, then they must be prepared to face "struggles."

> My male colleagues at Stanford had watched me struggle and had graciously accommodated many child-related complications over the previous three years. But while they had compassion, they were at a loss to say what they would do if their wives were sitting in my office chair. My husband, my former boss, and my athletics director encouraged me to ask for exactly what I needed to be successful. But I had already spent hours and hours dissecting these issues, writing plans, conceiving various scenarios, and ultimately failing to construct a cohesive life sturdy enough to withstand the stresses. . . . The team, having watched my pregnancies as one observes the results of a science experiment gone awry, accepted my limits (Evans, 2006).

And, noted in an article about a support network that helps women faculty in science and engineering:

> Some male faculty members in the sciences and engineering still hold negative stereotypes of women. . . . [For instance] a male member of the panel said the [search committee] needed to be cautious about recommending the woman because she had a family. (Sanoff, 2006)

The caretaker dimension of the woman leader's identity, then, is a part of one's self that must be accepted as a limitation. For some, it is a demographic footnote, a gender-blind view wherein an individual just "happened to be female." As asserted in one article, "I was succeeding in spite of my time away – in spite of having had children" (Segal, 2006). These characterizations construct caretaking as a private part of self, a role reserved for the private sphere (with children and husbands), outside of the workplace/academy.

In other instances, aspects of the caretaker identity are described as contributing to competencies in one's professional arena: "[When] the new department chairperson asked me if I could explain how I had become "such a good teacher" . . . I suggested that my having children might have something to do with it" (Segal, 2006). From this perspective, the caretaker identity, evident in characterizations of women leaders as helpful, supportive, and caring, shapes conceptions of women leaders as relational, collaborative, and empowering.

VULNERABLE LEADER

Another strand of the dominant discourse of femininity – vulnerability – contributes to shaping images of women leaders as fearful and threatened (Allan, 2003; Iverson, 2005, 2007). "Fear," "discrimination," "intimidation," "disrespect," "personal attacks," "pressure," and "numerous aggressive threats" are characterizations that produce the image of women leaders as vulnerable.

The following excerpts exemplify this strand:

> The medical dean ... resigned this month after three masked men attacked her husband and poodle, possibly in retaliation for her role in recent job cuts. Valerie M. Parisi, the medical school's first female dean, who also served as the university's chief academic officer, resigned "for personal reasons," effective immediately. (Mangan, Fogg, & Porter, 2006)

> Lynette M. Petruska, who had been the first female chaplain at Gannon University, ... sued the institution after she resigned under pressure, alleging that she had been discriminated against based on her gender. (Van Der Werf, 2006)

> Ms. Denton [chancellor] had begun to fear for her safety. . . . A window in her office was broken last year. And at 3 a.m. one night in June 2005, a parking barricade was used to break her bedroom window. During a campus protest on June 6 over staff wages and faculty diversity, students surrounded Ms. Denton in her car, sat on the trunk and hood, and struck it with placards . . . . "The atmosphere," said Ms. Irwin [university spokeswoman], "was intimidating and disrespectful." (Fain, 2006c)

> Celia May Baldwin, interim chair of the trustees, resigned from the board, citing emotional stress and "numerous aggressive threats". . . . (Bollag, 2006)

> I [professor of physical chemistry and materials science] had a lot of discrimination all the way up. I don't want to get into the war details, but in general: not being let into research groups even though I was one of the top students; being veered off into career directions that were more traditionally female-oriented; sexual advances that were completely unexpected; difficulties when I had my first child. (Richmond, 2006)

Since the dominant discourse of femininity has been so closely tied with womanhood, the vulnerability strand reminds us that all women, even those who hold positions of leadership, are vulnerable to discrimination, threats, and exclusion. If women push the boundaries a bit too much, they may even become victims, as illustrated by the following:

> Elizabeth Hoffman, who resigned under fire last year as president of the University of Colorado System ... is best known for her five years of leadership in Colorado, a time in which a perfect storm of controversies ended up wrecking her presidency. (Glenn & Fogg, 2006)

> Denice D. Denton came under fire immediately and often during her 16-month tenure as chancellor of the University of California at Santa Cruz, which ended with her apparent suicide late last month when she fell to her death from the roof of a San Francisco building. . . . Ironically,

n, 46, an accomplished electrical engineer and champion of
, science who had made diversity in academics a focus of her
,as also harangued recently by student protesters decrying
,ional racism and sexism." (Fain, 2006c)

The ... iage of the vulnerable (woman) leader as it is shaped by a dominant discourse of femininity highlights how professional and personal risks associated with leadership are shaped in gendered ways.

Discursive Tensions

DISCOURSES CONSTRUCT GENDER POLARIZATION
A dominant discourse of masculinity has long characterized ideas about acceptable performance of manhood (Kimmel, 2000; Wang, 2000). The social and behavioral traits that have long been considered "natural" expressions of maleness, but which many contend are socially constructed performances of gender, tend to be in opposition to that which is posited as feminine. Sandra Bem (1993) noted this modernist male/female divide as gender polarization "not only dictates mutually exclusive scripts for males and females ... it also defines any person or behavior that deviates from these scripts as problematic – unnatural, immoral, biologically anomalous, or psychologically pathological" (in Rothenberg, 2006, p. 51). Applied to this analysis of leadership, dominant constructions of gender contribute to the assumption that men are generally more competent than women. As noted by Biernat and Fuegen (2001), "the very essence of gender stereotypes defines men as instrumentally competent and agentic compared to women" (p. 707). Further, as Rudman and Glick (2001) illustrate, when women attempt to convey a competent impression through self-promotion, they are liked and hired less often than male counterparts.

DAMNED IF YOU DO; DOOMED IF YOU DON'T[2]
The discourse of femininity, in tension with the discourse of masculinity, gives rise to what is often referred to as "the double bind"; a situation in which a person cannot win no matter what she does (Appelbaum, Audet, & Miller, 2003; Estler, 1975; Oakley, 2000; Trinidad & Normone, 2005). Jamieson (1995), more specifically, identifies this as the femininity/competence bind, positing that women who are considered feminine will be judged incompetent, and competence is associated with masculinity, thus competent women are perceived as unfeminine. A dominant discourse of femininity reinforces cultural norms about how women "should" behave (Allan, 2003). "Good" women leaders, then, are compliant with these norms, adhering to the organizational rules, guidelines, and policies (Ridgeway & Correll, 2004). As one woman asserts, "I chose to respond as a diplomatic administrator rather than as a passionate feminist" (Chassiakos, 2006). Another "appears determined to choose her battles carefully

and keep a low profile" (Schmidt, 2006). Still another woman is "less outspoken than some of her colleagues. She prefers a quieter diplomacy" (Wilson, 2006b).

Conversely, when women seemingly fail to adhere to the norms of dominant femininity, they tend to be described as noncompliant, incompetent, disruptive, and controversial. The controversy adheres like glue, situating women leaders as the problem. For example, they are described as "controversial," "outspoken," having a "lack of bedside manner," and exhibiting "unwillingness to compromise." The following data excerpts illuminate this discursive strand:

> Ms. Gupta's career at Alfred was *controversial* even before the blog made its debut. Not long after taking office in 2003, she fired John Anderson, a long-serving vice president who had himself been considered for the college's presidency. By the time Ms. Gupta had been in office for a year, more than 20 college officials had quit or been fired. (Read, 2006, emphasis added)

> The University of Iowa has fired an *outspoken laboratory director who objected* to cutting the size of a proposed new laboratory building . . . . Mary Gilchrist, 62, director of the University of Iowa's Hygienic Laboratory, which investigates pathogens, says she was *fired because she went out on her own* and tried to raise money for the project herself, after the university made the cuts. (McCormack, Bartlett, & Fogg, 2006, emphasis added)

> A majority of the faculty attacked the [Western Michigan University] president [Judith Bailey] for her cost-cutting measures and for her "*lack of bedside manner.*" (Cotton, 2006, emphasis added)

> [Among posts to a blog criticizing Alfred State's then-President Uma Gupta was this comment:] "She has systematically destroyed the people and the institution through her incompetence, her unwillingness to compromise, and her inability to see any view but her own." (Read, 2006)

These characteristics, if ascribed to male leaders, would likely be interpreted as performing the role of a strong, agentic, autonomous leader (Allan et al., 2006; Biernat & Fuegen, 2001); yet, for women, being resolute, outspoken, and going out on one's own is typically depicted as "controversial" or "incompetent," and can carry swift consequences, including the termination of a woman leader. This double bind leaves women leaders with limited, conflicting, and at times unfavorable options; they feel damned if they do and doomed if they don't. Yet, many women leaders are legitimized as "ideal candidates to lead" (Fain, 2006c). We now illuminate the discursive construction of women as competent leaders.

CONSTRUCTING THE GENDERED PROFESSIONAL

The women who were depicted in our review of *The Chronicle* were also described with a focus on credentials earned, positions held, expertise gained, and other markers of achievement and authority. For instance:

> Michelle J. Anderson, a law professor at Villanova University since 1998, has been named dean of the City University of New York's School of Law. . . . She has focused on legal issues surrounding domestic violence and sexual assault throughout her career. A graduate of Yale University's law school, she has taught criminal law, criminal procedure, and feminist legal theory at Villanova. In a recent case involving child sexual abuse, the Massachusetts Supreme Court cited two of her published works. (Rainey & McCormack, 2006)

These characterizations are made visible by the discourse of professionalism that construct women leaders as *expert*. Their legitimacy is bolstered through emphases on credentials, positions of authority, and experience, as illustrated here: "the distinguished biologist from Spelman College who has just joined Drew as provost" (Weisbuch, 2006). Given recognition as expert, the discourse of professionalism positions women leaders as having access to "real power," as the following data excerpt exemplifies:

> *Real power, a $1-million budget, and a direct line to the president.* That's what persuaded Myra Hindus to take the newly created position of vice president for cultural diversity at Berklee College of Music, in Boston. Ms. Hindus, 56, spent the past six years as director of the Massachusetts Legal Services Diversity Coalition. Before that, she spent 20 years in higher education. That included nine years at the University of Connecticut and several at Princeton University. (Wilson & Fogg, 2006, emphasis added)

For many, the conflation of professionalism with upward mobility, progress, dependability – leadership – may appear natural. However, it is this taken-for-granted belief that professional advancement is inherently good or morally right (Allan, 2003) that this analysis seeks to uncover. The discourse of professionalism serves to produce status, rewards, and a prestige hierarchy (Allan, 2003) that can ultimately serve as "gatekeeping mechanisms" (Seddon, 1997) for leadership positions. The criteria by which individuals are measured for advancement, success, and access to leadership positions continue to benefit some more than others and constrains women's upward mobility. Further, a culture that tolerates gender discrimination may constrain women's advancement into leadership roles as noted in this data excerpt:

> A senior professor at a large public university . . . felt ignored, even disrespected, by her colleagues, despite making every effort to become a

more integral part of her department. Eventually she abandoned all attempts to "join" her department and, for 26 long years, hunkered down and concentrated on her research, producing groundbreaking scholarship. Despite her fame, her departmental colleagues continued to dismiss her accomplishments. It was only when her university conferred on her the status of "distinguished professor" that she felt part of the institution a full quarter of a century after she began her career there. (Olson, 2006a)

When images of women leaders are produced and supported by a discourse of professionalism with its emphasis on experience, rank, fame, and accomplishments, an inherent gender tension emerges as expectations about professionalism are largely shaped through the discourse of dominant masculinity; while expectations about how women should or ought to behave are shaped through a dominant discourse of femininity constructed as the antithesis of that which is masculine. Consequently, women leaders can find themselves caught in the "double bind" of being professional, competent, and demonstrating expertise while simultaneously becoming objects of critique or curiosity for being unfeminine and/or an exception to the normative assumptions that shape stereotypes about women and men. This point is illuminated in this example of a woman college president, a scholar of eighteenth-century British drama, who was described as being "an unlikely choice to lead Stony Brook in its quest for an identity. All three of the presidents who led the university before her were physicists – and men" (Fain, 2006b). Similarly, the polarity between these dominant discourses is illustrated by this excerpt about Laurel Thatcher Ulrich's selection as one of 19 distinguished university professors at Harvard University. Ulrich is described as a "well-behaved scholar" on an "unconventional career path" that led to an appointment as a professor at Harvard University.

She . . . spent her 20s and 30s as a faculty wife and mother of five children. She sewed quilts, made bread, and bottled pears, all while taking one course at a time toward her master's degree and then a doctorate in history. She is an accidental academic whose *unconventional career path* has landed her at the nation's most prominent university. (Wilson, 2006b, emphasis added)

These examples provide a glimpse of how dominant discourses of professionalism/masculinity and femininity shape images of women leaders and can operate to undercut and/or devalue experiences women have gained outside what has been deemed the "professional realm." This puts women leaders in a difficult position: should they act as people expect them to act as women – nurturing, supportive and gentle? Or should they behave as people expect a leader to act, exhibiting masculine behaviors such as aggressiveness and dominance (Paxton & Hughes, 2007)? In an effort to interrupt this double bind and challenge the male-normative system, some women leaders choose reconciliation, meaning working within the system for change while recognizing the limitation of the male norms, while others take a more resistance-oriented approach, meaning they engage in active opposition to the boundaries that male norms establish (Cooper et al., 2007; Tedrow, 1999). We will discuss resistance later in this chapter. Next, we examine how the subject position of the *relational leader* emerges from the tension between the discourses of professionalism and femininity.

RELATIONAL LEADERS

The discourse of professionalism, in tension with the caretaker strand of the discourse of femininity, produces the image of relational leader evident in the following statements of women leaders:

> "I provide a very supportive environment with an open-door policy." (Richmond, 2006)

> "The experience of so many of us *working together* on this project has illustrated what we can do if we bring many disciplines together." (Monastersky, 2006, emphasis added)

> "It's important to me to frame the issue in a way that bridges political divides." (Carlson, 2006)

The relational leader is characterized by mutuality, collaboration, co-operative interchange, and participatory leadership. Consistent with Henderson and Kesson's (2003) conception of a "decentralized participatory democracy," the relational leader calls for "a much higher level of participation and a deeper level of engagement" (p. 37). For example, women "may be seen as symbols of peace and reconciliation when they come to power" (Paxton & Hughes, 2007, p. 96). Less visible is the autonomous leader directing change; instead, leadership emerges as a process (Astin & Leland, 1991) or as a collaborative endeavor (Bensimon & Neumann, 1993), illuminating "a playful political practice that is not bound by rigid structures but is continually in the process of transformation" (Epstein, 1996, p. 128).

Applied to our understanding of leadership, this discursive tension gives rise to leaders who are relational and conciliatory, rather than heroes focused on visions (Woods, 2005). With an emphasis on groups and teams, the relational leader facilitates collective decision-making and shared responsibility. For instance, one woman president attributes "full credit for the above accomplishments . . . to a highly ethical, dedicated, and visionary team of senior leaders that I was privileged to be a part of" (DePree et al., 2006). Another leader, Sara Martinez Tucker, president and chief executive of the Hispanic Scholarship Fund, was initially "worried about all of us *staying together* through this entire process." ... But when members emerged from a closed-door meeting here two days later, Ms. Tucker was feeling more optimistic. She ... said members had reached *consensus* on many of the key issues facing the panel. (Field, 2006, emphasis added)

Linda Thor, Rio Salado College's president, an "efficiency-minded manager" with "a taste for M&Ms," describes how work at the Arizona community college gets done: "Part of the way we are, who we are, is that we can all get in one room – and we do – and work things out and get together behind an initiative" (Ashburn, 2006b). The relational leader is also evident in descriptions of collegial support for others, namely women. For example:

Geraldine L. Richmond, a professor of physical chemistry and materials science at the University of Oregon, has created a national support group where female scientists share war stories and learn to negotiate for resources and a better working environment. She has become a touch-stone for many women, and says she runs her career in a way that she hopes will show young female scientists that they can be mothers and professors. (Wilson, 2006a)

Finally, the relational leader emerges in descriptions of collective action, holding potential to empower people and change the organization. In the following excerpt, organizational changes occurred through the mutual empowerment of a group of women.

Coach [the Committee on the Advancement of Women Chemists] started when I kept hearing from my senior women colleagues the difficulties they were facing as they got older: In their research careers, in not getting recognition their male colleagues were getting, or getting their lab space taken away when they had a productive program, or in not being able to get grad students in their group for reasons that weren't obvious. . . . What I was hearing was when women were starting to be successful, that was when a lot of strange behavior from colleagues started to happen. We had this vision it would get easier when you got more successful, but actually it was getting a lot harder. That was what started Coach. ... [W]e suddenly realized, Oh my God. None of us are supposed to be having these stories. Our [Coach] facilitators told us how to go back home and deal with it. Within six months, *there were these incredible results from that.* So I thought if that could happen to us, imagine what could happen to all these other women out there who don't have a lifeline. So far, we've helped 300 women chemists and 1,000 women across the other scientific disciplines. (Richmond, 2006, emphasis added)

In this case, the relational leader utilized participatory and collaborative strategies to collectively act in the creation of a decentralized structure – that of a "Coach" – for promoting change from within. However, it is notable that "collaboration can also be seen as conspiracy, a move by an interest group to 'take over' and limit others' rights and choices" (Court, 1992, para 106). While limited in their visibility, this analysis illuminated descriptions of women leaders as "uppity," "outspoken," and "creating institutional change." Next, we describe the discursive construction of these change-oriented, activist leaders.

Counter-Discourse: Constituting Change

Throughout our analysis, we identified data examples illuminating women leaders' "commitment to social justice"; as a "champion of women . . . reputation for activism"; and promoting "radical structural change." With attention to inequities and injustice, and illustrating possibilities for resistance, we recognized a counter-discourse circulating and carrying the potential to interrupt dominant discursive practices. Characterized by critiques of existing social constructions for inequities that result from unequal power relationships and calls for (at times radical) social change to overcome these inequities (Furman & Gruenewald, 2004), we provisionally posit that these characterizations are shaped by a social justice strand of a liberal humanist discourse, giving rise to the image of *social justice leaders*. At times, the social justice strand intersects with feminist discourses that highlight structural inequalities and systems of oppression like patriarchy or sexism.

SOCIAL JUSTICE LEADERS

Social justice leaders are described as assuming responsibility for speaking out, providing advocacy, and engaging in social activism in order to achieve equal opportunities for and better treatment of marginalized groups, a commitment to social reform, and radical structural change. Principles of freedom, equality, and social justice are pronounced in data stretches describing social justice leaders as "fight[ing] over equal opportunities for female college athletes . . . and demanding better treatment" (Wolverton, 2006), "deal[ing] with issues essential to feminism, like the pressures on women to balance work with intimate relationships" (Ferriss & Young, 2006), "creating sustainable local economies" (Biemiller, 2006), collecting "the first national data showing that more women are earning doctorates in the sciences than are being hired as professors" (Wilson, 2006a), engaging in a program to "eliminate sweatshop labor" (June, 2006), and demonstrating "a commitment to social justice" (Wilson, 2005).

Women leaders as social justice leaders address problems of academic responsibility toward society by making informed decisions that balance the rights of an individual with those of the institution (Rawls & Kelly, 2001). The following quote exemplifies the woman leader as a change agent who is weighing options to make an informed decision that is just.

I [director of the Student Health Center and assistant clinical professor of pediatrics] needed time to consider the issue. My initial reaction was a vehement no. After struggling for years beside my feminist sisters and brothers to earn equal rights for women in the work force, how could I now comply with a request that essentially limited a health-care professional to the gender restrictions I had fought to demolish? And yet the words "cultural competency" quickly filtered through my passion .... In the end, ... I proposed a compromise that respected the student's religious views without promoting discrimination by our student-health center as a whole. (Chassokiakos, 2006)

Further evidence of the discursive strand of social justice is visible in the following data excerpts:

Deborah A. Shanley, dean of education at Brooklyn College of the City University of New York, says a *commitment to social justice* means that a teacher "deeply believes that all children should be treated fairly so that they can reach their potential." (Wilson, 2005, emphasis added)

Ms. Denton, 46, an accomplished electrical engineer and champion of women in science who had made diversity in academics a focus of her career, ... [said] she would help advance Santa Cruz's profile and long-standing reputation for activism. (Fain, 2006c)

The social justice strand of the liberal humanist discourse also shapes images of leaders working to change unjust institutional structures:

Candace de Russy, a trustee of the State University of New York ... , described aggressive changes that she said could improve universities' financial discipline and quality control. ... "We should have an open mind to *radical structural change*," Ms. de Russy said. (Fain, 2006a, emphasis added)

Ms. Hindus [vice president for cultural diversity] hopes to use her experience in gender, race, and class issues to put diversity at the center of the college's mission. "*It's really about creating institutional change.*" (Wilson & Fogg, 2006, emphasis added)

Additionally, as Grogan (2002) claims, social justice leaders must "interrupt the continued maintenance of the status quo" (p. 115). Such challenges to dominant ideology are depicted in the following data excerpt:

Debra R. Rolison, an analytical chemist with the U.S. Defense Department's Naval Research Laboratory, is an outspoken critic of academic science. ... "Isn't a millennium of affirmative action for white men sufficient?" she asks in a lecture that she has dubbed her "uppity woman" talk. Ms. Rolison was among the first people to call on the federal government to use Title IX of the Education Amendments of 1972 to investigate the scarcity of women in academic science. (Wilson, 2006a)

Discussion and Implications

This examination of women leaders depicted in *The Chronicle of Higher Education* provides a valuable opportunity to consider ways in which dominant discourses may contribute to shaping perceptions about women in leadership roles. Understanding the discursive constitution of these images is important because discourses, "as systematic sets of meanings, regulate how we understand who we are [and] . . . constrain and shape possibilities for action" (Blackmore, 1999, pp. 16–17). If social change is desired, understanding of how realities are discursively constituted can help women leaders become more aware of how their performance as leaders is negotiated, ambiguous, and shifting. Conceived in this way, women leaders are empowered to "perform" their leadership identity(ies) differently and therefore challenge and unsettle established understandings. "In viewing discourse as something that is actively chosen by subjects . . . [women leaders] have at their disposal an opportunity to subvert and resist prevailing and dominant understandings" of leadership (Osgood, 2006, p. 12).

Our analysis revealed that predominant images of women leaders were shaped by discourses of femininity, masculinity, professionalism, and liberal humanism. The dominant discourse of femininity positions women leaders as caretakers and vulnerable leaders. Tension between gender discourses of femininity and masculinity constructs a double bind for women leaders. A discourse of professionalism, reinforced by a dominant discourse of masculinity, constructs the images of the woman leader as expert, and, intersecting with the discourse of femininity, gives rise to the relational leader. Finally, a social justice strand of the liberal humanist discourse produces the image of social justice leaders.

The findings of this study offer a particular perspective that invites an opportunity for thinking differently about women and leadership. While perceptions of women leaders as experts, as relational leaders, and as social justice leaders are supportive of leadership effectiveness, the images of vulnerability and of being "damned" by the double bind of being female while leading under male expectations, challenge women's perceived leadership effectiveness. We contend that these negative leadership images arising from gendered discourses can become institutionalized cultural barriers, barriers that are compounded by the structural barriers of centralized bureaucracies that privilege traditional male-oriented conceptions of leadership (Bensimon & Newman, 1993; Kezar et al., 2006; Tedrow, 1999). In this environment, women leaders can take direction from the successes of some of the effective leaders described in the above quotes, for example, from the women chemists who formed the women's support group called Coach (Richmond, 2006). Building on the work of feminist scholars and activists, we offer the following initial suggestions for how decision-makers might engage new possibilities for thinking to enhance institutional leadership and improve practice for all:

1. Help others understand how dominant discourses support a narrow view of leadership. The findings of this study resonate with others who suggest that women's success in leadership positions is hampered by an organization that is male-centered (Kezar et al., 2006; Tedrow, 1999) and hierarchical. For example, Jablonski (1996) found that while women presidents espoused generative leadership processes, their effectiveness was hindered by college governance structures that did not support such a model. This investigation revealed how dominant discourses produce images of leadership that tend to align with or disrupt predominant views of leadership as qualities or behaviors possessed by charismatic individuals who attain some degree of formal authority in a hierarchical system. If discourses serve not only to reflect, but also shape reality, then it seems crucial to engage with different discourses that offer alternative conceptualizations of leadership. Wheatley (2005), for example, describes non-hierarchical, participatory, and generative approaches to leadership. Also, Bensimon and Neumann (1993) suggest redesigning collegiate leadership by employing team-oriented strategies. Dominant discourses are powerful because they have become so taken-for-granted that they are rarely called into question. We contend that the dominant discourses taken up to depict leaders and leadership are limiting for all, and for women in particular. One way to destabilize a dominant discourse is to expose it as one of many possibilities. In the case of leadership, critical awareness of the discursive shaping of leadership is a crucial step toward more inclusive images of leadership.

2. Support subject positions that draw upon alternative discourses. Non-traditional leadership development and experiential opportunities for women are valuable opportunities for nurturing expanded conceptions of what it means to be a leader. Amey (2005) suggests cultivating women as effective leaders through a cognitive orientation and cognitive team development processes. With such an orientation, leaders purposefully construct environments that engage multiple and differing perspectives in order to cognitively facilitate collective efforts to expose marginalized views, frame problems, think critically, empower others, and share leadership. For example, Kezar et al. (2006) posit that when decentralized leadership teams (those that break down hierarchical and bureaucratic structures) are used for policy/ procedural

development, the exploration of ideas, and task completion, leadership is experienced as a process rather than as a positional responsibility. Adopting a learning approach to leadership requires the cognitive effort of leaders and the preparation of the academy's members for engagement with leadership challenges (Amey, 2005; Bensimon & Neumann, 1993). We contend that the formation of alternative leadership practices will contribute to enhancing the prominence of non-dominant discourses supporting such approaches.

3. Design "chaotic" mentoring programs. Chaotic, as used here, refers to a process that resists the typical highly structured, hierarchic mentoring relationships. Professional development plans put great stock in mentoring programs, recommending that those in senior positions (students, faculty, or administrators) should be paired with those in similar junior positions. The assumption is that the senior persons hold knowledge and wisdom that can guide and encourage junior persons. While research supports these assumptions and attests to the benefits of such relationships (Boyle & Boice, 1998; Chesler, Single, & Mikic, 2003), we recommend the establishment of mentoring relationships that are lateral (peer-to-peer), bottom up (meaning the knowledge of junior persons is valued equally and/or more than senior persons' knowledge), and "irregular," meaning design and choice is open. As Stacey (1992) observes, such "chaotic interactions" and the creative tensions they inspire may facilitate empowering conversations and relationships within and among individuals and groups. In turn, these dynamics may contribute to making alternative or concealed discourses more visible, potentially giving rise to opportunities to think more strategically about the subject positions we take up when performing leadership roles.

4. Promote the strategic deployment of discourse. Building on recommendations made in Allan's (2003, 2008) policy discourse analysis of university women's commission reports, we argue that male-centered leadership models and status quo practices can be destabilized and interrupted through increased awareness of the ways in which policy and practice are discursively constituted. Through greater understanding and awareness of the discursive construction of leadership, and in particular the ways in which gender influences assumptions about competence and leadership, (women) leaders can become more strategic about ways their efforts (re)produce particular ways of thinking. As Weedon (1997) suggests, all discursive practices can be analyzed to examine "how they are structured, what power relations they produce and reproduce, where there are resistances and where we might look for weak points more open to challenge and transformation" (p. 132). The first step in this process is learning to identify

and examine the subject positions produced so they are less likely to be accepted without question. This process opens up greater potential for interruption and destabilization of discourses that tend to undermine women in leadership positions.

Summary

The findings of this study illuminate the importance of considering how dominant discourses may contribute to producing particular images and under-standings of leadership in the context of higher education. For instance, the tension between the gender discourses constructs a double bind for women leaders: while women leaders hold authentic positions of power, they suffer from the sexist attitudes of constituencies who judge their performance accord-ing to male-constructed norms of leadership (Jablonski, 1996; Rudman & Glick, 2001). Engaging in a critical examination of women leaders in academia will allow administrators, senior-level leaders, faculty, and academicians to identify the dissonance between goals for a participatory, collaborative, generative leadership approach and the existing organizational culture that continues to reward command-and-control, authoritarian leadership styles. A reconceptualization of leadership as process rather than positional creates space for the relational leader and potential for change-oriented collective action (Astin & Leland, 1991, p. 5).

When gender (as well as race and other identity formations) is positioned at the center of the question of what leadership means and who can be effective leaders, we begin to engage in a different dialogue about context rather than (in/effective) networking, modeling, and shadowing programs; we begin to interrogate the construction of (gendered) standards for defining and evaluating good leadership, rather than designing (more) developmental and compen-satory programs to help women achieve masculinist standards of leadership (Biernat & Fuegen, 2001; Blackmore, 1999). Knowledge of leadership dis-courses, and how they operate within higher education, provides leaders with understandings of how dominant discourses shape, and may constrain, possibilities for their performance of leadership. Scholars in higher education can draw upon these findings to re/consider how to think more strategically about the discourses we choose to take up when describing leadership and women in leadership roles. This research can serve as a platform for more critical dialogue and examination of the discursive shaping of women and leadership and the implication of these images for enhancing equity in higher education.

dle was responding to presidential candidate John Edwards' criticism of Hillary Clinton
ı she became emotional on the campaign trail.
s phrase, typically articulated as "damned if you do and damned if you don't" was pulled
ım the title of a report published by Catalyst (2007) on the double-bind dilemma for women
in leadership.

References

Allan, E. J. (2003). Constructing women's status: Policy discourses of university women's commission reports. *Harvard Educational Review*, 73(1), 44–72.

Allan, E. J. (2004). Hazing and gender: Analyzing the obvious. In Nuwer, H. (Ed.), *The hazing reader* (pp. 275–294). Bloomington, IN: Indiana University Press.

Allan, E. J. (2008). *Policy discourses, gender and education: Constructing women's status*. New York: Routledge.

Allan, E. J., Gordon, S. P., & Iverson, S. V. (2006). Re/thinking practices of power: The discursive framing of leadership in *The Chronicle of Higher Education*. *The Review of Higher Education*, 30(1), 41–68.

Amey, M. J. (2005). Leadership as learning: Conceptualizing the process. *Community College Journal of Research and Practice*, 29(9/10), 689–704.

Appelbaum, S. H., Audet, L., & Miller, J. C. (2003). Gender and leadership? Leadership and gender? A journey through the landscape of theories. *Leadership & Organization Development Journal*, 24(1), 43–51.

Ashburn, E. (2006a). The few, the proud, the professors. *Chronicle of Higher Education*, 53(7), A10–A12.

Ashburn, E. (2006b). An honors education at a bargain-basement price. *Chronicle of Higher Education*, 53(10), B12–B14.

Astin, H. S. & Leland, C. (1991). *Women of influence, women of vision: A cross-generational study of leaders and change*. San Francisco, CA: Jossey-Bass.

Baldridge, V. J., Curtis, D. V., Ecker, G. P., & Riley, G. L. (1977/2000). Alternative models of governance in higher education. *Governing academic organizations*. McCutcham Publishing. [Reprinted in Brown, M. C. (Ed.). (2000). *Organization and governance in higher education*, 5th ed. (pp. 128–142). ASHE Reader Series. Boston, MA: Pearson Custom Publishing.]

Barton, T. R. (2005). Feminist leadership: The bridge to a better tomorrow. In S. Harris, B. Alford, & J. Ballenger (Eds.), *Leadership: A bridge to ourselves* (pp. 178–190). Austin, TX: Texas Council of Women School Executives.

Baxter, J. (2003). *Positioning gender in discourse: A feminist methodology*. New York: Palgrave Macmillan.

Bem, S. (1993). *The lenses of gender: Transforming the debate on sexual inequality*. New Haven, CT: Yale University Press.

Bensimon, E. M. (1995). Total quality management in the academy: A rebellious reading. *Harvard Educational Review*, 65(4), 593–611.

Bensimon, E. M. & Neumann, A. (1993). *Redesigning collegiate leadership: Teams and teamwork in higher education*. Baltimore, MD: Johns Hopkins University Press.

Bensimon, E. M., Neumann, A., & Birnbaum, R. (1989). Higher education and leadership theory. *Making sense of administrative leadership. ASHE-ERIC Research Report*, No. 1. Association for the Study of Higher Education. [Reprinted in Brown, M. C. (Ed.). (2000). *Organization and governance in higher education*, 5th ed. (pp. 214–222). ASHE Reader Series. Boston, MA: Pearson Custom Publishing.]

Berquist, W. H. (1992). *The four cultures of the academy: Insights and strategies for improving leadership in collegiate organizations*. San Francisco, CA: Jossey-Bass.

Biemiller, L. (2006). At Penn, the White Dog Cafe feeds activists' hunger. *Chronicle of Higher Education*, 52(22), A56–A56.

Biernat, M. & Feugen, K. (2001). Shifting standards and the evaluation of competence: Complexity in gender-based judgment and decision making. *Journal of Social Issues*, 57(4), 707–724.

Birnbaum, R. (1988). *How colleges work: The cybernetics of academic organization and leadership*. San Francisco, CA: Jossey-Bass.

Blackmore, J. (1999). *Troubling women: Feminism, leadership, and educational change.* Philadelphia, PA: Open University Press.

Bollag, B. (2006). President-Elect at Gallaudet U. fails to win faculty support. *Chronicle of Higher Education,* 52(37), 1–3.

Bolman, L. G. & Deal, T. E. (2003). *Reframing organizations: Artistry, choice, and leadership,* 3rd ed. San Francisco, CA: Jossey-Bass.

Boyle, P. & Boice, R. (1998). Systematic mentoring for new faculty teachers and graduate teaching assistants. *Innovative Higher Education,* 22(3), 157–179. Retrieved November 15, 2005 from http://www.uvm.edu/~pbsingle/pdf/1998Boyle.pdf.

Braga, S. (2008). Transformational leadership attributes for virtual team leaders. In J. Nemiro, M. M. Beyerlein, L. Bradley, & S. Beyerlein (Eds.), *The handbook of high-performance virtual teams: A toolkit for collaborating across boundaries* (pp. 179–194). San Francisco, CA: Jossey-Bass.

Burns, J. M. (1978). *Leadership.* New York: Harper & Row.

Byerly, C. M. & Ross, K. (2006). *Women and media: A critical introduction.* Malden, MA: Blackwell Publishing.

Carli, L. L. (2001). Gender and social influence. *Journal of Social Issues,* 57(4), 725–741.

Carlson, S. (2006). In search of the sustainable campus. *Chronicle of Higher Education,* 53(9), 7.

Catalyst (2007). *The double-bind dilemma for women in leadership: Damned if you do, doomed if you don't.* New York: Catalyst. Retrieved July 18, 2008 from www.catalyst.org.

Chassiakos, L. R. (2006). Rights of passage. *Chronicle of Higher Education,* 52(32), B5.

Chemers, M. M. (1997). *An Integrative Theory of Leadership.* Mahwah, NJ: Lawrence Erlbaum.

Chesler, N., Single, P. B., & Mikic, B. (2003). On belay: Adventure education and peer-mentoring as a scaffolding technique for women junior faculty in engineering. *Journal of Engineering Education,* 92, 257–262. Retrieved November 15, 2005 from http://www.uvm.edu/~pbsingle/pdf/2003Single2.pdf.

Coates, J. (1996). *Women talk.* Cambridge, MA: Blackwell Publishers.

Conway, M. M., Ahern, D. W., & Steuernagel, G. A. (2005). *Women and public policy: A revolution in progress,* 3rd ed. Washington, DC: CQ Press.

Cooper, J., Eddy, P., Hart, J., Lester, J., Lukas, S., Eudey, B., Glazer-Raymo, J., & Madden, M. (2007). Improving gender equity in postsecondary education. In S. S. Klein, B. Richardson, D. A. Grayson, L. H. Fox, C. Kramarae, D. S. Pollard, & C. A. Dwyer (Eds.), *Handbook for achieving gender equity through education* (pp. 625–647). New York: Routledge.

Cotton, R. D. (2006). Why colleges should avoid abrupt terminations. *Chronicle of Higher Education,* 53(10), C1–C4.

Court, M. (1992). *Women teachers and discourses of leadership: A case study of job sharing.* Paper presented at The Australian Association for Research in Education. Retrieved July 18, 2008 from http://www.aare.edu.au/92pap/courm92469.txt.

Crenshaw, K. (1991). Mapping the margins: Intersectionality, identity politics, and violence against women of color. *Stanford Law Review,* 43(6), 1241–1299.

DePree Jr, C. M., Gupta, U. G., Iosue, R. V., Petrick, J., & Sciba, M. (2006). Bloggers vs. college administrators. *Chronicle of Higher Education,* 53(8), 48.

Eagly, A. H. (2005). Achieving relational authenticity in leadership: Does gender matter? *The Leadership Quarterly,* 16, 459–474.

Eddy, P. L. & VanDerLinden, K. E. (2006). Emerging definitions of leadership in higher education: New visions of leadership or the same old "hero" leader? *Community College Review,* 34(1), 5–26.

Epstein, B. (1996). *Radical democracy: Identity, citizenship, and the state.* New York: Routledge.

Estler, S. E. (1975). Women as leaders in public education. *Signs: The Journal of Women in Culture and Society,* 1(2), 363–386.

Evans, D. (2006). Going the distance and keeping the pace. *Chronicle of Higher Education,* 52(43), B8–B9.

Fain, P. (2006a). Conservative trustee group takes on the academy during annual meeting. *Chronicle of Higher Education,* 53(9), 32.

Fain, P. (2006b). Feisty president at SUNY Stonybrook has led a makeover of 'mudville'. *Chronicle of Higher Education,* 52(41), A23–A25.

Fain, P. (2006c). In apparent suicide, chancellor dies in a fall. *Chronicle of Higher Education,* 52(44), 1.

Ferriss, S. & Young, M. (2006). A generational divide over chick lit. *Chronicle of Higher Education,* 52(38), B13–B14.

Field, K. (2006). Uncertainty greets report on colleges by U.S. panel. *Chronicle of Higher Education*, 53(2), 1.

Fletcher, J. K. (2002). *CGO Insights, No. 13: The greatly exaggerated demise of heroic leadership: Gender, power, and the myth of the female advantage.* Boston, MA: Center for Gender in Organizations. Retrieved July 17, 2008 from http://www.simmons.edu/som/docs/centers/insights13.pdf.

Fletcher, J. K. (2004). The paradox of post heroic leadership: An essay on gender, power and transformational change. *Leadership Quarterly*, 15(5), 647–661.

Ford, J. (2006). Discourses of leadership: Gender, identity and contradiction in a UK public sector organization. *Leadership*, 2(1), 77–99.

Fullan, M. (2001). *Leading in a culture of change.* San Francisco, CA: Jossey-Bass.

Furman, G. C. & Gruenewald, D. A. (2004). Expanding the landscape of social justice: A critical ecological analysis. *Educational Administration Quarterly*, 40(1), 47–76.

Glenn, D. & Fogg, P. (2006). Manchester-Harvard project will serve as incubator for trans-atlantic policy debates; Emeritus professor at Yale is Connecticut's new poet laureate; Ex-President of Colorado system moves to Iowa. *Chronicle of Higher Education*, 53(8), 5.

Grogan, M. (2002). Guest editor's introduction: Leadership for social justice. *Journal of School Leadership*, 12, 112–115.

Henderson, J. G. & Kesson, K. R. (2003). *Curriculum wisdom: Educational decisions in democratic societies.* Upper Saddle River, NJ: Merrill/Prentice Hall Publishers.

Iverson, S. V. (2005). *A policy discourse analysis of U.S. land-grant university diversity action plans.* Unpublished doctoral dissertation. Orono, ME: University of Maine.

Iverson, S. V. (2007). Camouflaging power and privilege: A critical race analysis of university diversity policies. *Educational Administration Quarterly*, 43(5), 586–611.

Jablonski, M. (1996). The leadership challenge for women college presidents. *Initiatives*, 57(4), 1–10.

Jamieson, K. H. (1995). *Beyond the double bind: Women and leadership.* New York: Oxford University Press.

June, A. W. (2006). 8 colleges sign on to anti-sweatshop plan but worry over antitrust issues. *Chronicle of Higher Education*, 52(28), A38.

Kezar, A., Carducci, R., & Contraras-McGavin, M. (2006). Rethinking the "L" word in higher education: The revolution of research on leadership. *ASHE Higher Education Report*, 31(6). San Francisco, CA: Jossey-Bass.

Kimmel, M. S. (2000). *The gendered society.* New York: Oxford University Press.

Layton, L. (2004). *Who's that girl? Who's that boy? Clinical practice meets postmodern gender theory.* Hillsdale, NJ: The Analytic Press.

Lazar, M. (Ed.). (2005). *Feminist critical discourse analysis: Gender, power and ideology in discourse.* New York: Palgrave Macmillan.

Lorber, J. (2004). "Night to his day": The social construction of gender. In L. Richardson, V. Taylor, & N. Whittier (Eds.), *Feminist frontiers*, 6th ed. (pp. 33–51). Boston, MA: McGraw-Hill.

Lujan, L. (2006). Voices: 'I wanted to give something back'. *Chronicle of Higher Education*, 53(10), B21.

Mangan, K., Fogg, P., & Porter, J. R. (2006). Peer review: Had enough. *Chronicle of Higher Education*, 53(5), A7.

McArdle, M. (2008). Don't cry for me, New Hampshire. *The Atlantic* [online], January 8. Retrieved January 31, 2008 from http://meganmcardle.theatlantic.com/.

McCormack, E., Bartlett, T., & Fogg, P. (2006). Washington U. in St. Louis hires architecture dean; Embattled Baylor faculty member wins tenure on appeal; U. of Iowa fires outspoken lab director. *Chronicle of Higher Education*, 53(9), 4.

Mills, S. (1992). Negotiating discourses of femininity. *Journal of Gender Studies*, 1(3), 271–285.

Mills, S. (1997). *Discourse.* New York: Routledge.

Monastersky, R. (2006). A new science breaks down boundaries. *Chronicle of Higher Education*, 53(9), 13.

Oakley, J. G. (2000). Gender-based barriers to senior management positions: Understanding the scarcity of female CEOs. *Journal of Business Ethics*, 27, 321–334.

Olson, G. A. (2006). Praising you as we should. *Chronicle of Higher Education*, 52(39), C2–C3.

Osgood, J. (2006). Deconstructing professionalism in early childhood education: Resisting the regulatory gaze. *Contemporary Issues in Early Childhood*, 7(1), 5–14.

Paxton, P. M. & Hughes, M. M. (2007). *Women, politics, and power: A global perspective.* Thousand Oaks, CA: Pine Forge Press.

Rainey, A. & McCormack, E. (2006). Peer review: Mission convergence. *Chronicle of Higher Education*, 52(35), A10.

Rawls, J. & Kelly, E. (Eds.). (2001). *Justice as fairness: A restatement*. Cambridge, MA: The Belknap Press of Harvard University Press.

Read, B. (2006). Attack of the blog. *Chronicle of Higher Education*, 53(4), A35.

Reynolds, A. L. & Pope, R. L. (1991). The complexities of diversity: Exploring multiple oppressions. *Journal of Counseling and Development*, 70, 174–180.

Richmond, G. (2006). People are as important as results. *Chronicle of Higher Education*, 52(38), A12.

Ridgeway, C. L. (2001). Gender, status, and leadership. *Journal of Social Issues*, 57(4), 637–655.

Ridgeway, C. L. & Correll, S. J. (2004). Unpacking the gender system: A theoretical perspective on gender beliefs and social relations. *Gender & Society*, 18(4), 510–531.

Rothenberg, P. S. (Ed.). (2006). *Race, class and gender in the United States: An integrated study*, 7th ed. New York: Worth Publishers.

Rudman, L. A. & Glick, P. (2001). Prescriptive gender stereotypes and backlash toward agentic women. *Journal of Social Issues*, 57(4), 743–762.

Sanoff, A. P. (2006). At U. of Southern California, a support network helps women in science and engineering. *Chronicle of Higher Education*, 53(6), 58.

Schmidt, P. (2006). The Bush White House picks its civil-rights fights carefully. *Chronicle of Higher Education*, 52(37), 22–28.

Seddon, T. (1997). Education: Deprofessionalised? Or reregulated, reorganised and reauthorised? *Australian Journal of Education*, 41(3), 228–246.

Segal, C. F. (2006). Having it all . . . over all. *Chronicle of Higher Education*, 52(19), B5.

Stacey, R. D. (1992). *Managing the unknowable: Strategic boundaries between order and chaos in organizations*. San Francisco, CA: Jossey-Bass.

Strout, E. (2006). Author calls for a college course on the art of conducting meetings. *Chronicle of Higher Education*, 52(21), A27.

Tedrow, B. (1999). A qualitative study of women's experiences in community college leadership positions. *Community College Review*, 27(3), 1–18.

Tierney, W. G. (Ed.). (1991). *Culture and ideology in higher education: Advancing a critical agenda*. New York: Praeger Publishers.

Trinidad, C. & Normone, A. H. (2005). Leadership and gender: A dangerous liaison? *Leadership & Organization Development Journal*, 26(7), 574–590.

Van Der Werf, M. (2006). Federal appeal yields win for Gannon U. *Chronicle of Higher Education*, 53(5), A26.

Wang, A. (2000). Asian and white boys' competing discourses about masculinity: Implications for secondary education. *Canadian Journal of Education*, 25, 113–125. Retrieved July 17, 2008 from http://www.csse.ca/CJE/Articles/FullText/CJE25–2/CJE25–2-wang.pdf.

Weedon, C. (1997). *Feminist practice and poststructuralist theory*, 3rd ed. Cambridge, MA: Blackwell Publishers.

Weisbuch, R. A. (2006). Avoiding a sophomore slump. *Chronicle of Higher Education*, 53(8), 66.

West, C. & Fenstermaker, S. (1995). Doing difference. *Gender & Society*, 9(1), 8–37.

Wheatley, M. J. (1992). *Leadership and the new science: Learning about organization from an orderly universe*. San Francisco, CA: Berrett-Koehler Publishers.

Wheatley, M. J. (2005). *Finding our way: Leadership for an uncertain time*. San Francisco, CA: Berrett-Koehler Publishers.

Wilson, R. (2005). We don't need that kind of attitude. *Chronicle of Higher Education*, 52(17), A8–A11.

Wilson, R. (2006a). The chemistry between women and science. *Chronicle of Higher Education*, 52(38), A10–A12.

Wilson, R. (2006b). A well-behaved scholar makes history. *Chronicle of Higher Education*, 52(29), A12–A15.

Wilson, R. & Fogg, P. (2006). Peer review: Diversity at Berklee. *Chronicle of Higher Education*, 52(41), A9.

Wolverton, B. (2006). Crying foul over postseason opportunities. *Chronicle of Higher Education*, 52(47), A26.

Woods, P. A. (2005). *Democratic leadership in education*. London: Paul Chapman Educational Publishing.

Part 2
Subjects and Objects of Policy

Feminism has long been concerned about the positioning of women and men with diverse identities and experiences as subjects (or agents) and objects (those acted upon). And, while FPS resists the firm positioning of people, concepts, or strategies as statically situated within discourses, it nevertheless offers the possibility that there are ways that are more or less effective in shifting (or maintaining) current discourses. Yet, it pushes beyond more structural framings and asks: In what ways are individuals and groups both subjects and objects, both agents and recipients of discursive functioning? In this book, several chapters' analyses have implications for the ways in which policy positions certain individuals or groups as subjects and objects of policy in particular ways. In this section, we consider Susan Talburt's interpretation of the experiences of students through their engagement with a Gay Lesbian Straight Alliance, and Jennifer Hoffman, Susan Iverson, Elizabeth Allan, and Rebecca Ropers-Huilman's chapter on representations of student athletes as constructed and reinforced by enactments and interpretations of Title IX policy. Finally, we review Jeni Hart and Jennifer Hubbard's analysis of how institutional policies intending to more equitably serve students with fewer economic resources structure those students' experiences.

Susan Talburt's chapter focuses on both the discursive framing of lesbian, gay, bisexual, and transgendered college students, as well as on the possibilities of qualitative research to inform educational policy related to these students and other important aspects of education. The purpose of her research is to consider "how the young people are made – and make themselves – subjects" (p. 114). In this sense, Talburt's research focused on the ways in which students framed themselves as "becoming" – becoming individuals, becoming visible as a group, and becoming integrated into campus life. They also hoped that their campus community would become more accepting and tolerant. In this way, they articulated a clear desire to be subjects who influenced their environments and the terms through which they were seen. Yet, they also struggled with moving too clearly in that direction since they were aware of how they were objectified by dominant discourses in the larger society and sought to "express socially intelligible behaviors" (p. 120). Students struggled to determine their roles as objects of university norms and societal expectations and, simultaneously, as subjects who make meanings of their own experiences. This chapter raises the question: How can policy research inform students' experiences and sense-making processes? And an equally important and parallel question is: How can students' experiences and sense-making processes inform both policy and research? As Talburt suggests, "Rather than refining predictable narratives whose beginnings, middles, and endings must be administered by experts and institutions, research might complicate ideas about identities and thus cease to participate in disciplining and normalizing subjects through ideals of needs and successes" (p. 126).

The chapter focusing on Title IX by Jennifer Hoffman, Susan Iverson, Elizabeth Allan, and Rebecca Ropers-Huilman points out how Title IX policy shapes student-athletes' experiences primarily in two ways: through marketplace and self-development discourses. The tension between marketplace and developmental discourses produces competing subjectivities for student-athletes both institutionally and as related to individual players' lives, resulting in gender differentiation, despite the policy's intent to equalize the playing field for men and women. Men's involvement in certain sports was seen as meeting marketplace demands (and therefore worthy of greater institutional support), while women's involvement in sports was seen as being part of participants' holistic development. Hoffman and colleagues point out that while both discourses were tapped in various ways to meet perceived institutional or social needs, it is important to note that they were called upon in different ways – and were available in different ways – based on the gender of student-athletes. Thus, despite rhetoric that suggests otherwise, the discursive construction of student-athletes remains gendered and privileges males. Further, while gender is the focus of Title IX, Hoffman et al. acknowledge the implications for other marginalized groups, i.e. racial and sexual minorities within athletics.

Finally, Jeni Hart and Jennifer Hubbard's chapter on the multiple costs associated with attending postsecondary education focuses on "how policies related to social class experiences and identities in a women's college contribute to reproducing a cycle of oppression" (p. 148). Hart and Hubbard provide multiple examples showing how the "object" of financial aid policies (women with few economic resources) is affected by those policies in unintended ways. For example, financial aid policies are meant to equalize the experiences of women from different economic strata. However, given their implementation at this particular women's college (and, likely, many other colleges of different institutional types), the enactment of institutional financial aid policies privileges applicants with greater economic means and students without family responsibilities, despite rhetoric that suggests otherwise. Additionally, while students may want to ignore the implications of their financial status, their work study assignments to particular types of jobs identify them as having fewer economic means early in their enrolment and reminds them and others of their less powerful and objectified status within the collegiate environment. In their analysis, Hart and Hubbard poignantly suggest that "there is more that needs to be done, since those paying the price for many of the policies are those the policies were intended to help" (p. 163). Their chapter provides a powerful example of the ways in which "objects" of policy are simultaneously "subjects" in making meaning of their experiences. Participants' framings of subjective experience provide important insights about the ways in which policies have unintended and potentially counter-intuitive implications.

The chapters in this section, like others in the book, have clear implications for policy analysis. Specifically, who are the objects and subjects in and of educational policy? How are they simultaneously the same and different? How closely should the two be aligned? How are they mutually formed by the discourses that structure educational and social understandings? If a policy is constructed by one group to shape the behavior of another – without taking seriously the subjective experiences of both self and others – it is extremely likely that the policy effects will be surprising and, in many cases, harmful to educational experience. We urge readers to take seriously the ways in which the objects of policy are also subjects in their own lives.

6

Developing Students

Becoming Someone But Not Anyone

SUSAN TALBURT

In this chapter, I have two motivating and interrelated desires. One is to inquire into the actions and interactions of student members of a Gay Lesbian Straight Alliance (GLSA) at a public university. The other is to explore the potential for knowledges created through qualitative inquiry to illuminate the categories that frame university policy and practice. I describe a research project that started with some clear predispositions. First, I entered the inquiry wary of discourses that frame lesbian, gay, bisexual, and transgender (LGBT) youth as primarily at-risk, isolated, lacking resources, and in need of social and academic support. Second, I began with a skepticism of universities' increasing emphases on developing "successful students" through curricular and extracurricular programming. The promotion of "involvement" and "belonging" to enhance student retention can constitute a normalizing technology to address students' presumed needs and develop their social and academic skills. Extracurricular student groups, such as a GLSA, are one location in which discourses of developing "successful students" converge with minoritizing "multicultural" discourses to address particular sets of needs. Thus, I was interested in understanding how a group of students at one university lived out their social and institutional identities as "LGBT students." This chapter, then, offers a glimpse of my fieldwork and theorizing, focusing on the limits and possibilities of my research.

Throughout this inquiry, I was conscious of theoretical tensions related to creating knowledge, particularly between the unified subjects of modernism on which much qualitative inquiry depends and the decentered subjects with non-linear trajectories of various poststructural theories. For example, my inquiry began with humanistic research questions comprehensible to the teleologies and coherences privileged by Institutional Review Boards, including the motivations of individual group members, the group's impact on campus, the meanings of participating in the group for individual members, and the campus' impact on the group. Hoping to disrupt these modernist linearities that presume coherent subjectivities and causal relationships, I drew on feminist poststructural (e.g., Butler, 2004; Grosz, 1994), queer (Jagose, 1996), and Deleuze-and-Guattarian (1987) thought to ask to what extent my inquiry could offer nuanced understandings of subjects' positionings in relation to social and institutional discourses.

I begin with a brief discussion of the framing of LGBT college students and of my research. I then present some scenes from my fieldwork and the initial discourses I constructed to understand the positioning of the young people I encountered. Finally, I consider how feminist poststructural, queer, and Deleuze-and Guattarian thinking hint at alternative ways of thinking and return to my data to posit hints of "lines of thought" that are not readily visible but that suggest something beyond the coherence institutions increasingly demand of subjects. In structuring my discussion this way, this chapter engages in what has come to be called "reflexivity," but not of the authorizing sort. I follow Pillow's (2003) suspicion of reflexivity as a means to position the self as a part of accomplishing research goals, whether to gain authority, demonstrate empathy, or claim authenticity. In this sense, this is not a reflexivity that seeks to bolster the accuracy of my data or my credibility to readers; rather it is a de-authorizing reflexivity that may work against a project of creating authoritative knowledge.

Logics Related to LGBT College Students

Throughout the twentieth century in Western societies, adults have defined adolescence as a critical transitional period, a dangerous developmental passage from childhood innocence to adulthood (see Lesko, 2001; Patton, 1996). By such logic, adults must monitor and guide youth through this period of "storm and stress" in order to support a healthy and proper transition to adulthood. As Nancy Lesko (2001) has argued, a dominant discourse positions adolescence as a transitional narrative segment:

> [S]ince the end of the story matters, and adults know what the correct and happy ending is (increasing maturity and responsibility, school achievement, full-time employment, marriage and children, property ownership, in that order), only deviations or pitfalls along the prescribed plot merit attention. (p. 132)

A normative lens defines youth as at risk of improper development and in need of adult and institutional support.

In the case of young LGBT people, this developmental narrative entails heightened risk and thus additional needs for support and protection. As a counter to the pathologizing of same-sex sexuality and gender diversity, research and personal narratives over the past several decades have argued that difficulties LGBT youth face are due to society's oppression. This argument offers an important discursive shift in terms of the locus of a "problem," but continues to reproduce the discourse of "problem" by defining dominant understandings of LGBT youth in terms of victimization. LGBT youth come to be framed in terms of verbal harassment and physical violence, increased rates of drug and alcohol abuse, dropping out, homelessness, sexually transmitted diseases, low self-esteem, depression, and suicide. While these can be very real issues for some LGBT youth, a discourse that situates them as at-risk creates a singular narrative of needs for safety and social support in order to promote healthy identity development and "resilience" (see Rofes, 2004, and Talburt, 2004, for critical discussions of the limitations of these discourses).

Following this zeitgeist, much antihomophobic research and practice, which informs university policy and practice, encourages the provision of support systems that enable young people to develop their LGBT identities in a safe environment so that they can successfully enter LGBT adulthood. Many college campuses have responded by encouraging and/or implementing Safe Zone programs, LGBT-inclusive multicultural programming, and student groups. These extracurricular activities are premised on an idea that with appropriate support and resources, LGBT students will build community; create visibility; participate in and contribute to a positive educational climate; and develop leadership skills, coping strategies, and positive identities (see, for example, Evans & Wall, 1991; Sanlo, 1998). While well-intentioned, such practices rely on narrow ideas of who LGBT youth are and what they need. Barry (2000), for example, offers an interesting account of an LGBT student group's negotiations to create a space free of the assumptions and control of "sympathetic" adults seeking first to create a support group and later an activist group. Moreover, these practices rely on ossified ideas of linear development that ignore more "queer" understandings of identity, time, and space in which subjects may "develop" according to "other logics of location, movement, and identification" (Halberstam, 2005, p. 1), disrupting normative accounts of adolescence-to-adulthood as a linear narrative.

Programming to promote tolerance and diversity intersects with campus efforts to foster student success. Research into "successful students" advises that institutions can work against risks of "premature departure" or "under-performance" by promoting student involvement and a sense of campus "belonging" (see Astin, 1984, 1993; Tinto, 1998). Universities, then, develop curricular and extracurricular programming aimed at fostering academic and social integration (see Kuh, Kinzie, Buckley, Bridges, & Hayek, 2007, for a comprehensive overview of models for success). These practices are bolstered by "student development theory," which includes psychosocial and identity development theories, cognitive-structural theories, and typology theories (see Dilley, 2002, for an overview) as well as consideration of socio-cultural dimensions related to development (see, for example, Evans, 1998; Wilson & Wolf-Wendel, 2006). Psychosocial theories, which are frequently stage models that name developmental tasks that inform the logic of extracurricular programming (e.g., Chickering and Reisser, 1993), delineate processes by which students resolve "questions of identity and purpose in life" (Dilley, 2002, p. 24). Authoritative social scientific discourses support institutional policies and practices that ask college students to exercise a seeming autonomy as they "are expected to measure up to finely attuned assessments of productivity, learning, morality, and achievement" (Lesko, 2001, p. 129). Research, policy, and practice seek to make college students' needs and social and academic developmental outcomes knowable and known, positioning them in adults' and institutions' ideas of success, ideally mobilizing them to behave in certain ways.

Institutional responsibilities to support student success and to create supportive learning environments for LGBT students might appear curious ideas to question. Indeed, they have gained the status of common sense. Yet, given institutions' facile adoption of development as a predictable, linear process of arrival at mature adulthood and dominant discourses of LGBT youth as "at-risk," I wished to understand the positionings of actors caught in these discourses. In this sense, my concern with the intersections of LGBT needs and university success is aligned with Bacchi's (1999) exploration of how policy constructs and represents problems. A problematization, or the way something is made to become a problem, necessitates asking how a problem is defined and what is left out (p. 1). This inquiry is not, however, a study of processes of university policy construction or a discourse analysis of policies themselves. Rather, I take these pervasive discourses as "givens," and focus on one group of students' actions in and articulations of the meanings of affiliating with a GLSA as they relate to perceptions of LGBT needs and student success. By taking up discourse, I follow poststructuralism's gesture as it:

> dis-assembles the *humanist subject* – the thinking, self-aware, truth-seeking individual ('man'), who is able to master both 'his' own internal passions, and the physical world around him, through the exercise of reason. Poststructural theorists argue that subjects are constituted within discourses that establish what is possible (and impossible) to 'be' – a woman, mother, teacher, child, etc. – as well as what will count as truth, knowledge, moral values, normal behaviour and intelligible speech for those who are 'summoned' to speak by the discourse in question. (MacLure, 2003, p. 175)

In effect, I ask how the young people are made – and make themselves – subjects.

Entering the Inquiry; Or, the Meeting of Different Logics

My qualitative study of the GLSA began with these guiding research questions:

1. What are the organization's purposes and activities?
2. How do members work together to achieve these purposes?
3. How do participants describe the organization and their membership in it?

4. How do participants describe their contributions to and the benefits they derive from the group?

During most of an academic year, I attended the majority of the group's meetings, went to numerous events it sponsored or participated in, and conducted one-on-one semi-structured interviews with ten group members and the GLSA's faculty advisor. My approach to thinking about these young people and their organization comes from a desire to understand possibilities for subjects to create spaces of opening, or practices that do not conform to dominant logics of identity or development, within university policy and practice.

Although this research was predicated on LGBT identity (in that it relied on finding *identifiable LGBT people*), my theoretical and political affinities question mainstream LGBT politics, which seeks recognition and rights for those claiming LGBT identities (see Vaid, 1995). I align my thinking with queer politics, which eschews identity as fixed or stable, questions the homo/hetero binary, and seeks to analyze and disrupt ideological and material processes of hetero- and homonormalization (see Duggan, 2003; Jagose, 1996).

My orientation to theories that question identity's political utility seemed somewhat at odds with the lesbian- and gay-identified (no Bs or Ts were in evidence) young people I came to know. Indeed, the GLSA members' "ordinariness" and "niceness" struck me immediately. They were predominantly white, clean-cut young people who just wanted to do "normal" things – date, do volunteer work, have fun, create campus visibility, and be accepted as gay men and lesbians. Yet the group members demonstrated a self-conscious energy in transgressing local norms, particularly in their willingness to "put themselves out there" on a notoriously conservative campus in a notoriously conservative county, famous for insistently keeping on the books an antiquated law that its citizens must own a gun. Even the institutional space functioned for me as a constant reminder of normalcy. The campus, suburbanly pristine, with new buildings, paths, and plantings, contrasted starkly to my urban, semi-crumbling campus. Polite young white males wearing caps often held doors open for me as I entered buildings. As an example that may illustrate different worlds of thought between me and the students, noteworthy as I reviewed my interview transcripts was my persistent, faltering use of the word "queer" in asking questions. There are hesitations, self-corrections, where I stop the word, "Qu—," and shift to "gay and lesbian." Not once, except in a reference to the TV show *Queer Eye for the Straight Guy*, did I hear the young people articulate the word "queer." A question arose in the process of the research: How do theoretical and political stances that disavow identities and categories enter into dialogue with an institution, student organization, and individual young people, not to mention a research project, all of which are invested in and predicated on identities and categories? Unable to answer my ruminations, I continued my fieldwork, observing order and breakdown in meetings, hanging out at GLSA events, and asking students to narrate their understandings and experiences of the GLSA. My data included interview transcripts, fieldnotes, and a research journal I kept during and after interviews and observations.

While I did not follow a specific, canonized "method" of analysis, my orientation to interpreting the data centered largely on identifying salient topics and developing categories from the interviews and observations, through which I created themes that linked and gave them meaning (e.g., Seidman, 1991). Despite a poststructural theoretical spirit that rejects the coherence of categories and themes, I followed dominant logics of analysis, coding my data topically, looking for patterns and divergences across interviews and observations, trying to understand individual and collective positionings of the group's members. This first reading of the data offered a portrait of converging lines, a representation whose narrative of progress and purposefulness, I suspect, would hearten universities and activists alike. The central analytic theme was *becoming*. The students articulated desires to *become* someone as individuals, to *become* visible as a group, and to *become* integrated into campus life. In this way, they would develop and the campus community would *become* more tolerant. Thus, I organized my initial analysis of individual and collective actions and reflections in terms of several framing discourses related to *becoming*: a discourse of a developmental narrative of psychosocial formation, a discourse of campus involvement and belonging, and a discourse of individual and collective LGBT progress through visibility. As I present these discourses, I offer examples from my interviews and observations less to put the actors into motion than to illustrate these discursive positions.

Converging Discourses of Becoming

The first discourse entails a developmental narrative of youthful transition to responsible adulthood within an institutional space. Roger told me, "We are all finding ourselves. That's why we're here at college." Indeed, a cover story in the student newspaper identified the GLSA as "A place where students can grow and learn from each other either through volunteer activities or social activities." As Joe described the importance of the GLSA's social functions, volunteer activities, and educational work, he explained, "We want to have a good time. It is part of college life. Having a good time and to learn at the same time, that's the system of college life." Tameka narrated her development in the context of the GLSA: "I know when I first started with the GLSA it was a lot about the social events that we did. And it has moved towards the politics and everything because I am learning more about it. And I am of age to vote." College and the GLSA, then, offered resources for pleasure and for "becoming," or developing the self.

This self-conscious development of self is consonant with practices of Western societies, in which youth are individualized to take on new forms of responsibility, or to govern themselves, as they work toward their future adulthood. As Kelly (2001, p. 30) points out, "experts" and society alike narrate youth as intrinsic transition:

> as an artefact of expertise, youth is principally about becoming; becoming an adult, becoming a citizen, becoming independent, becoming autonomous, becoming mature, becoming responsible. There is some sense in which all constructions of youth defer to this narrative of becoming, of transition.

One could understand this discourse in the context of Lesko's (2001) formulation of "panoptic time," in which young people are aware of social and institutional expectations regarding their development and self-consciously develop themselves within narrative segments created by others. Indeed, the students understood that the academic and the social serve complementary pedagogical functions of enabling their developmental trajectories.

The second discourse involves social "common sense" of young people's need for peer groups in order to support their development, particularly in college. "Belonging" and "fitting in," particularly for students pertaining to "minority groups," were significant discourses throughout my interviews. Greg described what the GLSA offered:

> I came out when I was a freshman in high school, but I'm independent and strong-willed. Not everyone is like that, and some people need a group they can belong to and feel like they fit in. . . . I think most of them join because it is a group that they can automatically be part of . . . . If you're gay, you can come right on in. And you'll fit right in, and you'll make new friends, and you can relate to other people.

Roger echoed this sentiment, telling me, "I went straight to the GLSA to basically find people, to find friends, just people that you like." Julie found that the GLSA offered both belonging and support: "people you can turn to, that have the same issues that you do . . . . I mean, in [this] county, there is a lot of discrimination. And so at least being in a group of people, you know you don't have to be alone in that."

As I suggested earlier, a discourse of students' needs for belonging, involvement, and integration into campus life supports institutional interests in creating "successful students" (e.g, Astin, 1984, 1993; Kuh et al., 2007; Tinto, 1998). Moreover, this belonging is linked to the first discourse, of transitioning to adulthood, in that social and educative peer group activities are thought to support successful (normative) development. Yet involvement and belonging also entailed a spatial factor of separation, as suggested by the students' assumptions that the enclosure of the GLSA would provide them with people with shared interests and concerns. Not only was sameness at work but difference. Students were conscious of real and imagined boundaries between the GLSA and others, mentioning the placement of the group's cubicle in the student group area. Sam explained, "You can't talk about sex too much because we've had complaints," to which Chuck responded, "Well, across the room from us is the Catholic cubicle." In another discussion about the upcoming Student Group Fair, one member commented, "Yeah, we'll be next to the Christian group again. Last time they said they were praying for us." This spatialization of groupness, particularly when understood in relation to the students' essentializing assumptions about shared interests among group members, conjures Clarke, Harrison, Reeve, and Edwards' (2002) image of a postsecondary institution as an assemblage that "might be represented as a space of enclosure, in which people are subject to disciplinary constraints and in which they enjoy a sense of belonging" (p. 288).

The third discourse entailed using individual and collective visibility as a means of creating acceptance and equality so that the university would become a more tolerant, equitable place. In meetings and interviews, group members reiterated the importance of campus visibility. The group's vice-president explained,

> One of our goals is to promote equality on campus. And last semester we were invited to speak to a class about not just the GLSA, but about gay life. A goal is just to make the group wider, more known, and with that make more people on campus know about gay life, and accept it in a way.

Within this discourse, LGBT students benefit developmentally from representing the self and from positive representations, and "straight" students benefit from increased contact with and understanding of difference. Tameka described this logic: "We're having a large impact on individuals, which is where it starts. People are coming to meetings, coming out, and then speaking up on campus." These students echoed dominant narratives that assume that gay and lesbian visibility creates political progress, that individual "coming out" and collective representation lead to understanding, tolerance, and social change (Talburt, 2000).

This educative desire to work for campus tolerance projected the group from its isolated spatiality outward to the campus. In an interview in the campus newspaper, one member explained, "We make people aware just by being out, being active in school and being active in more than just the GLSA." The group's signature event of the season was its sponsorship of a talk by a popular local radio disc jockey who had recently come out as lesbian. As the group's vice-president explained to members at a meeting,

> She was a graduate of [this university], one of the first open lesbians on radio, and their ratings have skyrocketed. She wants to do a casual Q & A, to talk about how to succeed in the corporate world you need to diversify your mind.

Another student explained excitedly, "We want straight people to come and this will be a good time to get our name out there." In another meeting, as the group deliberated participating in a project with Habitat for Humanity, which was recruiting student groups to work on houses, the first question a student asked was, "Will [the president of the university] know the GLSA did it?" The students tacitly expressed a goal of progressively normalizing gayness on campus through a repeated (and positive) presence.

These discourses of becoming intersect to define the logic within which these young people negotiated their activities. The students had a goal of "becoming meaningful" on campus through social and educational activities, yet these meanings were constrained by linear narrative trajectories laid out for them by institution and society. Becomings through development, involvement, integration, and progressive visibility converge to constitute a logic of "straight lines" that can be understood in advance. Students' developmental needs, LGBT progress, and institutional success meet happily.

And here I pause. Such a neat reading seemed incomplete.

My dissatisfaction with these converging lines led me to wonder whether there might be another way to approach the data. In other words, I wondered not only what institutional logic left out, but what my research left out. To press no further than a critique of these logics of becoming as normative technologies that produce "good" lesbian and gay students (who are largely desexualized and mostly involved in wholesome volunteering or corporate-style diversity talk) on a campus shedding its conservatism (at least in relation to "good gays") did not seem to offer an alternative vision. I thus posed for myself an analytic challenge to rethink openings in the data. My goal was to read the data in a way that would enable me to create "unstraight" lines that break with conventional developmental narratives of progress that insist on and produce desires for a singular trajectory with a beginning, middle, and ending. A second, less thematized, reading of the data focused on interruptions in reflections and actions that might suggest detours. Two elements stood out. First were the group's actions and interactions, which, though framed by a purposeful rhetoric of becoming, suggested that a trajectory was not in evidence, except as a desire, a motivating force. Second were ambivalent, yet provocative, challenges to identity injected into the group by Roger. Before turning to this "other reading," I offer some theoretical ruminations that enabled this different thinking.

Different Becomings

Feminist literary theorist Jane Gallop (2002) opens her book *Anecdotal Theory* by telling readers, "Dynamic ideas are definitely more to my liking" (p. 1). She valorizes less what ideas and texts *mean* and more what they *do*, a spirit consonant with Deleuze's (1990, p. 25) seductive proposition that philosophy is trying to invent or create concepts. . . . We . . . are interested in the circumstances in which things happen: in what situations, where and when does a particular thing happen, how does it happen, and so on? A concept, as we see it, should express an event rather than an essence.

As acts of creation, concepts relate to "circumstances rather than essences" (p. 32). Such thinking reminded me that my inquiry was in danger of reproducing the logic of essences (or essential becomings) rather than constituting *doings*.

Although this reading does not take up an explicitly feminist poststructural or queer analysis, it is informed by their displacement of binary logic (such as homo/hetero, youth/adult), questioning of mainstream LGBT politics' identitarian will-to-recognition, and play with the relations of *being* and *doing* (see Butler, 1990, 2004; Sedgwick, 1990). Queer theory rejects the idea of a discrete, stable (sexual) identity, arguing that the homo/hetero division is constituted by a power/knowledge regime that organizes the normal and the abnormal and orders social and institutional relations. Queer theory studies processes of differentiation of "normal" and "deviant," disrupts these categorizations as natural, and seeks to foster new forms of affiliation. Because binary categories are effects of a system of compulsory heterosexuality, the claiming of a marginalized identity, such as "gay" or "lesbian," reinforces categories that support heteronormative regimes. Judith Butler (1990) argues that compulsory heterosexuality regulates the continuity of a subject's sex-gender-desire as coherent, demanding that subjects express socially intelligible behaviors. To "be" or "become" gay or lesbian, then, is an effect of power, a series of regulated "doings" or actions. One cannot "become" a gender. Rather, one must repeat gender in order for it to seem real. In this sense, "becoming" something is not predictable or linear, but is a doing, "a practice of improvisation within a scene of constraint" (Butler, 2004, p. 1). And improvisation is open to detours within constraints.

This anti-essentialistic thinking is consonant with Deleuze and Guattari's anti-foundationalist emphasis on non-linear connections, circumstances, and relations. In fact, a number of feminist poststructural educational researchers have drawn on Deleuze and Guattari's metaphors of the nomad, rhizomes, the fold, and lines of flight to enact new forms of qualitative research (e.g., Leach and Boler, 1998; St. Pierre, 1997a, b). St. Pierre (1997a) has described her efforts to "deterritorialize the linearity and coherence of the ethnographic text" (p. 283) by drawing on the image of the fold. Like the rhizome, which exists in the middle and has no beginnings or endings, the fold does not stand alone and suggests other sides that might constantly change. It breaks apart the reified logic of binary categories, subverting the order representation can impose on its subjects.

Of particular interest to me, Deleuze's (1990) idea of becoming is distinctly opposed to the narrative predictability of *evolving*. In other words, becoming may entail repetition but it is not predictable and does not occur in the straight line many would equate with development and evolution. Rather, becoming entails unpredictable connections and the "positive movement of differentiation" (Leach and Boler, 1998, p. 153). In *Difference and repetition,* Deleuze (1994) argued that repetition is essential to difference, but repetition occurs in relation to something new; hence, his emphasis on circumstances and connections. Parallel to Butler's (2004) thinking about the repetition of gender in new contexts, Deleuzian repetition is not a "copy," but actions with the potential to produce something different. Becoming entails nonteleological directions and movements even as it depends on repetition (of, for example, developmental narratives).

Deleuze and Guattari's (1987) metaphor of the rhizome enables an understanding of becoming that is not predicated on straight lines, teleologies, or essences. Unlike the hierarchy of the tree, with its foundational roots and predictably directed growth, the rhizome represents an uncentered series of lines that spread and proliferate and can connect with any other line. To think rhizomatically is to be concerned with relations, linkages, and surface connections rather than wholes, hidden depths, or latencies (Grosz, 1994). The rhizome opens understandings of subjects, events, or entities that might seem coherent, unified, or singular, to conceptualize them as "temporary assemblages of elements, composites that follow abstract lines of development and organization" (Roy, 2003, p. 87) without beginnings or endings. In the context of the GLSA, the becoming of the students becomes other than the repetition of a developmental order.

Grosz (1994) synthesizes Deleuze's distinction between two sorts of lines, molar unities and molecular becomings, which she equates with minoritarian and majoritarian groupings. The molar "is a rigidly segmented line, the line that divides, orders, hierarchizes, and regulates social relations through binary codes" (p. 203), such as "the divisions of classes, races, and sexes" (p. 203). In contrast, a molecular becoming "forms connections and relations beyond the rigidity of the molar line. It is composed of fluid lines, which map processes of becoming, change, movement, and reorganization" (Grosz, p. 204). The molecular is in relation to the molar, yet disrupts its certainty, traveling through and beyond it (Marks, 1998, p. 100). Leach and Boler (1998) explain that molar lines give rise to identity politics and "help explain how we become fixed; (molecular) lines of flight how we can interrupt the trajectories of molar lines" (p. 160). In the context of my research with the GLSA, molar lines might be understood as institutional(ized) desires, exemplified by linear narratives for developing identity, the spatialization and integration of the group, and progress through visibility and education. And the molecular was less visible.

My goal in rereading my data was to think rhizomatically, or to understand the possibility of molecular lines of becoming as potentialities, capacities, or movements. I traced actions and perceptions as they revealed the interplay of the molar and molecular, finding places in which linear individual and collective trajectories were not in evidence.

Unstraight Lines

Despite the students' clear statements of purpose, the GLSA's meetings frequently ended without a conclusion or destination. In contrast to declarations of educational, social, and political goals and seemingly purposeful activities, the students' actions and interactions were often suggestive of a subversion of their own stated trajectories. In other words, the students primarily engaged in "hanging out," using institutional resources and structures as sources of pleasure. When I asked the outgoing president what she would do differently, she noted a disjuncture between goals for purposefulness and desires for less direction, saying, "We talked about that, we should do more social stuff. . . . We have these meetings to do stuff, but it turns more social." When I asked Joe his impressions of members' desires for activities, he said, "A lot of them, when they offer ideas for things to do, it's always for like an event or some kind of activity. It's not really an activity that promotes equality on campus. . . . It's more a hanging out kind of thing, meeting people they can relate to."

My fieldnotes offer an interesting example of intersecting lines. The scene was a Wednesday night in a side room of the university cafeteria, where some 30-plus students were eating pizza and drinking sodas at a GLSA meeting. The group's leaders were outlining possible events and recruiting volunteers to form organizing committees. In the midst of selecting activities for the remainder of the semester, the following exchange began:

Bob: I thought S was Student. I didn't know straights were welcome. You might want to change your advertising.
Pamela: If you want to get technical, it should be LGBTS.
Alicia: We don't want to change our name because people are just getting to know the GLSA.
Bob: What's the point? If you want to attract people, your name needs to tell them what you do.
Joe: We have a mission statement on our website.
Bob: No, your name. I have to be looking for information, but if you want to reach people who aren't looking, who're walking down the quad. The name tells me that it's a bunch of people, but it doesn't tell me anything, like a mission.
Tameka: In the student hall, everyone puts up posters. Could we put up a poster saying what we do?

Roger: Our point, what is our point?

Bob: What is the purpose, that you want people to know you want to be part of the community?

Cory: Five words, you need five words.

Roger: What do you want our moral to be? Do you want it to be a gay clique?

Scott: From a student viewpoint, I don't see the GLSA out there. I know gay people on campus who don't know about this group. I'm in poli sci and it's hard to speak as a gay man. They're talking about Bush and stuff. You gotta break the barrier.

Roger: If we're going to be comfortable on campus, we've gotta make the group visible. I'm for all of us getting along.

Angela: The mission statement says we should educate the campus, and we can't get along if most of the campus doesn't know us and they're afraid of us.

Gary: We're talking about all of this. Let's pick times and places and get things done. A banner, a mission statement, and let's do things.

Roger goes to the board and solicits five words to get picked for a banner. Tameka grabs the chalk to write them down. Group members offer words that she writes carefully on the board.

Education	Community	Pride
Diversity	Acceptance	Unity
Fun	Outreach	

As the word choice continues, the meeting degenerates into conversations among different groups. A few participate in this originally central conversation, some chat in small groups, and others plan a social event and a fundraising carwash in the city's "gay neighborhood."

There are a number of ways to think about this scene, one of the more engaging moments I witnessed in my time with the GLSA. Briefly, a number of the discourses of "becoming" that I identified earlier are present: members' perceptions of a need for integration into a larger community, an idea that group visibility will enable the individual to speak as a gay person, a belief that group visibility will foster campus tolerance and acceptance. The galvanizing question of borders of who is in or out was present in but not central to my initial analysis. And this question of "who" relates to the group's spatialization as a site of sameness (or identity), which makes possible its purpose, its desire for recognition in and integration into a larger sphere of the university.

The breakdown of order and ferment of this meeting contrasted with the predictability of most of the GLSA's meetings. Usually, Joe, the group's vice-president, would open the meetings by handing out a calendar for the month, during which he would announce upcoming events and solicit volunteers for fundraising activities such as a bake and T-shirt sale, banner-making, or a Student Groups Fair exhibit. This would usually be followed by suggestions for how to undertake these activities or brainstorming sessions for other activities. Some members would suggest social activities; others wanted political discussions and activism at the local and state levels; and still others desired discussion of "everyday issues," such as the effects of coming out. The meetings tended to end with light, social discussion.

This meeting, "disrupted" by a straight-identified student visiting the GLSA as an extra credit assignment for his psychology class (which several GLSA members had recently visited to offer a panel on "Gay and Lesbian Issues"), brought to the fore questions of "who" and "what for" in a way that initially seemed to focus the group. But the group members could not sustain a purposeful trajectory related to defining their collective identity and goals. The turn to various forms of sociality suggests that other connections and desires were at work. With little evidence, I want to suggest that on the one hand these young people were "attached" to their identities: being "someone," in this case lesbian or gay, offered a space and set of reasons to come together, including the ostensible "duties" and "obligations" (see Patton, 1993) to seek rights and recognition that come with a minoritized identity. Yet these institutionalized (or molar) unities were disrupted by molecular becomings that were not in evidence as tangible goals but as micro-resistances to a singular purposeful becoming. Rather than enacting a unitary collective identity or a singular goal, the students appeared to be exploring affiliations within the group.

The second disruptive moment I turn to entails Roger's more overt challenges to identity and purpose. This example comes from my research journal:

> At the safe space training offered to faculty, staff, and students, Roger asked questions that clearly annoyed a few of the faculty members and the faculty advisor who had organized the training. After a fill-in-the-blank sentence completion activity, "Being GLBT at [this university] means _____," participants answered "being second class," "being ignored," "nothing," "negotiating safe space." Roger jumped out of his chair and declared, "My race is human and we're putting gay people in a group." After a few people responded to him that they didn't feel safe in their environments, Roger asked, "What are you going for, acknowledging people or working for a loving environment?" Someone says, "It's about all kinds of allies for all kinds of minorities, like international students, and different kinds of minorities." Roger: "I don't want to form another minority, another group of people with purple skin."

Roger's query about acknowledgment of a specific group functioned as an opportunity to take up the purposes of LGBT visibility on campus, yet it was an opportunity largely ignored. For example, the group's faculty advisor commented that Roger wanted the GLSA to be a "happy people's organization, with no focus; great for a university without homophobia, but not here." In an interview a few days later, Roger described his discomfort with the group's identitarian segregation. The GLSA had offered him a place to find friends, yet it was a space he wanted to open up:

> They [the GLSA's officers] want it to be exclusively gay, you know, 'we're gay people and we want people to know that we are gay,' but I don't want it to be exclusively gay. It's almost like saying, we need the gay club so that people feel accepted, but then we are also saying no one else is allowed in there.

He was developing a nascent critique of the GLSA leaders' adherence to institutionalized logic:

> They want to get as many members so they can say we have five hundred members even though they never show up. Who cares about the membership? I want to get people involved. What's a number? It's like society, all they want is numbers. School, all they want is a good test score. They could care less if they are actually teaching their students, that they are learning anything, as long as they have good test scores.

Although his protests did not appear to be taken seriously (at least not in the context of my empirical research), Roger was a charismatic young man who remained in the GLSA despite repeated warnings that he would drop out. As I was completing my fieldwork, I learned that he had become increasingly active in the organization (and had begun a relationship with Joe, the vice-president) and headed up the Design Committee. On my last visit, I arrived to find a new look for the GLSA. A couple of group members told me that Roger's group had undertaken a "de-gaying" of the GLSA's cubicle. They appeared pleased with the change, smiling as they saw me look. Gone were the rainbow flag and the Human Rights Campaign poster. In their place was a banner:

Gay Lesbian Straight Alliance

Education	Community	Diversity
Acceptance	Unity	Fun

With the "S" publicly clarified and multiple goals announced, Roger had participated in making a move toward defining a "who" and a "what for." While the change continued to be attached to an institutional logic of identities and development, it also suggested possibilities for new forms of affiliation and multiple trajectories.

The Messiness of Becoming

My research is unable to "explicate" the molecular, perhaps due to a lack of data, which could be attributed to the research's initial linear orientation or to happenstance in fieldwork. Regardless, my sense is that this lack of explication can point to alternative directions for research into higher educational policy and practice. If a project of education is to encourage the development of potentialities, capacities, and movements – and I believe it is – research needs to move beyond reproducing the logic of molar unities, such as elaborating models undergirding student development, success, or resilience. Rather than refining predictable narratives whose beginnings, middles, and endings must be administered by experts and institutions, research might complicate ideas about identities and thus cease to participate in disciplining and normalizing subjects through ideals of needs and success.

Puar (2005) writes against stabilizing identities in time and space by naming and making them knowable and draws instead on a Deleuzian idea of assemblage "as a series of dispersed but mutually implicated networks" (p. 127) that is beyond the logic of "diversity management [and] liberal multiculturalism" (p. 128). The idea of assemblage shifts attention to intensities and affect, acknowledging becomings that cannot be known as pertaining to something or someone specific. Her thinking is consonant with an emphasis on molecularities that seeks spaces of play that institutional policy and practice cannot identify, prescribe, or predict. In my research, the students' deviations of becoming could be qualified as relatively "small" or "minor"; nonetheless, their non-teleological and non-linear practices point to the possibility that students can put institutional and social discourses and resources to new (if not in this case, radical) uses. Although discourses circumscribe what is possible to say, do, be, or become, and even as subjects depend on discourses and norms to become recognizable to themselves and others, discourses and norms are "socially articulated and changeable" (Butler, 2004, p. 2).

If research is to move away from predicting and controlling and toward focusing on possibilities of becoming, research must take care not to insistently privilege the potentiality of "becoming" over individuals' sense of and desires for "being someone." Research must be mindful of the power of discourses to attach subjects to desires for identity, community, and "correct" development. As Tatman and Rasmussen (2003) have rightly argued, "'becoming' (as the promise of our theoretical salvation) becomes rather problematic when it is presented independently of the messiness and intractability of 'being'" (pp. 1–2). They point to a romantic strain in theorizations of "becoming" that contrast possibility, potentiality, and openness to the stasis of "being." Yet, given subjects' affective attachments to "being," they caution that theory and research cannot "privilege 'doing' over 'meaning,' particularly when the subjects in question [such as youth] . . . have a long history of being precluded from the realm of meaning-making" (p. 3). To return to the idea of repetition, they follow Butler's thinking that subjects may be attached to their subjection (as a source of subjecthood), but may also repeat their subject positions "incorrectly," thereby producing something new yet recognizable. "Becoming" is not a free-floating promise, but takes place within the constraints of socio-historical "facts" of designating individuals and groups, the materiality of bodies, and the bifurcation of sexes and genders. Thus, Tatman and Rasmussen (2003) say, "Like it or not our becoming is limited. We may become someone but we cannot become *anyone*" (p. 4).

As GLSAs and other entities function as social and political formations in universities, and as they interact with university policy and university policy interacts with them, researchers might ask: If subjects must act and affiliate with others in certain ways in order to be recognized as someone, what new ways of acting and affiliating do young people create? To what extent do students use these organizations and other university formations to chart new registers of community and connection? And, as institutions and their policies mediate possibilities for subjects, how do students rewrite these possibilities? What degrees of freedom to "become someone" do students create?

References

Astin, A. W. (1984). Student involvement: A developmental theory for higher education. *Journal of College Student Personnel*, 25(5), 297–308.
Astin, A. W. (1993). *What matters in college? Four critical years revisited*. San Francisco, CA: Jossey-Bass.
Bacchi, C. L. (1999). *Women, policy, and politics: The construction of policy problems*. London: Sage.
Barry, R. (2000). Sheltered "children": The self-creation of a safe space by gay, lesbian, and bisexual students. In L. Weis & M. Fine (Eds.), *Constructing sites: Excavating race, class, and gender among urban youth* (pp. 84–99). New York: Teachers College Press.
Butler, J. (1990). *Gender trouble: Feminism and the subversion of identity*. New York: Routledge.
Butler, J. (2004). *Undoing gender*. New York: Routledge.
Chickering, A. W. & Reisser, L. (1993). *Education and identity*, 2nd ed. San Francisco. CA: Jossey-Bass.
Clarke, J., Harrison, R., Reeve, F., & Edwards, R. (2002). Assembling spaces: The question of 'place' in further education. *Discourse: Studies in the Cultural Politics of Education*, 23(3), 285–297.
Deleuze, G. (1990). *Negotiations 1972–1990*. Trans. M. Joughin. New York: Columbia University Press.
Deleuze, G. (1994). *Difference and repetition*. Trans. P. Patton. New York: Columbia University Press.
Deleuze, G. & Guattari, F. (1987). *A thousand plateaus: Capitalism and schizophrenia*. Trans. B. Massumi. Minneapolis, MN: University of Minnesota Press.
Dilley, P. (2002). *Queer man on campus: A history of non-heterosexual college men, 1945–2000*. New York and London: RoutledgeFalmer.
Duggan, L. (2003). *The twilight of equality? Neoliberalism, cultural politics, and the attack on democracy*. Boston, MA: Beacon Press.
Evans, N. J. (1998). *Student development in college: Theory, research, and practice*. San Francisco, CA: Jossey-Bass.
Evans, N. J. & Wall, V.A. (Eds.). (1991). *Beyond tolerance: Gays, lesbians, and bisexuals on campus*. Lanham, MD: University Press of America.
Gallop, J. (2002). *Anecdotal theory*. Durham, NC and London: Duke University Press.
Grosz, E. (1994). A thousand tiny sexes: Feminism and rhizomatics. In C. V. Boundas & D. Olkowski (Eds.), *Gilles Deleuze and the theater of philosophy* (pp. 187–210). New York and London: Routledge.
Halberstam, J. (2005). *In a queer time and place: Transgender bodies, subcultural lives*. New York and London: New York University Press.
Jagose, A. (1996). *Queer theory: An introduction*. New York: New York University Press.

Kelly, P. (2001). Youth at risk: Processes of individualisation and responsibilisation in the risk society. *Discourse: Studies in the Cultural Politics of Education*, 22(1), 23–33.

Kuh, G., Kinzie, J., Buckley, J. A., Bridges, B. K., & Hayek, J. C. (2007). *Piecing together the student success puzzle: Research, propositions, and recommendations.* ASHE Higher Education Report 32(5). San Francisco: Jossey-Bass.

Leach, M. & Boler, M. (1998). Gilles Deleuze: Practicing education through flight and gossip. In M. Peters (Ed.), *Naming the multiple: Poststructuralism and education* (pp. 149–170). Westport, CT: Bergin & Garvey.

Lesko, N. (2001). *Act your age! A cultural construction of adolescence.* New York: Routledge.

MacLure, M. (2003). *Discourse in educational and social research.* Buckingham, UK and Philadelphia, PA: Open University Press.

Marks, J. (1998). *Gilles Deleuze: Vitalism and multiplicity.* London and Sterling, VA: Pluto Press.

Patton, C. (1993). Tremble hetero swine! In M. Warner (Ed.), *Fear of a queer planet* (pp. 143–177). Minneapolis, MN: University of Minnesota Press.

Patton, C. (1996). *Fatal advice: How safe-sex education went wrong.* Durham, NC: Duke University Press.

Pillow, W. S. (2003). Confession, catharsis, or cure? Rethinking the uses of reflexivity as methodological power in qualitative research. *International Journal of Qualitative Studies in Education*, 16(2), 175–196.

Puar, J. K. (2005). Queer times, queer assemblages. *Social Text*, 84–85(23, 1–2), 121–139.

Rofes, E. (2004). Martyr-target-victim: Interrogating narratives of persecution and suffering among queer youth. In M. L. Rasmussen, E. Rofes, & S. Talburt (Eds.), *Youth and sexualities: Pleasure, subversion, and insubordination in and out of schools* (pp. 41–62). New York: Palgrave Macmillan.

Roy, K. (2003). *Teachers in nomadic spaces: Deleuze and curriculum.* New York: Peter Lang.

Sanlo, R. L. (1998). *Working with lesbian, gay, bisexual, and transgender college students: A handbook for faculty and administrators.* Westport, CT: Greenwood.

Sedgwick, E. K. (1990). *Epistemology of the closet.* Berkeley, CA: University of California Press.

Seidman, I. E. (1991). *Interviewing as qualitative research: A guide for researchers in education and the social sciences.* New York: Teachers College Press.

St. Pierre, E. A. (1997a). An introduction to figurations: A poststructural practice of inquiry. *International Journal of Qualitative Studies in Education*, 10(3), 279–284.

St. Pierre, E. A. (1997b). Methodology in the fold and the irruption of transgressive data. *International Journal of Qualitative Studies in Education*, 10(2), 175–189.

Talburt, S. (2000). *Subject to identity: Knowledge, sexuality, and academic practices in higher education.* Albany, NY: SUNY Press.

Talburt, S. (2004). Intelligibility and narrating queer youth. In M. L. Rasmussen, E. Rofes, & S. Talburt (Eds.), *Youth and sexualities: Pleasure, subversion, and insubordination in and out of schools* (pp. 17–39). New York: Palgrave Macmillan.

Tatman, L. & Rasmussen, M. L. (2003). Becoming someone (but not anyone). Paper presented at the Cultural Studies Association of Australasia, Christchurch, Aotearoa/New Zealand.

Tinto, V. (1998). Colleges as communities: Taking research on student persistence seriously. *The Review of Higher Education*, 21(2), 167–177.

Vaid, U. (1995). *Virtual equality: The mainstreaming of gay and lesbian liberation.* New York: Anchor.

Wilson, M. E. & Wolf-Wendel, L. (Eds.). (2006). *ASHE Reader on College Student Development Theory.* Boston, MA: Pearson.

7

Title IX Policy and Intercollegiate Athletics

A Feminist Poststructural Critique

JENNIFER LEE HOFFMAN, SUSAN V. IVERSON,
ELIZABETH J. ALLAN, AND REBECCA ROPERS-HUILMAN

Few policies in higher education garner as much attention from campus leaders, students, parents, government agencies, and the general public as Title IX. This legislation was originally developed by Edith Green (D-OR) and Patsy Mink (D-HI) (later joined by advocate Birch Bayh, D-IN) to ensure women equity in medical and law school admissions. Since its inception in 1972, Title IX policy has also removed barriers to women's participation in intercollegiate athletics. Yet, its application in college sports continues to receive mixed responses. It is praised for the opportunities given to women student-athletes, but is also largely viewed as a policy that takes athletic opportunity away from men to make room for women. Often the dialogue in the press, on campus, and in the courtroom is focused on monitoring the number of participants and gauging interest in athletic participation among women students. The impact of Title IX policy on intercollegiate athletics is more complex than simply "counting ponytails" to maintain a proportional balance between student-athletes and the student body based on gender (Suggs, 2007). This chapter describes how the use of a feminist poststructural (FPS) analysis of Title IX illuminates the ways in which Title IX policy can simultaneously reinforce and disrupt the relationship between athletic programs' mission and purpose and those of universities.

Illustrating the "institutional ties between sports and schools" (Boutilier & SanGiovanni, 1994, p. 14), Title IX amplified the argument that participating in intercollegiate athletics has an inherent educational value and is integral to the mission of higher education. This policy has also been proposed as a strategy to rein in "big-time" sports, by replacing the commercial, professional model with one based on educational values (Lazerson & Wagener, 1996; Porto, 2003) or with an amateur athletic model (Sack & Staurowsky, 1998). Complying with Title IX is suggested as an occasion for university Presidents and Boards to examine the athletic budget, providing a "golden opportunity to address the chronic corruption of college sports" (Lazerson & Wagener, 1996, p. 52). From this perspective, the policy is seen as a chance to promote women's sports while reforming men's college athletics. Using Title IX to exert more institutional control over the professionalized college football model is an attempt to minimize the commercial aspects of intercollegiate athletics, replacing it with a developmental model more closely aligned with the academic goals of colleges and universities.

Conversely, the College Sports Council and the Independent Women's Forum view this federal gender equity policy as an additional economic burden and quota system that prompts schools to add programs for women regardless of demonstrated interest and to eliminate some men's sports (Gavora, 2002). Complying with Title IX means providing equitable access and resources which often entails adding women's programs, updating facilities, hiring additional coaches, and providing scholarships so that opportunities and support for female students is at, or approaching, the same level as it is for male students. Annual costs for each women's team average $500,000 per year at Division I-A athletic programs (Moore, 2005). Adding women's programs increases the demand for resources within a department and this demand is criticized because of the perception that it forces a loss of athletic opportunity for men. The addition of women's programs or cuts to men's sports disrupts the status quo of intercollegiate athletics. There is an assumption that to make room for women's programs, men's programs must either be eliminated or men's programs must share resources that belong only to them.

These educational and economic perspectives are situated within broader discourses that have shaped Title IX policy. College football and men's basketball garner wide spectator appeal and are thought to operate separately from the academic mission of teaching, learning, and research (Toma & Cross, 2000). Yet, Title IX "leaves unquestioned the educational value of athletics and the proper role of sports in schools" (Boutilier & SanGiovanni, 1994, p. 14). This chapter describes a conceptual analysis of Title IX policy that draws on feminist poststructural perspectives to examine discourses circulating in intercollegiate athletics, illuminate tensions between marketplace and developmental discourses, and discuss implications for educational administrators.

A Feminist Poststructural Critique

Building on historical analyses of women's intercollegiate athletics, this chapter describes the contemporary implementation of Title IX and the policy discourses that shape predominant understandings of this legislation. Then, the policy is examined through an FPS lens which differs from other approaches in that it illuminates "ways of constituting knowledge, together with the social practices, forms of subjectivity and power relations which inhere in such knowledges and the relations between them" (Weedon, 1997, p. 105). A poststructural analysis of policy considers how knowledge is constituted and how meaning is inscribed (Ropers-Huilman, 1998). The meaning produced by Title IX policy goes beyond the 37 words of the federal statute or textual definitions of policy guidelines. Rather, Title IX policy is a "meaning-constituting system" (Scott, 1990, p. 135) and a type of discursive practice that both reflects and shapes culture.

Specific statements, terms, categories, and beliefs about Title IX have historical, social, and institutional context and meaning (Scott, 1990; Weedon, 1997) for intercollegiate athletics and educational institutions. Within these contexts, they play an "important determining role in the development, maintenance, and circulation of discourses" about women in athletics (Mills, 1997, p. 11). From an FPS view, these discourses are "forms of knowledge or sets of assumptions, expectations, and explanations" that govern mainstream social and cultural practice in college sports (Baxter, 2003, p. 7).

This chapter highlights how assumptions, expectations, and explanations that influence intercollegiate athletics are discursively shaped. In organizations and social relationships, language, customs, practices, and policy are constituted via discourse (Weedon, 1997). Baxter describes how discourses shape and distribute knowledge and power by producing and sustaining "systematic ways of making sense of the world" (2003, p. 7). As such, Title IX policy and the discourses shaping it are an important way in which power in intercollegiate athletics is produced and transmitted.

A FPS perspective of Title IX policy discourses also draws attention to the multiplicity of power relations between women and men and among women (Baxter, 2003). Women of color have not benefited from the athletic opportunities as participants, coaches, or administrators in the same way as white middle-class women. The discourses shaping intercollegiate athletics and women's sports in general tend to highlight a distorted view of women as a universal group based on a white, middle-class, heterosexual social and cultural experience. Yet, within Title IX policy, and athletic departments alike, power struggles are often rooted in gender, class, ethnic, and sexual orientation identity categories.

While much of our discussion of women in athletics will be premised on a provisional acceptance of women as a universal category, we want to acknowledge that difference among women is re/produced by the discourses circulating in intercollegiate athletics. Social power in athletics manifests differently for women and is often linked with other identity statuses (e.g., race, sexual identity, social class); thus, the impact of Title IX is not consistent for all women. In 2004–2005, 70.5 percent of women participating in Division I intercollegiate athletics were white. Women of color, mainly African-American women, participate largely in basketball and track and field. In all other Division I sports, African-American women make up only 15.4 percent of participants, Latinas 3.3 percent, and Asian women 2.2 percent (Lapchick, 2005). Women of color are also scarce in coaching and administration. Among Division I women's teams, 35.3 percent of coaches were white women, 3 percent African-American women, and only 1.3 percent all other minority categories combined; men comprised the remainder (Lapchick, 2005). Nor were a critical mass of women of color able to engage in the early fight over Title IX due to previous limits in accessing predominantly white higher education institutions. Likewise, lesbian women have suffered additional discrimination in athletics, and all women, regardless of sexual identity, have been victims of homophobic stereotyping in promoting women's sports (Griffin, 1992; O'Reilly & Cahn, 2007). This negative stereotyping only intensifies amidst advocacy for Title IX. Today, the policy dialogue is based on a normative standard constructed as white, heterosexual, and middle class.

Before Title IX, women's opportunity for participation in individual sports exceeded team sports, especially in colleges and universities. It was not until after Title IX that the shift back to team sports "at a highly competitive level" occurred (Grant & Darley, 1993, p. 256). Changes in women's athletics were consistent with this shift. For example, before Title IX, women's athletics emphasized the student-athlete and her ability to develop "knowledge of self and values that pertained to self" in informal and organized sport (Grant, 1984; see also Grant & Darley, 1993, p. 256). After Title IX, women's athletics, consolidated with men's programs, took on the characteristics of programs that cater to the interests of power, profitability, and a spectator audience (Bouttilier & SanGiovanni, 1983).

Dominant in shaping contemporary conceptions, implementation, and interpretation of Title IX is a competitive, commercially oriented understanding of intercollegiate athletics (Grant & Darley, 1993). An alternative understanding, focusing on self-development, is also visible in Title IX policy, constructing athletics as an opportunity for individual growth among the student-athletes who participate in college sports. This analysis of marketplace and self-development discourses proceeds in three stages. We begin with a historical perspective on women's intercollegiate athletics to explain the shift from informal and organized women's sports, a shift that began with a focus on the self-development of individual women and moved to a corporate sport model that emphasizes team sports in a broader marketplace. Next, we describe marketplace and self-development discourses and how they shape Title IX policy in intercollegiate athletics. Finally, we consider the discursive tension between these discourses and implications for policy and practice.

But first, a few words regarding method. Unlike traditional forms of inquiry that rely upon empirical tools to systematically investigate gender equity, this analysis employs a conceptual approach to pose questions about assumptions related to Title IX and the value of women's participation in intercollegiate athletics. The conceptual argument that follows draws on the lead author's previous history and knowledge about women's participation in intercollegiate athletics, relying on her experiences as a white woman working among an expansive array of college athletic teams at predominantly white institutions. From the intense sideline of a bowl game to the triumphant exhaustion at a women's cross-country finish line, I (Hoffman) acquired a unique insider perspective. This insider status gives me a rich awareness relevant to the theories of race, gender, and social class related to intercollegiate athletics. My (Hoffman's) involvement in college athletics, joined with feminist poststructural perspectives, informs the interrogation of evidence linked to assumptions shaping perceptions about Title IX. The intent of this analysis is to raise different kinds of questions about how women's participation in intercollegiate athletics is valued.

Historical Perspective on Title IX Policy in Athletics

Title IX policy reinforced the ties between intercollegiate athletics and higher education due in part to the historical legacy of women's athletics prior to Title IX and the legal interpretation of the policy after its passage in 1972. A historical analysis sheds light on the way in which particular discourses have shaped perceptions about Title IX within the context of college athletics.

Title IX policy marks a shift in the purpose of educating women. Before Title IX, women and men educated in coeducational institutions were prepared for different roles (Bashaw, 2001; Glazer & Slater, 1987). These institutions differentiated the purpose of education for students based on gender; thus, women's athletics were shaped by the separate purpose of educating women students. After Title IX mandated equity for women students, norms associated with education for separate spheres gave way to a valuing of gender equity. The coeducation philosophy in higher education and the shift to a gender equity philosophy is an integral component in understanding the historical legacy of women's athletics and Title IX.

Coeducation: Separate Purpose for Women's Athletics

At the start of the Progressive Era in 1890, most women college students attended coeducation institutions (Newcomer, 1959). The influx of women students challenged previously all-male institutions and renewed questions about the purpose of higher education for women. Coeducation meant women and men were *coeducated*, attending the same institutions but preparing for different roles (Bashaw, 2001; Glazer & Slater, 1987). "Men and women students proceeded along separate although parallel paths, establishing a separate, but parallel purpose for educating women" (Gordon, 1990, p. 3). As more women students were admitted, there was also growing concern about "feminization" of the university. "When at the beginning of the century, there was a sudden influx of women students into the university, top-level administrators began to fear that these new women students would drive men out" (Nerad, 1999, p. 10). Institutions limited women in admissions, built separate coordinate colleges, and created segregated classes (Gordon, 1990).

The rise of intercollegiate sport competition coincided with the rise of coeducation in the Progressive Era. Intercollegiate athletics grew quickly and became an important feature of the extracurriculum. Institutions built football stadiums and Olympic-size swimming pools (Clifford, 1983; also Porto, 2003). Women's basketball quickly gained popularity among women students, but there were immediate concerns from university officials about their involvement in competitive athletics. At coeducational institutions men's sports were used to increase prestige and status of the institution. As early as 1900, Oberlin College used football to promote institutional reputation and bolster men's enrollment (Horger, 1996). The men's athletic program also helped counter fears over the feminization of higher education as more women attended coeducation institutions.

After an initial interest in competitive sports among women students, intercollegiate sports had developed into gender-differentiated opportunities by 1930 at most institutions. Assumptions about the effect of involvement in competitive sports on femininity, a belief in biology as destiny, maintaining separate spheres, fear of unwomanly behavior, and medical implications shaped discursive practices in women's intercollegiate sport (Hult & Trekell, 1991). For example, varsity basketball competitions were replaced with "play days." Play days were interschool events that mixed players for friendly recreation instead of head-to-head play. Play days emphasized moderation and the social aspects, often hosting teas or dances as part of the play day activities (Grundy & Shackelford, 2005; Suggs, 2005).

The highly competitive, commercially oriented men's athletic model continued to emerge and women took on a distinctly recreational, social model. This was due, in part, to a backlash that all women students and faculty faced throughout higher education in the 1920s. This backlash altered the initial gender-differentiated, *separate but parallel* purpose of educating women. Separate classes and colleges such as women's medical schools were replaced with women-specific fields such as nursing and home economics (Cott, 1987; Gordon, 1990; Nerad, 1999).

Women in physical education, such as Senda Berenson, Mabel Lee, and Clelia Mosher, responded by creating separate departments to retain their role in coeducation institutions and discouraged strenuous, competitive activity for women students. Women leaders in physical education were astute at taking control of women's athletics based on specific feminized philosophy of women's physical activity, emphasizing participation and minimizing competition (Grundy & Shackelford, 2005). By the 1930s, women students participated in non-competitive activities such as play days and sports days that were highly resistive to competition with strong leadership by faculty from the women's physical education department (Cahn, 1994; Hult & Trekell, 1991; Sack & Staurowsky, 1998).

There were alternatives to the women's physical education model. Outside of higher education, women's industrial leagues, Olympic development, and the American Athletic Union (AAU) all continued to promote a competitive model for women's athletics (Festle, 1996; Suggs, 2005). Other exceptions occurred in high schools, some colleges, and in particular institutions that served women of color. African-American women also participated in intercollegiate athletics during the Progressive Era. As was consistent with white institutions, most elite black colleges and universities "abandoned their earlier commitment to women's intercollegiate basketball" during the backlash at the end of the Progressive Era (Liberti, 1999, p. 567). However, while some black institutions were dismantling programs, others were introducing competitive teams. For example, at Bennett College, competitive athletics for women complemented the academic mission of contributing back to the black community. Women who had played competitive basketball at black institutions gained jobs teaching and coaching basketball at black elementary schools. Competitive basketball provided an outlet for black women to fulfill their duty of giving back to the community and their obligations of maintaining high moral standards. Although competitive basketball was offered at black institutions such as Bennett through the late 1930s and early 1940s, most competitive programs eventually followed the dominant women's physical education movement. Competition was de-emphasized in favor of non-competitive activities that promoted play days and "sportsmanship among the colleges" (Liberti, 1999, p. 578).

Until the late 1950s, the purpose of higher education for women was still highly differentiated by gender (Horowitz, 1987). The differentiation between women's and men's roles throughout coeducation shaped the separatist strategies faculty used to develop gender-specific athletic opportunities for women. Women leaders throughout the coeducation period created a separate, feminized subspecialty of physical education that minimized competition in contrast to the competitive, often commercialized men's intercollegiate model (Glazer & Slater, 1987; Nidiffer, 2000). Play days and sports days continued to provide a recreational model with an educational focus that countered the competitive, commercial men's athletic model.

It was not until the late 1950s and 1960s that women students and faculty began to challenge the gender-differentiated restrictions in higher education. In physical education a new generation of students, faculty, and athletic leaders prompted the re-emergence of competition in schools and colleges (Cahn, 1994; Festle, 1996; Hult, 1999; Hult & Trekell, 1991). The Association for Intercollegiate Athletics for Women (AIAW) evolved out of women's physical education and women's higher education organizations from this period. During the transformation of women's athletics after Title IX, the AIAW became the national governing body for women's competitive athletics in colleges and universities. Even as the change in the purpose of educating women in the years preceding Title IX ensued, the AIAW's philosophy for women's competition drew heavily on the heritage of women's athletics from coeducation. The AIAW promoted a separate women-led model of women's competitive sport that emphasized the educational aspects of women's sport, distinct from the commercial aspects of men's sport.

Gender Equity: Transforming Women's Athletics

Changes in higher education and the later feminist movement in the 1960s and 1970s challenged the separatist strategy that emphasized women-specific athletic programs. The method of educating women transformed from coeducation to a gender-combined model of higher education characterized by equity. The purpose of educating women changed from a separate, distinct purpose based on gender, to a purpose of education for women based on civil and legal equality. Separatist strategies to maintain women's athletic programs and governance of competition in previous generations were challenged. When Title IX went into effect on June 23, 1972, athletic programs were not specifically mentioned. Title IX simply states:

> No person in the United States shall, on the basis of sex, be excluded from participation in, be denied the benefits of, or be subjected to discrimination under any educational program or activity receiving Federal financial assistance. (Carpenter & Acosta, 2005, p. 3)

The National Collegiate Athletic Association, the men's governing organization, immediately challenged the application of Title IX in college athletics. Women leaders in the AIAW were integral in fighting the NCAA's challenge to Title IX and continued to promote a separate women's governance model of intercollegiate athletics.

The Department of Health Education and Welfare (HEW) clarified how Title IX applied to athletics in its guidelines published on June 19, 1974. The guidelines stated that, "although few athletic departments *directly* received federal funding, sports *would* be covered by Title IX" (Festle, 1996, p. 166, emphasis in the original). In this same year, the Tower Amendment was introduced to "exempt coverage under Title IX any sports that do or may provide gross receipts, noting that the purpose of this amendment was to preserve the revenue base of intercollegiate activities [so that] it will provide the resources for expanding women's activities in intercollegiate sports" (United States Commission on Civil Rights, 1980, p. 7). The Tower Amendment was unsuccessful in exempting revenue-producing sports in determining equity under Title IX (Carpenter & Acosta, 2005; Hogshead-Makar & Zimbalist, 2007). In December 1979, the Department of Health, Education and Welfare, via the Office of Civil Rights (OCR), issued a final policy interpretation providing a language that specifically included intercollegiate athletic programs, but many institutions were still out of compliance (United States Commission on Civil Rights, 1980).

Women student-athletes continued to demand more athletic opportunity in the 1980s, yet the only choices were options based on the men's model.

Intercollegiate athletics was a distinctly masculinist enterprise, with a strong, commercially oriented, marketplace-driven foundation. In 1981, the NCAA started offering women's championships and many member institutions began combining separate women's athletic departments under the oversight of the men's athletic director into one program. Women who had been Director of Women's Athletics under the separate program model were assigned a new title in the combined department arrangement. The AIAW's fight to retain a distinct women's philosophy for athletics and governance failed. The women's athletic governing organization was unable to resist a takeover by the NCAA and the AIAW ceased operations in 1982 (Washington, Forman, Suddaby, & Ventresca, 2005).

The women's leadership and funding structures were dismantled and there was little change in the model of men's athletics, but women's athletics continued to disrupt the resources of the established intercollegiate athletic program model. Few resources were available for women's programs and progress in meeting the demands of women's athletics was slow. Despite the OCR clarification in 1979 that regulated Title IX's application in higher education, the interpretation of the policy moved to the courts.

On February 28, 1984, the U.S. Supreme Court ruled in *Grove City College v. Bell* that Title IX only applied to programs within an institution that *directly* benefited from Federal funds. Under this interpretation Title IX did not apply to intercollegiate athletics. The *Grove City* court found that "program" was interpreted as a subunit of the institution and only those subunits were subject to Title IX jurisdiction, not the entire institution. Only programs receiving Federal funding must comply with Title IX. Since athletic programs did not receive any Federal subsidy, they were exempt under this interpretation. The *Grove City* decision eliminated Title IX's application in women's athletic programs. "Within weeks of the decision, scholarships for female athletes were canceled at several colleges across the nation, women's teams were slated for termination at others, OCR complaints were closed, and lawsuits were dismissed" (Carpenter & Acosta, 2005, p. 121).

Congress intervened after *Grove City* and passed the Civil Rights Restoration Act in 1988, reinstating Title IX's application to the entire institution, not subunits within institutions. The term "program" was clarified to apply "to the entire institution, not merely the subunit that actually receives federal funding" (Carpenter & Acosta, 2005, p. 126). This clarification reinstated intercollegiate athletics' compliance with Title IX. After the reversal of *Grove City* the OCR was still slow to respond to Title IX violations.

In 1996, *Cohen v. Brown University* reinforced proportionality as the "safe harbor" for Title IX compliance. In *Brown* the court found in favor of the plaintiffs, citing the 1979 OCR guidelines for achieving gender equity in athletics. The "three-pronged" test, as it is known, requires institutions to meet one of the following: (1) provide opportunity for athletic participation in numbers "proportional" to the undergraduate enrolment, (2) demonstrate a history of continued program expansion for the under-represented gender, or (3) demonstrate that the interest and ability of the under-represented gender have been effectively accommodated. *Cohen* rebuked the idea of "relative interest" to achieve compliance and the court recognized that a "lower rate of participation in athletics reflects women's historical lack of opportunities" (Carpenter & Acosta, 2005, p. 125). With successful legal enforcement of Title IX, athletic departments were ill-prepared to quickly construct an infrastructure for expansion of women's athletics. Many institutions addressed Title IX program requirements by making economic cuts in one program area to fund another. After Cohen the intense focus on Title IX "diverted attention from the escalating costs of football as the primary threat to men's Olympic sports" (Estler & Nelson, 2005, p. 53). Quick solutions to complying with Title IX left men's programs that didn't appeal to a large spectator audience vulnerable, forcing them to give up resources and opportunity (Anderson & Cheslock, 2004; Elliott & Mason, 2001).

Title IX Policy Discourses and Intercollegiate Athletics

Today, participation models in intercollegiate athletics fall loosely into three categories: the informal model, the organized model, and the corporate model (Boutilier & SanGiovanni, 1983). These categories are constituted through discourses that shape the way power is reflected and reproduced in athletics. The informal model exemplifies the recreational emphasis found in women's play days and interclass competition or contemporary intramural programs open to women and men. Although institutions build elaborate student recreation centers and offer extensive intramural and club athletic programs, the informal model receives little attention in the Title IX debate.

The organized model suggests more structure, reflecting the mission of the AIAW, fostering broad programs consistent with educational objectives. Today, women and men participate in organized college athletics, but women's participation is framed in self-development terms. Women's participation in college sports is assumed to be "beneficial, but not as serious as men's participation" (McDonough & Pappano, 2008, p. 239). The self-development discourse shapes the perception that women's participation in intercollegiate athletics benefits individual student-athletes who compete "for the love of the game" (McDonough & Pappano, 2008, p. 239).

The corporate model, exemplified by men's football and basketball, is a "structured and commodified one in which winning and making money (are) central goals" (Grant & Darley, 1993, p. 255). This model, made visible by a marketplace discourse, shapes beliefs that men's sports are valued more than women's athletics and men's intercollegiate programs garner more resources and attention (McDonough & Pappano, 2008). A seemingly dichotomous relationship between the organized and corporate model amplifies debate about the goals and purpose of intercollegiate athletics. Before discussing this tension, we will describe the discursive context from which these models gain currency.

Marketplace Discourse

The dominant discourse circulating around and within Title IX policy is characterized by economic aspects of intercollegiate athletics, such as cutting teams to manage budget overruns or as a model for controlling the commercialization in men's football and basketball. These characterizations are made visible by a marketplace discourse that shapes college sports as commercially oriented and competitive, and gives rise to images of the athlete as a commodity. The willingness of universities to profit from intercollegiate athletics is not limited to college sports. Bok (2003) defines commercialism in the academy as the "efforts within the university to make a profit from teaching, research, and other campus activities" (p. 3).

The dominant marketplace discourse is evidenced by descriptions of escalating financial costs and the commercial nature of college sports. Terms such as "big time," "commercialized," and "revenue-generating" describe the dominant college football and men's basketball model, keeping the attention squarely on economics and the fiscal benefits to sports as entertainment. Specifically, the term "revenue-generating" implies that these sports generate profit (Priest, 2003). There is an assumption that all revenue-generating sports produce a profit, and that they support other sports and program activities within a department.

In the pre-Title IX era, the athletic department consisted only of men's sports and it was not uncommon for men's football to provide financial support to other programs in the department. When women's and men's athletic departments were separate, funds generated by men's football were distributed to other men's sports and the financial demands from these sports were modest. Before Title IX, scholarships and other high-cost expenses were usually limited to football, basketball, baseball, and track (Thelin, 2000). Women's sports received little, if any, funding. Later, when women's and men's programs were combined, the gendered practices of resource allocation often remained. The gendering of resources in athletics remains a proxy for the gendered culture of intercollegiate athletics.

Football prevails as a vehicle to generate resources that help support other programs. However, this is often limited to a few institutions at the Division I-A level with very prominent football programs that regularly play in front of national and regional television audiences. Women's programs at these institutions also have capacity to generate revenue. It is not surprising that athletic programs at Division I-A institutions also fare better in compliance with Title IX (Cheslock, 2007).

Emphasis on the revenue-generating (and thus profit-generating) characteristic of the dominant college football model creates a standard – "revenue-generating" or "self-sustaining" – against which all sports will be measured. Thus, teams that fail to meet this standard (e.g. swimming, track) have less value and are faced with the dilemma of either being sub-par within athletics (and vulnerable to cuts) or mimicking the structure and operation of the football model.

The football model, made prominent through the marketplace discourse, appears race- and gender-neutral. Yet, the "benchmark" it creates is based on a normative standard of socially constructed values related to commercialism that favor men. This conceals inequities related to gender and ethnicity experienced by student-athletes, staff, administrators, and spectators. In *Play-by-play: Radio, television, and big-time sport*, Ronald Smith (2001) notes, "Not only intercollegiate athletics but also higher education, in many ways, reflects the commercial aspect of America's free enterprise system" and colleges and universities "have prospered, in part, because of their ability to sell themselves to the public" (p. 2). Institutional rivalry and increased competition for students, top faculty, and resources all prompted greater entrepreneurial activity. Institutions regularly participate in a "technologically sophisticated, knowledge-based economy" by selling specialized knowledge (Bok, 2003, p. 15). Although these capitalist and commercial elements of higher education are positioned as gender- and race-neutral, higher education continues to be modeled after a "male worker or capitalist" (Acker, 2006, p. 5).

Intercollegiate athletics is dominated by the activities of men's teams and men hold far more coaching and leadership roles. Women tend to serve in the advising and support roles within a department. Only 42 percent of women's teams and less than 2 percent of men's teams are coached by women (Acosta & Carpenter, 2006). Lower numbers of women in coaching and administration are thought to be due to extreme workloads, family-unfriendly work practices, and a masculinist culture in athletics. When men and women in coaching are compared to other professions, women coaches are less likely to be married or rearing children than men (Drago et al., 2005). The schedule of games, travel, planning, practice, and recruiting favors the traditional male worker who is not constrained by raising children and caring for others. Like all of higher education, intercollegiate athletics is a "gendered organizational environment, one that favors men's interests" (Forman, 2001, p. 6). The gendering of intercollegiate athletics, visible in the marketplace discourse, is also evident in the self-development discourse.

Self-Development Discourse

Another discourse, the self-development discourse, shapes perceptions of Title IX as well. It is characterized by images of athletics promoting individuals' identity development, social, and emotional growth as part of students' educational progress and success. This discourse underscores the value of college sport in terms of its ability to facilitate vocational knowledge and skills and psycho-social development among participants. These characterizations, made visible by a self-development discourse, give rise to descriptions of the developmental benefits to participation in sports and the ways in which intercollegiate athletics facilitates students' growth. The stated purpose of the National Collegiate Athletic Association (NCAA) is to "integrate intercollegiate athletics into higher education so that the educational experience of the student-athlete is paramount" (NCAA, n.d.). Furthermore, among the NCAA core values is to promote "the collegiate model of athletics in which students participate as an avocation, balancing their academic, social and athletics experiences" (NCAA, n.d.). The alignment with maturation and self-growth of the participants is constructed through Title IX policy and intercollegiate athletics.

Most intercollegiate competitions – teams not competing in football or basketball – focus on the "self-development of the participants" (Toma, 2003, p. 21). These less commercialized women's and men's programs are often referred to as "non-revenue," "minor," or "Olympic" sports. For most student-athletes participating in intercollegiate sports, such as tennis, golf, soccer, and lacrosse, the focus is on the participants, not commercial interests, institutional prestige, or entertainment. These contests occur without much notice except by a handful of highly interested friends and family and very little attention by media or other institutions (Toma, 2003).

Less commercial sports, often characterized by women's athletics, typically generate less revenue, lack visibility, and garner modest attention from a regional and national pool of spectators. Rationales for sports that focus less on spectators and more on the growth and benefit to individual student-athletes are shaped by the self-development discourse in intercollegiate athletics. Intercollegiate sports are promoted as part of the educational mission due to the self-development of the student-athlete. Consistent with other extra-curricular and out-of-classroom experiences, participation in sports that do not (appear to) serve the commercial interests of the university are justified for their development benefits, such as hard work, being part of a team, and leadership development. Fostering these skills, particularly among sports that receive less spectator attention and commercialized marketplace demand, fuels arguments that college sports are amateur and nurture individual growth.

Women's sports, in particular, have fewer commercial interests and professional counterparts. This leads to the perception that women's teams exemplify the opportunity for gaining knowledge, leadership abilities, problem solving, and interpersonal skills that are integral to the self-development discourse. Because women's sports appear less professionalized, they can be used to counter the dominant football model of college sports with amateur and educational characteristics such as the emotional, social, and intellectual self-development of individual student-athletes (Toma, 1999, 2003). In the dialogue related to Title IX, the self-development discourse of college sport that favors the growth of the athlete is positioned as opposite to, or in conflict with, the marketplace discourse of athletics.

Discursive Tension

While there are many discourses that could be drawn upon to mediate understandings of Title IX, some are more prominent and tend to eclipse other possibilities. As a consequence, a dichotomous relationship between commercial and developmental goals – a tension between marketplace and self-development discourses – comes to the fore within the context of intercollegiate athletics. The marketplace discourse, dominant in shaping our view of athletics, gives rise to characterizations of intercollegiate sports as revenue-generating, competitive, commercialized, and status-enhancing. Alternately, the self-development discourse shapes our views of college athletics as contributing to student-athletes' growth, identity development, increased involvement, and overall satisfaction with the collegiate experience.

Deploying non-revenue-generating sports, often women's teams, to achieve developmental goals, requires resources for scholarships, coaches' salaries, travel, and equipment. The greater weight of the marketplace discourse shapes a discursive space in which women's teams must position themselves as a valuable commodity or risk consequence as a "cost" to the men's program. Often, administrators shift money from men's programs to women's programs, rather than generate new resources.

Teams that fail to generate revenue have less value and are more vulnerable to elimination. However, taking up the developmental discourse enables non-revenue-generating sports to promote their educational value to the university. For example, the Washington State Supreme Court found that football is not to be considered separately, under "business principles," in calculating gender equity in intercollegiate athletics. Rather, football is considered part of the educational institution, regardless of its capacity to generate revenue (*Blair v. Washington State University*, 1983, 1987; see also Hoffman, Hoffman, & Kotila, 2007). This decision reinforces the argument that despite the corporate characteristics of many football programs, participating in intercollegiate athletics provides opportunities for individual growth similar to those found in the classroom and campus life.

Thus, characterizations of intercollegiate athletics are situated dichotomously – they either contribute to the marketplace discourse or the student-athlete self-development discourse. The inclusion of women's sports in intercollegiate athletics is discursively constituted as counter to men's football and basketball; women's sports, perceived as contributing solely to developmental goals, are viewed as not contributing to (and even undermining) a university's economic interests. Yet, Title IX has secured resources for the emergence of a women's program that has been instrumental in developing opportunities for women student-athletes.

In 1991, Chris Voelz, then president of the National Association of Collegiate Women Athletic Administrators (NACWAA), with Elaine Dreidam, Judy Sweet, and Charlotte West, drafted an equity statement to guide program development in intercollegiate athletics (personal communication with Voelz, April 25, 2007). It asserts, "An athletics program is gender equitable when the men's sports program would be pleased to accept as its own, the overall participation, opportunities, and resources currently allocated to the women's sports program and vice versa" (NACWAA, 1992). Grant and Darley (1993), too, call for "new directions for intercollegiate sport that can someday supplant the destructive elements of the present system" (p. 259). More specifically, they assert the need to "whittle away at the existing structure to make it fit the ideal" and to "work politically to bring more women into positions of power" (p. 259). A critical mass of women in positions of influence holds the potential to shift the power in athletics to benefit women and men (Maurer, 1999); and Moss (1997) observes that a key to equity in athletics is to involve women at all levels of governance. However, numbers alone are not likely to shift the dominant characterizations of athletics from "Big Time" to "gender equitable."

Gender hierarchy exists. Revenue-generating sports, shaped by the marketplace discourse, are typically men's teams (football, basketball), whereas non-revenue-generating sports, shaped by the self-development discourse, are typically women's teams. Men's sports hold greater potential for commercial returns and are perceived as more valuable than women's sports. Further, both the marketplace and self-development discourses erase socially constructed differences among student-athletes.

Viewing intercollegiate sports through only these two discourses narrows the possibilities for change. Non-revenue-generating sports, typically women's teams, are faced with (1) situating themselves as a commodity, (2) accepting their performance as deficient compared with men's, revenue-generating, teams, and (3) continuing to promote their importance and presence in intercollegiate athletics as fulfilling the educational mission of the institution. However, strategically facilitating a discursive shift toward equity can, as Bensimon (2005) suggests, shift attention to institutional practices and the production of unequal educational outcomes.

Summary

The discursive tension between marketplace and self-development discourses situates educational benefits in opposition to the potential economic gains of institutions. An FPS perspective on intercollegiate athletics illuminates how this tension re/produces power inequities in intercollegiate athletics. FPS provides a lens through which to examine how policy discourses circulating in intercollegiate athletics re/produce a gendered system of power; a lens that promotes the commercial interests of revenue-generating (men's) sports and relegates non-revenue-generating (women's) sports to fulfill developmental goals. However, athletic administrators and higher education leaders are not confined to choose between economic or developmental interests. Such a narrow view risks shifting power relations based on "new systems of oppression and domination" (Ropers-Huilman, 1998, p. 9), meaning women's interests trump men's. Elevating both – economic *and* developmental interests – may contribute to recognition, valuing, and respect of all athletes. However, it may continue to conceal the normative standards against which athletic performance is measured, and that continues to privilege some groups (males, white women) over others.

In intercollegiate athletics there tends to be a reluctance to discuss difference. Institutions fear repercussions for not complying with Title IX and advocates for women's sports fear loss of women's opportunity if difference is acknowledged. Yet, the erasure of difference forecloses opportunities for acknowledging inequities based on difference. Our aim with this analysis was to raise awareness of conditions that produce particular discursive effects and practices. Athletic administrators and policy-makers are called to acknowledge and potentially disrupt how dominant discourses constitute particular gendered hierarchies. Further, this inquiry challenges administrators to "unpack" dominant characterizations of athletics to discover new and different possibilities and limitations for equity in intercollegiate sports.

References

Acker, J. (2006). *Class questions: Feminist answers*. Lanham, MD: Rowman and Littlefield.

Acosta, R. V. & Carpenter, L. J. (2006). *Women in intercollegiate sport: A longitudinal study twenty-seven year update 1977–2006*. New York: Brooklyn College.

Anderson, D. & Cheslock, J. (2004). Institutional strategies to achieve gender equity in intercollegiate athletics: Does Title IX harm male athletes? *American Economics Association Journal*, 94(May), 307–311.

Bashaw, C. T. (2001). Reassessment and redefinition: The NADWC and higher education for women. In J. Nidiffer & C. T. Bashaw (Eds.), *Women administrators in higher education: Historical and contemporary perspectives* (pp. 157–182). Albany, NY: State University of New York Press.

Baxter, J. (2003). *Positioning gender in discourse: A feminist methodology*. New York: Palgrave Macmillan.

Bensimon, E. M. (2005). Closing the achievement gap in higher education: An organizational learning perspective. *New Directions for Higher Education*, 131, 99–111.

Blair v. Washington State University, No. 28816 (January 3, 1983).

Blair v. Washington State University, 740 2nd 1379 (Washington State Supreme Court 1987).

Bok, D. (2003). *Universities in the marketplace: The commercialization of higher education*. Princeton, NJ: Princeton University Press.

Bouttilier, M. & SanGiovanni, L. (1983). *The sporting woman: Feminist and sociological dilemmas*. Champaign, IL: Human Kinetics.

Bouttilier, M. & SanGiovanni, L. (1994). Politics, public policy, and Title IX: Some limitations of liberal feminism. In S. Birrell & C. Cole (Eds.), *Women, sport, and culture* (pp. 97–118). Champaign, IL: Human Kinetics.

Cahn, S. (1994). *Coming on strong: Gender and sexuality in twentieth-century women's sport*. New York: Maxwell Macmillian, International.

Carpenter, L. J. & Acosta, R. V. (2005). *Title IX*. Champaign, IL: Human Kinetics.

Cheslock, J. (2007). *Who's playing college sports? Trends in participation*. East Meadow, NY: Women's Sports Foundation.

Clifford, G. J. (1983). "Shaking dangerous questions from the crease": Gender and American higher education. *Feminist Issues*, 3(2), 3–62.

Cott, N. (1987). *The grounding of modern feminism*. New Haven, CT: Yale University Press.

Drago, R., Hennighausen, L., Rogers, J., Vescio, T., & Stauffer, K. D. (2005). *Final report for CAGE: The coaching and gender equity project*. Retrieved August 26, 2005 from http://lsir.la.psu.edu/workfam/CAGE.htm.

Elliott, S. & Mason, D. (2001). Gender equity in intercollegiate athletics: An alternate model to achieving Title IX compliance. *Journal of Legal Aspects of Sport*, 11, 1–24.

Estler, S. E. & Nelson, L. (2005). *Who calls the shots? Sports and university leadership, culture, and decision-making*. ASHE Higher Education Report. San Francisco, CA: Jossey-Bass.

Festle, M. (1996). *Playing nice: Politics and apologies in women's sports*. New York: Columbia University Press.

Forman, P. (2001). *Contesting gender equity: The cooptation of women's intercollegiate athletics*. Unpublished dissertation, University of California, Davis.

Gavora, J. (2002). *Tilting the playing field: Schools, sports, sex, and Title IX*. San Francisco, CA: Encounter Books.

Glazer, P. M. & Slater, M. (1987). *Unequal colleagues: The entrance of women into the professions, 1890–1940*. New Brunswick, NJ: Rutgers University Press.

Gordon, L. D. (1990). *Gender and higher education in the progressive era*. New Haven, CT: Yale University Press.

Grant, C. (1984). The gender gap in sport: From Olympic to Intercollegiate level. *Arena Review*, 8, 31–48.

Grant, C. & Darley, C. (1993). Equity: What price equality? In G. Cohen (Ed.), *Women in sport: Issues and controversies* (pp. 251–263). New York: Sage Publications,

Griffin, P. (1992). Changing the game: Homophobia, sexism, and lesbians in sport. *Quest*, 44, 251–265.

Grundy, P. & Shackelford, S. (2005). *Shattering the glass: The remarkable history of women's basketball*. New York: The New Press.

Hoffman, J., Hoffman, H., & Kotila, A. (2007). Athletics gender equity in the State of Washington: The 20th anniversary of Blair v. Washington State University. *Journal for the Study of Sports and Athletes in Education*, 1(3), 273–294.

Hogshead-Makar, N. & Zimbalist, A. (2007). *Equal play: Title IX and social change*. Philadelphia, PA: Temple University Press.

Horger, M. (1996). Basketball and athletic control at Oberlin College, 1896–1915. *Journal of Sport History*, 23(3), 256–283.

Horowitz, H. L. (1987). *Campus life: Undergraduate cultures from the end of the eighteenth century to the present*. New York: Knopf.

Hult, J. (1999). NAGWS and AIAW: The strange and wondrous journey to the athletic summit, 1950–90. *Journal of Physical Education, Recreation & Dance*, 70(4), 24–31.

Hult, J. & Trekell, M. (1991). *A century of women's basketball: From frailty to the final four*. Reston, VA: American Alliance for Health, Physical Education, Recreation, and Dance.

Lapchick, R. (2005). *The 2005 Racial & Gender Equity Report Card: College Sports*. Retrieved April 24, 2007 from www.bus.ucf.edu/sport.

Lazerson, M. & Wagener, U. (1996). Missed opportunities: Lessons from the Title IX case at Brown. *Change*, July/August, 46–52.

Liberti, R. (1999). "We were ladies, we just played basketball like boys": African American womanhood and competitive basketball at Bennett College, 1928–1942. *Journal of Sport History*, 26(3), 567–594.

Maurer, R. (1999). *An inductive case study of women leaders of athletics at Northern Illinois University: Learning, leadership, and transformation*. Ph.D. dissertation, Northern Illinois University.

McDonagh, E. & Pappano, L. (2008). *Playing with the boys: Why separate is not equal in sports*. New York: Oxford University Press.

Mills, S. (1997). *Discourse.* New York: Routledge.

Moore, R. (2005). Title IX: Opening doors for female athletes [electronic version]. *University of Minnesota News*, Spring. Retrieved June 10, 2009 from http://www1.umn.edu/umnnews/Feature_Stories/Title_IX_Opening_doors_for_female_athletes.html.

Moss, S. (1997). *Gender equity in intercollegiate athletics: A case study of a Title IX compliance effort at a Division I-A public university.* Ph.D. dissertation, University of Wisconsin-Madison.

National Association of Collegiate Women Athletic Administrators. (1992). Gender equity. Retrieved November 17, 2008 from http://www.nacwaa.org/.

National Collegiate Athletic Association (n.d.). Our Mission. Retrieved September 13, 2008 from http://www.ncaa.org/wps/ncaa?ContentID=1352.

Nerad, M. (1999). *The academic kitchen: A social history of gender stratification at the University of California, Berkeley.* Albany, NY: State University of New York Press.

Newcomer, M. (1959). *A century of higher education for American women.* New York: Harper and Row.

Nidiffer, J. (2000). *Pioneering deans of women: More than wise and pious matrons.* New York: Teachers College Press.

Porto, B. L. (2003). *A new season: Using Title IX to reform college sports.* Westport, CT: Praeger.

Priest, L. (2003). The Whole IX Yards: the impact of Title IX: The good, the bad and the ugly. *Women in Sport & Physical Activity Journal*, 12(2), 27.

Ropers-Huilman, B. (1998). *Feminist teaching in theory and practice: Situating power and knowledge in poststructural classrooms.* New York: Teachers College Press.

Sack, A. & Staurowsky, E. (1998). *College athletes for hire: The evolution and legacy of the NCAA's amateur myth.* Westport, CT: Praeger.

Scott, J. (1990). Deconstructing equality-versus-difference: or, the uses of poststructuralist theory for feminism. In M. Hirsch & E. Fox Keller (Eds), *Conflicts in feminism* (pp. 134–148). New York: Routledge.

Smith, R. A. (2001). *Play-by-play: Radio, television, and big-time college sport.* Baltimore, MD: Johns Hopkins University Press.

Suggs, W. (2005). *A place on the team: The triumph and tragedy of Title IX.* Princeton, NJ: Princeton University Press.

Suggs, W. (2007). Counting ponytails: The Title IX debate has gotten truly tedious. *Inside Higher Education*, July 19. Retrieved June 9, 2009 from http://www.insidehighered.com/views/2007/07/19/suggs.

Thelin, J. (2000). Good sports? Historical perspectives on the political economy of intercollegiate athletics in the era of Title IX, 1972–1997. *The Journal of Higher Education*, 71(July/August), 391–410.

Toma, J. D. (1999). The collegiate ideal and the tools of external relations: The uses of high profile intercollegiate athletics. *Reconceptualizing the Collegiate Ideal*, 105, 81–90.

Toma, J. D. (2003). *Football U.: Spectator sports in the life of the American university.* Ann Arbor, MI: University of Michigan Press.

Toma, J. D. & Cross, M. E. (2000). Contesting values in American higher education: The playing field of intercollegiate athletics. *Higher Education Handbook of Theory and Research*, 15, 406–455.

Washington, M., Forman, P., Suddaby, R., & Ventresca, M. (2005). Strategies and struggles: The governance of U.S. collegiate athletics. In K. D. Elsbach (Ed.), *Qualitative organizational research: Best papers from the Davis Conference on Qualitative Research* (pp. 113–138). Greenwich, CT: Information Age Publishing.

Weedon, C. (1997). *Feminist practice and poststructuralist theory*, 2nd ed. Cambridge, MA: Blackwell Publishers Incorporated.

United States Commission on Civil Rights. (1980). *More hurdles to clear: Women and girls in competitive athletics* (Clearinghouse Publication, No. 63, July 1980). Washington, DC: U.S. Government Printing Office.

8

Consuming Higher Education

Who Is Paying the Price?

JENI HART AND JENNIFER HUBBARD

> The land before them would need competent rulers
> and, of course, a learned clergy . . . the colleges were all
> essential to reinforce the proper moral precepts in the
> American elite and to demonstrate the separation of the
> American upper class from the raw nature and
> barbarism. (Mandell, 1977, in Bogue & Aper, 2000, p. 19)

Since its inception, higher education in the United States has perpetuated social connections among the privileged that stratified students by social class. Historically, those who have benefited most were white, economically privileged, and male. In many respects, higher education, like many social institutions, continues to privilege those same groups (Bogue & Aper, 2000; Vine, 1997). While today higher education includes more demographic diversity, which ultimately broadens the social networks that can be developed, problems related to social class (Vander Putten, 2001), race (Watson et al., 2002), gender (Glazer-Raymo, 1999, 2008; Rich, 2000), and privilege (Langston, 1993) still remain obscured or sometimes even ignored.

Historically, the complexity of social forces within and outside higher education have influenced postsecondary institutions in ways that maintained the social status of the elite and upper-middle class. For example, women's colleges were established in part to respond to the need of "an educated citizenry and that this in turn required the nurturing of the young by more educated mothers" (DeBra, 1997, p. 2). Establishing women's colleges created separate arenas for women and men; however, it also continued to stratify students based on social class because it failed to provide equal access to those from less privileged social classes. While inequities existed in terms of access by sex,[1] and when efforts were made to redress those inequities through the establishment of women's colleges, sex was often used to divert attention from social class (Ollenburger & Moore, 1992). Decisions to increase access did benefit women; however, the collateral outcome was the continued reproduction of an economically elite citizenry. This educational outcome replicated broader social phenomena where "race and gender [were] used as screens to deflect attention away from the harsh realities class politics exposes" (hooks, 2000, p. 7).

Miller-Bernal (2000) argued coeducation and even the establishment of women's colleges (both practices centered on increasing access in higher education for women) did little to address other disadvantages related to other aspects of identity (e.g., race, class, sexual orientation) that mutually shape individual student experiences. While women gained access to higher education, the system of higher education remained largely unchanged, rendering the participation of women from less privileged economic backgrounds an uncommon occurrence. This is to say that coeducation and the establishment of women's colleges served to perpetuate the cycles of privilege and oppression (Bishop, 2005).[2] Thus, progress and access in the broadest sense were only partially attained (i.e., more women were able to go to college than prior to these events).

Purpose of the Study

The study described in this chapter emerged from the recognition that despite often well-meaning efforts to address sex and social class[3] inequities and biases, such inequities in higher education persist (e.g., Allan & Madden, 2006; Brady & Eisler, 1995; Rodriguez, 1997; Vander Putten, 2001; Volk, Slaughter, & Thomas, 2001). More specifically, this chapter examines how policies related to social class experiences and identities in a women's college contribute to reproducing a cycle of oppression at one women's institution. In this study, social class was selected as an important focus because it is often excluded from the existing literature about academe (Vander Putten, 2001). Further, it could be argued that class is less visible, thus making it easier for those in institutions to mask or disregard it. Until recently, higher education institutions have done little to remedy the increasing gap between the "haves" and "have-nots" (Selingo & Brainard, 2006, p. A1). It is uncertain whether these recent efforts (e.g., eliminating tuition for low-income students) at institutions like Rutgers, Harvard, and Stanford will truly improve access and graduation rates of lower-class and working-class students.

By focusing on social class, it is not our intent to eclipse the salience of other identities. Rather, we are including social class, in addition to sex, as one of many social identities contributing to the lived experience – one that is often overlooked (Langhout, Rosselli, & Feinstein, 2007). In addition, we are using a feminist poststructural (FPS) lens to analyze the policies and practices related to social class and sex, as understood by women students at this institution, which contribute to shaping their realities. This lens will help us think about how power influences policy creation, and how that power can be reproduced through policy implementation. The voices of women at one women's college will amplify the consequences of policies on campus related to class. Specifically, we hope to shed light on how such policies and practices are understood and help educators and policy makers consider better ways to address the quiet, yet powerful classism faced by women at one single-sex institution. By exploring how policies and practices are understood through a FPS lens, we demonstrate how policies may have unintended consequences on this campus, and likely many others.

The identification of how a system, like higher education, reproduces privilege and power affords the opportunity for analysis. Such an analysis not only illuminates how that power and privilege influences individuals who are part of that system, but it offers the possibility to re/define the system to stop the cycle of oppression. The "educational system fulfills a function of legitimation which is more and more necessary to the perpetuation of the 'social order' as the evolution of the power relationship between classes" (Bourdieu, 2000, p. 60). Said differently, educational systems are structured to benefit the people they serve. We contend that many of the policies and practices described throughout this chapter replicate and sustain a caste system based on sex and social class, just as Bourdieu suggested. Our intent in the sections that follow is to analyze the policy narratives at Women's College (a pseudonym), aided by the counter-narratives of women students on this campus, in order to begin to more fully explore the systems of domination and privilege. What follows is a discussion of our theoretical framework and brief review of the literature to provide a context for our study. Then, after a description of the research design, we discuss our findings and consider their implications of those findings.

Theoretical Framework

Social class and sex are two of several identity characteristics, or subject positions, that are used as markers of demographic diversity. Our study centers on the lives of women and is informed specifically by experiences (including policies and practices) related to social class, and thus, we draw on these dimensions of identity to frame our study. Our use of an FPS lens helps us to see how policies and practices contributed to the social reality on college and university campuses. Policies and practices, typically created and implemented by institutional leaders, "reflect and transmit a dominant interpretation of the campus culture" (Allan, 2008, p. 5), and its dominance can conceal that alternatives are available. Often, this dominant interpretation informs other decisions and practices, and consequently shapes the experiences of students.

Discursive practices, often carried through policies and practices, have some institutional force, which means "they have a profound influence on the way that individuals act and think" (Mills, 1997, p. 62). Thus, they shape prevailing images of particular identities. Further, attention to one dimension of identity (i.e., gender) may conceal other dimensions (i.e., race, social class), and erase the complexities and multidimensionality of identities (Reynolds & Pope, 1991). For example, a university policy may require all students to live in student housing, all of which comprise two-person same-sex rooms and common bathrooms. This policy is rooted in normative assumptions about students' identities, thus failing to consider ways in which various dimensions of one's identity (e.g., mother, transgender student) may collide with such housing policy. Recognizing and appreciating the multidimensionality of students' identities is central to their ability to contribute to the construction of their own subjectivity. However, if the dominant discursive practices on a college or university campus fail to recognize the complexity of identities, campus policy risks constraining the possibilities for (full) participation and may contribute to erasing the multidimensionality of who students are and can become.

We believe it is critical to examine the dominant discourses carried by policies in higher education in order to better understand how they may shape and/or limit the subject positions available. By doing so, administrators, faculty, and students can become more aware of the unintended consequences of dominant policy discourses and can help campus communities rethink their policies and practices. We are not suggesting that policies and practices are inherently bad. On the contrary, many policies have had a liberating and equalizing affect for some, or even many, individuals. For example, since the passage of the Higher Education Act of 1972, women have enrolled in programs from which they have been excluded in the past. Now women comprise nearly 60 percent of all undergraduate students in higher education (Glazer-Raymo, 2008). However, FPS research has highlighted how even policies and practices intended to be liberatory or equalizing may have the unintended consequence of reinforcing the status quo (Allan, 2003; Buzzanell & Liu, 2005). As such, we approach this investigation by examining the discourses carried by college policies and practices that convey a desire to explicitly address inequities due to socio-economic realities at Women's College. We examine aspects of women's lives at an elite college that are shaped by messages the college communicates about social class (through formal policies and policy practices). Informed by poststructuralism, we examine the dominant discourses of policies and practices, and alternative discourses circulating in women students' experiences in order to better understand the consequences, intended and unintended, of these policies and practices. Further, through a feminist lens, we highlight how power and knowledge can and does maintain certain discourses, and hope that through our exploration, policy makers can rethink the construction of policies and practices.

Review of Literature

For college students, social class and sex, as well as many other aspects of identity, often intersect. This interplay can result in inequities and challenges for students related to, for example, where to attend college, buying textbooks versus checking them out in the library, and working to continue the educational process (hooks, 2000). As a result, institutional leaders create policies (both formal and informal) leading to practices in higher education intended to address those challenges and inequities. We approach our analysis from an FPS perspective that recognizes the power of policies, but argues that power is socially constructed and may have differing influences and interpretations for each individual within the system. Additionally, we are interested in the discourses informing policy because how the discourses are understood can shape norms that keep structures intact (Foucault, 1980).

Policies, such as student aid, claim to resolve financial issues for all students; however, upon further review, these policies may not remove barriers, and may, in fact, perpetuate the cycle of oppression, particularly for students from lower socio-economic statuses [SES] (Heller, 2002). In the brief review of the literature, we attempt to contextualize how policies, like access and student aid, contribute to institutional practices of classism and sexism. In addition, we want to enable more complex understandings of how sexism and classism intersect. To do so, we examine policies that affect women without economic resources as they illustrate power relations and reproduction of power within a higher education policy context.

"From the establishment of the first college in America in 1636, there has been an understanding that higher education, though it clearly provided private benefits, also served important community needs" (Newman, Couturier, & Scurry, 2004, p. 3). Neither past nor current policies and practices fully meet community needs, leading to questions about whether higher education is or has ever been truly a public good (Bok, 2003). As one example of how complexities of policy adapt to meet community needs, policies such as tuition discounting shift institutional resources to meet increasing fiscal demands and competition for students (Newman et al., 2004); yet, the results are making college access more difficult for some due to the perception of increasing costs (and the real increasing costs for those who have the economic means). Institutional leaders often view students for what they contribute to the campus in terms of money and academic talent. As such, colleges and universities are redesigning financial policies and marketing strategies that emphasize their dependency on student tuition and rising student fees (Long, 2004; Newman et al., 2004), further reinforcing higher education as primarily a private benefit (and cost).

Cultural Capital

Social class is a learned position (Fay & Tokarczyk, 1993), influenced by policies and practices and normalized assumptions about what class should mean. Even if we were to embrace higher education as a meritocracy as Trow (1984) suggested it should be, classism (and many other oppressive systems) would prevent many students who have the ability to succeed in higher education from applying, let alone matriculating. If education is the "ticket" to class mobility

(Newman et al., 2004), it appears that only some of us can access the ticket. Having the ability to access the ticket, or even talk about the ticket, is often helped or hindered based upon one's access to cultural capital.

"Cultural capital is the knowledge, skills, education, and other advantages a person has that make the educational system a comfortable, familiar environment in which he or she can succeed easily" (Oldfield, 2007, p. 2). For example, students from wealthier socio-economic groups, including those whose parents are college-educated, have access to academic tools and resources, as well as social knowledge to support them in school (Perna & Titus, 2005). For those with cultural capital, it becomes a "taken for granted" that they know to fill out financial aid forms, to register for the SAT or ACT, to take college preparation coursework in high school, to be involved in community service, among other things that facilitate going to college. These students have access to more information, and more resources generally result in advantage. Students who do not have parents, siblings, or other mentors who attended college often find it difficult to understand or even find out about university policies, traditions, and expectations. Some of the disparity is not only knowledge- and culturally based but class-based (i.e., economic capital matters too) when parents are able to provide "financial support . . . internet access, and tutors, all of which have the potential to maximize educational performance" (Rothman, 2005, p. 229). All of these differences acknowledge that current policies and practices tend to privilege particular students within the educational system. While it is true that some policies and practices do exist to help students facing challenges due to gender, race, social class, or other issues, cultural capital is associated with the ability to navigate institutional resources. So, even with policies in place to benefit those who lack economic or other capital, the lack of cultural capital makes it increasingly less likely that those potential students will be able to access those resources.

Bourdieu (2000) stated that the "academic market tends to sanction and to reproduce the distribution of cultural capital by proportioning academic success to the amount of cultural capital bequeathed by the family" (p. 61). This means institutional leaders can claim they have resources aimed at reducing disparate experiences but actually have to provide very few of those resources if those who need them lack the necessary capital to know about them and request them. This means the institution appears to be a champion of social justice, despite the fact that the resources rarely get used. Ultimately, the responsibility falls on the student, instead of the institution, to maximize the use of available institutional resources. If students do not have the requisite knowledge or capital related to these resources, including policies, then the resources are not used. If these resources have financial costs, the institution saves money, which may be one of the reasons cultural and economic capital issues remain ill-addressed. But in the end, this practice comes at a very high cost for the students who need the resources but lack the capital.

Cultural Reproduction in Education

"Systems organized around privilege have three key characteristics. They are *dominated* by privileged groups, *identified* with privileged groups, and *centered* on privileged groups" (Johnson, 2006, p. 90, emphases in original). In systems that maintain privilege, the policies themselves are crafted by those who are in privileged positions. Policy makers within higher education (e.g., administrators, state and federal governments) create and implement policies that seem to assume all students are, in some aspects, the same. While policies and practices such as need-based financial aid, open access, and the establishment of single-sex institutions and classrooms were often created to address difference and erase inequities, the policies are often predicated upon an assumed homogeneity within the group for whom the policy was intended, making it difficult for the policies to benefit all who may need them.

For example, financial aid policies are often considered one way to provide access to students who may not have the ability to pay full tuition. However, instead of eliminating hierarchies, these policies can, and often do, contribute to the financial gap for students. Specifically, money was once provided to students as a means to close the gap between the cost of attending an institution and ability to contribute. However, now the amount available for needs-based students is not adequate. For example, according to Symonds (2003), "even with financial aid the average poor student falls $3800 short of covering expenses at a public university" (pp. 66–67). Thus, loan and grant policies are insufficient and continue to reduce, instead of increase, access to higher education (Wax, 2007). "While tuition continues to rise, family incomes at the lower ends of the income hierarchy do not. Various forms of financial aid are designed to lessen the impact of class inequality, but they do not eliminate it" (Rothman, 2005, p. 234), creating a situation where students are less focused on institutional fit and learning opportunities and more focused on finding a funding source. In the end, the policies and practices socially reproduce the status quo, maintaining the existing power balance that sustains systems of privilege and oppression.

Research Design

The analysis in this chapter is taken from a larger qualitative study of campus climate that included faculty and staff. While the voices of faculty and staff are critical to the overall understanding of campus climate, for this study, we focus on the experiences of students at Women's College.

Site

Women's College is a single-sex highly selective college with over 2,000 students. Using Pell Grant recipients as a proxy to reflect the percentages of low-income undergraduate students at Women's College, the college reports that approximately 25 percent of its students are Pell Grant recipients. Women's College is among the 75 wealthiest private colleges in the U.S. that, upon average, award Pell Grants to 13.1 percent of their undergraduate students (Fischer, 2008).

Due to the dwindling numbers of women's colleges in the U.S. and our ethical commitment to maintain the confidentiality of our participants, we have chosen not to share any other identifying characteristics about the institution. While this may limit transferability of our findings, our commitment to the confidentiality of those who gave of their time and valuable perspectives to participate in our study was more important.

Sample

The campus population comprises women from around the United States and world. The college registrar randomly generated a sample of 300 undergraduate students that intentionally included a representative sample of each academic class (first year through senior) and oversampled under-represented minorities to help ensure the participation of these women. Invitations to participate in the study were sent to these 300 students and 117 women students agreed to and did participate in either a focus group or an individual interview. One limitation to collecting much of the data in focus groups is that we only have demographic variables (e.g., class year, race, ability) in the aggregate, rather than linked to each individual participant in a group. For example, we know that one focus group included six seniors and two sophomores, but we do not know if a particular comment in the focus group was made by a senior. However, whenever possible, we tried to provide some context about the participants sharing their voices within this chapter.

Data Collection

We used a semi-structured protocol for all individual interviews and focus groups. The protocol contains one probe that specifically mentions social class; however, even without asking directly, issues around social class emerged throughout the interviews. Participants discuss how they feel about class on campus, policies and practices intended to eliminate markers of lower socio-economic status, and how individuals are treated based on social class status. Since social class issues were more often raised by the participants without prompting from the facilitator, we believe our findings are robust and credible. Interviews, transcribed verbatim, were conducted over a four-month period.

Analytic Process

We used a FPS lens as an analytic framework through which to examine students' experiences around social class at Women's College. Drawing upon established qualitative methods of coding and categorizing, we looked for patterns and common themes to generate image categories and identify identity positions that emerged from these images. We then reanalyzed the data looking for contradictions within and between our participants' narratives and these college policies (Reinharz, 1992). Finally, we identified discourses that were most prominent in constituting identity positions related to social class and sex. The women with whom we spoke provide a "counterhegemonic" (Personal Narratives Group, 1989, p. 7) perspective to a dominant policy discourse about social class.

Our analytic decisions were, in part, based upon our own positionalities as feminist researchers and on the nature of the emergent themes about social class that emerged in our field notes. Students' positionality as women and as students within the academy gives them unique insight into policies and practices created and implemented by those in power, much like that described by feminist standpoint theory (Hartsock, 1983). We believe it is important to pay attention to women's points of view and experiences, and to recognize that these experiences in turn can shape women as subjects (Goodman & Martin, 2002).

Findings and Discussion

Through analysis of stories shared by students, we identified how some current institutional policies draw upon discourses that reinforce status hierarchies. We begin by sharing some examples of policies and practices employed at Women's College. We believe these policies and practices, at their core, are created to improve the quality of students' lives. However, in practice, these policies can serve to highlight class differences as they seek to redress socio-economic inequities. Interwoven in this discussion of policies and their consequences are the individual voices of women students who shared their perceptions of class and experiences of classism as women on a college campus.

Policies and Practices

Student voices illustrate how the Women's College administration is aware of some of the complexities of women's lives. By virtue of the college's mission, women students are central to the purpose of the institution. In addition, institutional policies and practices intended to provide resources aimed at access, affordability, and equity demonstrate that those creating the policies and practices are aware that women students come to the college with varying financial resources. Nevertheless, as we describe next, policy makers may fail to recognize the limitations and the unintended consequences of well-meaning policies.

The current financial aid policy at this institution seeks to provide educational opportunities for qualified women, knowing that many of them will require financial assistance. According to the college's website, Women's College has a needs-based aid program. Further, this program begins with a consistent, yet personalized assessment of each applicant's ability to pay for college expenses. The financial aid policy describes how the college meets the full documented need of all admitted students who apply for aid by the published deadlines, and states that some admission decisions may include an assessment of the student's level of need. What remains unclear from the public explanation of the policy on the Women's College website is who benefits from the assessment of need, the student or the institution. That is, will a student who has more need be less likely to be admitted, despite other qualifications, in order to create a more diverse student body, or will that student be rejected for someone of the same ability, but with the financial means to attend? The de facto policy (i.e., as demonstrated by practice, but not in writing) answers that question. The practice is as follows:

> The institution does not designate aid for the consideration of low SES [Socio-Economic Status] prospective students, nor does it recruit lower SES students per se. Instead, all admission applications are read and ranked. The class is shaped on admission criteria alone, but if there is not enough aid available to meet the need of all the students in the top priority group, students are subsequently "swapped out." This means that some who would have been admitted at the lowest admit ratings are placed on the wait list. If spaces are not completely filled in the class after that exercise, full pay students from the top of the wait list are then put in the admit group. (Financial Aid Officer, Women's College, personal communication, October 23, 2006)

It appears that the institutional budget remains a driving force behind policy development, advantaging some women more than others. In this case, Women's College may seek out full-pay students to help subsidize the other forms of merit-based aid it provides, making it similar to other institutions where "the purpose of the admissions office is shifting from selecting a balanced class to maximizing tuition revenue" (Newman et al., 2004, p. 12). However, this knowledge is not well-publicized, which gives the financial aid officers and other college administrators the power to admit students who can pay full tuition, sometimes at the expense of academically able students who do not have the resources to pay the going rate of tuition.

What may not be considered in the policies around admission and financial aid is how the admission decisions may affect the academic and social experiences once students are on campus. For example, this woman shared how social class and her learning disability led to feelings of marginalization by the institution, including the faculty; not only was she a token, but she was stereotyped and reminded of circumstances that could disempower her.

> I feel like somehow I got in because I am from a lower income class and don't know how to spell very well or read because I have a learning disability. Professors treat me a certain way like, "Oh, you got in somehow. You are getting really good grades in my class, but I don't know how."

Women's College specifically designed a program for women who want to re-enter college after stopping out or after having completed an associate's degree at another institution. This program, which we will call the Returning Scholar Program, explicitly acknowledges that life circumstances can hinder women from being able to complete a four-year degree between the ages of 18 and 24. The program is highly regarded and unique in its attention to the complexities of women's lives. Only women 25 and older who have completed some college can be in this program. Tuition and fees are covered by the college and women who may never have considered themselves as likely candidates of a degree from Women's College are welcomed into the community. However, the program is primarily focused on admission. Several women in the program shared that they had to leave their families in another state while they completed their degrees. Some came to the college with their partners and/or children, but there were few resources in place to assist them with family housing or family care issues. One of our participants even brought her daughter to the interview because she did not have childcare. She remarked that she had to play a "balancing act" in order to do what was expected of her as a student and a mother. Another shared:

> [Traditional] students seem extremely well-prepared, but in the Returning Scholar Program, there is a real problem of picking appropriate people. And people who have extremely young children are less likely to be successful here because they don't have time.

These policies do not consider the inherent complexities for students who are not part of the majority student population at Women's College (i.e., 18–24-year-olds). In such cases, life factors that may influence a Returning Scholar's academic success are often neglected. Another Returning Scholar Program student shared how the policies were centered on the experiences of a traditional student. She shared how class and sex intersected with her role as a mother and student, but that lived experience was rarely taken into account by others.

> Educational loans do not cover new winter boots and they don't cover sneakers when your child's shoes are too small and they are pinching and

you have to say you need to wait another three weeks because I don't have the money. There are a lot of things set up for [traditional students] when you come to college and you live in a house where food is cooked for you. Your room isn't cleaned for you, but the bathrooms are cleaned for you and the dishes are done for you. [That is not the experience of the Returning Scholars.] [W]e have to go home and we have to buy the groceries and we have to prepare the food and whatever.

Some of the policies, like those highlighted above, illustrate awareness and consideration for unique student experiences in the admission process; however, once students arrive on campus, the policies and practices are often inadequate at addressing how students experience life at Women's College. Moreover, they serve to reinforce the hidden gendered domestic economy. For the students in the residential housing, the cooking and cleaning is completed for them primarily when the students are in class and out of the houses (and it is a reasonable assumption that it is most often completed by women who are invisible or hidden from the students). For the Returning Scholars, they have a "second shift" when they return from classes, and by and large, the college seems to forget this aspect of these women's lives (Hochschild & Machung, 1990). In the end, these inadequacies reinforce the overarching position of institutional power, privilege, and of the idealized Women's College student, making it difficult for those who do not fit that "ideal" to truly feel a part of the community.

Perceptions about Class and Experiences of Classism

Once students are admitted to Women's College, resources are available to assist students with basic needs such as financial support for health care, winter coats, discounts and waivers for books, and free eyeglasses. In order to benefit from these resources, students must not only self-disclose their class background, but they must also know how to navigate the system in order to access the resources. Ultimately, the system reinforces institutional power at the expense of those (i.e., the women students) with less power, because students are less likely to use resources that they do not know about or that they must publicly identify their lack of power (i.e., their lower social class, in this case) in order to access. From a Foucauldian (1979) perspective, students discipline their behaviors (e.g., do not self-disclose class status, do not seek out resources) partly in response to messages (implicit or explicit) from the administration.

The administration has explicit policies and practices focused on class, but one African student articulated a subtext that contradicted the formal institutional/administrative messages about class.

The administration takes a blind eye to class. For example, we have to pay for printing at 5 cents per copy. There are still students without computers and it really adds up if you have to pay. When you have readings on Blackboard [an on-line system for classes], we have to print it out. While [Blackboard] is supposed to save us copyright costs, it is still expensive. I have 40–60 pages to print. And we have to pay for laundry; it adds up.

Information about how the institution provides support to students is not readily available. Rather, students are the messengers about policies around social class, and in many ways, students are expected to serve as activists for the issue. In so doing, they are both resisting the administrative discourse around class-based policies and practices and are reconstituting those policies in a way that makes them accessible for those who need them. For example, out of necessity, a student group created a resource guide (a counter-discourse) to highlight the variety of services and benefits available to students who are financially challenged. One of its members said:

Then you go to the classroom and everyone will try to rid themselves of markers of class. I think it is a conscious thing because people are very uncomfortable about it. I think my most common experience is guilty women; [those without class privilege feel] guilty.

Although the woman above points out that some women in her classes are aware of their privilege, their guilt serves as a reminder of class privilege.

Similar to the reminder of class status in the classroom, settings like student activities, work opportunities, and athletics also served as reminders of social class. A student-athlete shared:

I do crew and [a] spring break trip is mandatory; it's $600 per year, all four years. There are ways through the teams that you can try to spend your weekend working traffic [to help pay for the trips], but of course that kind of gets in the way. So that can be an issue.

Moreover, certain work study positions can remind the community of a hierarchy of privilege. The following quotes from three students exemplify how social class stratification is perpetuated by the financial aid practice of work study.

You want to keep your financial status out of it, [but] you can't do that because you are in the kitchen and everyone else can see you in your house and you have to clean up after your other peer groups. (students with disabilities focus group member)

All first-year work study students have to work in the kitchen. So they are beginning with a huge class marker right there. (students of color focus group member)

I look at how dishwashing is problematic for students who are on work study. She is a student and kind of a housekeeper and has to face students in her own house. (students of color focus group member)

In addition to formal college activities and employment, even the informal activities become markers of one's class status. Students illustrated how social opportunities (e.g., going out to eat) and campus involvement (e.g., participating in student organizations) are reminders that one's class identity plays a role in student life.

> There are a lot of students in my hall who order take-out at night. I choose not to because I am already paying for my food [with my meal plan] and I don't really need to pay for it twice. (student-athletes focus group member)
>
> When I was a first year, I remember my roommate felt very uncomfortable speaking to a girl because they were [from] different socioeconomic classes. I was too. It was really interesting because she would invite us to restaurants that were a little expensive for the rest of us; but to a majority of her friends, it was OK and it was a good price range. (students of color focus group member)
>
> I have been told that you can't be poor because you go to [Women's College]. So, there is this ideology that if you go to [Women's College] you must have money, even if you don't have money and are on full financial aid. It doesn't matter because there is a blind assumption that everyone here is pretty well-off or at least middle class, which is well-off to me. (social class awareness student organization focus group member)

From these stories, it is clear that class hierarchies exist. Discourses that advantage those from middle- and upper-class backgrounds are reflected in remarks and behaviors that contribute to maintaining a hierarchy of power and privilege. Administrative leaders largely employ the dominant discourse of class privilege and it is shared at times by students who adopt that discourse. For those who try to challenge that discourse, there are consequences, including a lack of access to resources and constant reminders of their less privileged status. Moreover, classism can serve to reject the complexity of the women who experience it, as it reduces them to one subject position – social class – and it often rejects their subject position as women, lesbians, feminists, etc., which could, in other ways, empower them.

Sometimes even the subject positions of lower or working class can be ignored by peers, administrators, and faculty. The following narrative reinforces a perceived assumption of sameness among the students at Women's College.

> Students are of an assumed social class. I think if I were from a lower income class, I might be treated differently because Women's College is a wealthy school and a lot of wealthy people go here. I can see that it would be difficult not having that privilege because of the culture here . . . . People's parents pay for them and support them and they support them very much financially. It allows them to spend more time devoted to

studying or have more trips downtown to eat out with friends. (senior student)

A lot of professors, if not all of them, think you are a student and you have everything else taken care of for you and you don't have to worry about your bills and you don't have to cook your food. . . . It is really an issue when you have to work almost full-time to go to school. (social class awareness student organization focus group member)

Even with attempts from the institution to be conscious about social class, these stories demonstrate an assumption that all students are the same and have the necessary cultural and economic capital to be a certain kind of Women's College student (e.g., do not have to work, only have to study and socialize, can afford to shop and eat downtown). As such, those who do have cultural capital continue to be privileged by the administration and the existing policies and practices. Student experiences differ and it is important for college communities to understand and consider those differences, particularly as policies are created and implemented. Without such consideration, the implications of cultural reproduction and a dominant discourse that serves to maintain hierarchy and privilege can be further marginalizing for those who do not experience the same social class privileges.

Implications

Transforming the culture of an institution is a slow and difficult process; this women's college is beginning to include social class issues as part of the broader conversations about diversity. We laud this process, but do so tentatively. We hesitate because we must ask: Who benefits and who really pays the price for policies and practices related to social class?

Women's College, as an institution, may experience some benefits due to class-based policies and practices including: having few students take advantage of costly resources like free books, eyeglasses, and coats due to the lack of publicity around this policy; privileging applicants who can pay full tuition over those who may not be able to do so; and being able to publicly claim increased access to lower-income students, due in part to the Returning Scholars Program. However, these benefits come at a cost to others, particularly students, and particularly those students these policies were intended to serve. The policies and practices have maintained a dominant discourse that reinforces status hierarchies of social class at the college which assumes that all students are the same and when differences are self-disclosed (like being from a lower socio-economic class), those differences are considered problematic. Further, in many cases, those differences must be self-disclosed if students want to take advantage of policies; yet, such self-disclosure provides opportunities for the admini-stration, faculty, staff, and students to remind those students of their lack of privilege and power. Ultimately, the dominant discourse at this institution maintains and reinforces institutional power related to economics and class, and any counterhegemonic discourses are unwelcome. We look at the institutional policies and practices in this study in order to identify the dominant discourse about social class and we highlight several women's narratives that reinforce the dominant narrative, but more often create a counterhegemonic discourse about social class. We believe it is essential to dismantle class discrimination, and one way to begin to do so is to identify unintended consequences of the dominant discourses and simultaneously listen to the counterhegemonic discourses. Moreover, we argue that it is imperative to include the intersectionality (Collins, 1991) or interlocking of all aspects of identity in institutional policies and practices. As a women's college, there is an assumption that sex is central – and it is in terms of admission. Yet, this does not mean that every policy and practice is feminist or even considers diverse women's identities. In this study, we did not explicitly examine policies related to sex. In fact, other than the fact that the college only admits those who are women at the time of matriculation, there are few policies and practices that are explicitly intended to improve the quality of women's lives. Further, we noted that the college fell short in providing resources for mothers, suggesting that from a feminist perspective, this practice has unintended consequences for women. However, we argue that each policy at Women's College has implications for women, and this should never be taken for granted. Doing so only serves to reinforce institutional and administrative power at the expense of women. We hope, through our analysis, other colleges and universities may be able to learn from the well-intended policy efforts and practices of this institution that strive to raise class-consciousness and eradicate classism and sexism, but may actually contribute to reinforcing what they seek to eliminate.

Conclusion

Students, like those who attend Women's College, live in a space where classism is reinforced, despite well-meaning policies and practices that appear class-neutral or try to compensate for economic inequalities. As a result, students are placed in a position where they "are forced to acquire the ability, like a chameleon, to change colors when the dangers are many and the options few" (Anzaldúa, 1990, p. xv). In order for these women to have access to and participate fully in an institution like Women's College, they are forced to advertise their lack of privilege in order to receive benefits or hide their classed culture to avoid being targeted by administrators, professors, or peers.

In this time of increasing attention to demographic diversity on campus, we must move from increased consciousness to increased agency. We hope that institutions can create and implement policies that address discrimination and bias related to social class and sex, that also address other multiplicities of students' lives. This means that the dominant discourses around social class and sex must be challenged and discursive shifts must be facilitated. This is not an easy task. Bensimon (2005) described how individuals can cognitively reframe language from deficit to equity. For example, rather than blaming students for their lack of preparedness for college work because they went to an underfunded high school, we now recognize that by admitting students we have a respon-sibility to facilitate their academic success. Cognitive reframing may be one way to potentially contribute to a discursive shift, but it does stop short, much like what seems to be happening at Women's College. Women's College has made a well-meaning start, but as we have shown, there is more that needs to be done, since those paying the price for many of the policies are those the policies were intended to help. Further, even in our critique, we used concepts like cultural and economic capital and presented the challenges related to a "lack" of such capital. That language is a language of deficit. We need to work harder at finding language that identifies privilege and oppression, but does not imply that a difference is an inadequacy. Using such language only seeks to maintain a system of power and privilege. However, a tool such as an FPS analysis of policies and practices can be another step toward considering the intended and unintended consequences of policies for each individual, with her multiple subject positions.

Notes

1   Sex is used throughout this chapter because it refers to a student's biological designation and there are policies in place at Women's College, as a single-sex institution, where admission is based on biological birth designation.
2   Racism, classism, sexism, and heterosexism are historically and geographically specific, socially constructed systems of oppression, whereby certain races, classes, sexes, and sexual orientations have power and others do not (Weber, 2001). These power relationships will continue over time and the oppression is reinforced by the dominant ideas about race, class, sex, sexual orientation, and other aspects of identity (Bishop, 2005).
3   We use social class to refer to a socially constructed idea about one's economic status. Often individuals and colleges and universities will adopt a culture associated with a particular social class (e.g., working class, lower socio-economic status, middle class, upper-middle class). However, each individual creates his or her own definition such that a parent's income level may suggest a middle-class background, even if previous experiences and value systems led to an identification as working class.

References

Allan, E. J. (2003). Constructing women's status: Policy discourses of university women's commission reports. *Harvard Educational Review*, 73(1), 44–72.

Allan, E. J. (2008). *Policy discourses, gender, and education: Constructing women's status.* New York: Routledge.

Allan, E. J. & Madden, M. (2006). Chilly classrooms for female undergraduate students: A question of method? *The Journal of Higher Education*, 77(4), 684–711.

Anzaldúa, G. (1990). *Haciendo, caras, una entrada.* In G. Anzaldúa (Ed.), *Making face, making soul: Creative and critical perspectives by feminists of color* (pp. xv–xxviii). San Francisco, CA: Aunt Lute Books.

Bensimon, E. M. (2005). Closing the achievement gap in higher education: An organizational learning perspective. *New Directions for Higher Education*, 131, 99–111.

Bishop, A. (2005). *Beyond token change: Breaking the cycle of oppression in institutions*. Black Point, Nova Scotia: Fernwood.

Bogue, E. G. & Aper, J. (2000). *Exploring the heritage of American higher education: The evolution of philosophy and policy*. Phoenix, AZ: Oryx Press.

Bok, D. (2003). *Universities in the marketplace*. Princeton, NJ: Princeton University Press.

Bourdieu, P. (2000). Cultural reproduction and social reproduction. In R. Arum & I. R. Beattie (Eds.), *The structure of schooling: Readings in the sociology of education* (pp. 56–68). Boston, MA: McGraw Hill.

Brady, K. L. & Eisler, R. M. (1995). Gender bias in the college classroom: A critical review of the literature and implications for future research. *Journal of Research and Development in Education*, 29(1), 9–19.

Buzzanell, P. M. & Liu, M. (2005). Struggling with maternity leave policies and practices: A poststructuralist feminist analysis of gendered organizing. *Journal of Applied Communication Research*, 33(1), 1–25.

Collins, P. H. (1991). *Black feminist thought: Knowledge, consciousness, and the politics of empowerment*. New York: Routledge.

DeBra, E. (1997). Women's Colleges in the United States: A historical context. In I. Harworth, M. Maline, & E. DeBra (Eds.), *Women's Colleges in the United States: History, issues and challenges* (pp. 1–20). Washington, DC: National Institute on Postsecondary Education, Libraries, and Lifelong Learning and the U.S. Department of Education.

Fay, E. A. & Tokarczyk, M. M. (1993). Introduction. In M. M. Tokarczyk & E. A. Fay (Eds.), *Working-class women in the academy: Laborers in the knowledge factory* (pp. 3–24). Amherst, MA: The University of Massachusetts Press.

Foucault, M. (1979). *Discipline and punish: The birth of the prison*. New York: Vintage.

Foucault, M. (1980). *Power/Knowledge: Selected interviews and other writings, 1972–1977*. New York: Pantheon Books.

Fischer, K. (2008). Top colleges admit fewer low-income students: Pell Grant data show a drop since 2004. *The Chronicle of Higher Education*, 54(34), A1.

Glazer-Raymo, J. (1999). *Shattering the myths: Women in academe*. Baltimore, MD: Johns Hopkins University Press.

Glazer-Raymo, J. (2008). The feminist agenda: A work in progress. In J. Glazer-Raymo (Ed.), *Unfinished agendas: New and continuing challenges in higher education* (pp. 1–34). Baltimore, MD: Johns Hopkins University Press.

Goodman, J. & Martin, J. (Eds.). (2002). *Gender, colonialism and education*. London: Woburn Press.

Hartsock, N. (1983). The feminist standpoint: Developing the ground for a specifically feminist historical materialism. In S. Harding & M. Hintikka (Eds.), *Discovering reality* (pp. 283–310). Dordrecht, Germany: Kluwer Academic.

Heller, D. E. (Ed.). (2002). *Condition of access: Higher education for lower income students*. Washington, DC: American Council on Education.

Hochschild, A. R. & Machung, A. (1990). *The second shift*. New York: Avon Books.

hooks, b. (2000). *Where we stand: Class matters*. New York: Routledge.

Johnson, A. G. (2006). *Privilege, power, and difference*, 2nd ed. Boston, MD: McGraw Hill.

Langhout, R. D., Rosselli, F., & Feinstein, J. (2007). Assessing classism in academic settings. *Review of Higher Education*, 30(2), 145–184.

Langston, D. (1993). Who am I now? The politics of class identity. In M. M. Tokarczyk & E. A. Fay (Eds.), *Working-class women in the Academy: Laborers in the knowledge factory* (pp. 60–72). Amherst, MA: The University of Massachusetts Press.

Long, B. T. (2004). How do financial aid policies affect colleges? The institutional impact of the Georgia HOPE Scholarship. *Journal of Human Resources*, 39, 1045–1066.

Miller-Bernal, L. (2000). *Separated by degree: Women students' experiences in single-sex and coeducational colleges*. New York: Peter Lang.

Mills, S. (1997). *Discourse*. New York: Routledge.

Newman, F., Couturier, L., & Scurry, J. (2004). *The future of higher education: Rhetoric, reality, and the risks of the market*. San Francisco, CA: Jossey-Bass.

Oldfield, K. (2007). Welcoming first-generation poor and working-class students to college. *About Campus*, 2(6), 2–12.

Ollenburger, J. C. & Moore, H. A. (1992). *A sociology of women: The intersection of patriarchy, capitalism, and colonization*. Englewood Cliffs, NJ: Prentice Hall.

Perna, L. W. & Titus, M. A. (2005). The relationship between parental involvement as social capital and college enrollment: An examination of racial/ethnic group differences. *The Journal of Higher Education*, 76(5), 485–518.

Personal Narratives Group (1989). *Interpreting women's lives: Feminist theory and personal narratives.* Bloomington, IN: Indiana University Press.

Reinharz, S. (1992). *Feminist methods in social research.* New York: Oxford University Press.

Reynolds, A .L. & Pope, R. L. (1991). The complexities of diversity: Exploring multiple oppressions. *Journal of Counseling and Development*, 70, 174–180.

Rich, A. (2000). Toward a women-centered university. In J. Glazer-Raymo, B. K. Townsend, & B. Ropers-Huilman (Eds.), *Women in higher education: A feminist perspective*, 2nd ed. (pp. 3–15). Boston, MA: Pearson.

Rodriguez, S. (1997). Detour from nowhere: The remarkable journey of a re-entry community college woman. *Initiatives*, 58(1), 1–10.

Rothman, R. A. (2005). *Inequality and stratification: Race, class, and gender*, 5th ed. Upper Saddle River, NJ: Pearson.

Selingo, J. & Brainard, J. (2006). The rich–poor gap widens for colleges and students. *The Chronicle of Higher Education*, 52(31), A1.

Symonds, W. C. (2003). College admissions: The real barrier is class. *Business Week*, April 14. Retrieved March 31, 2008 from http://www.businessweek.com/magazine/content/03_15/b3828071_mz021.htm.

Trow, M. A. (1984). The analysis of status. In B. R. Clark (Ed.), *Perspectives on higher education: Eight disciplinary and comparative views* (pp. 132–164). Los Angeles: University of California Press.

Vander Putten, J. (2001). Bringing social class to the diversity challenge. *About Campus*, November–December, 14–19.

Vine, P. (1997). The social function of eighteenth century higher education. In L. F. Goodchild & H. S. Wechsler (Eds.), *The history of higher education*, 2nd ed. (pp. 115–124). Boston, MA: Pearson Custom.

Volk, C., Slaughter, S., & Thomas, S. (2001). Models of institutional resource allocation: Mission, market, and gender. *Journal of Higher Education*, 72(4), 387–413.

Watson. L. W., Terrell, M. C., & Wright, D. J. (2002). *How minority students experience college: Implications for planning and policy.* Sterling, VA: Stylus.

Wax, A. L. (2007). Engines of inequality: Class, race, and family structure. *Family Law Quarterly*, 41, 567–599.

Weber, L. (2001). *Understanding race, class, gender, and sexuality: A conceptual framework.* Boston, MA: McGraw-Hill.

Part 3
Discursive Constructions of Change

While some feminists have issued strong critiques of poststructuralism because of its lack of ability to move purposefully toward change, others have embraced a tentative theoretical partnership with poststructuralism because its discursive tools present a poignant opportunity to engage the underlying structures of social institutions and relations. Whereas this book furthers our collective understandings of educational policy, especially as it is gendered, most chapters also point out pathways for change at some level. In this section, we focus on Rebecca Ropers-Huilman's analysis of the discourses that student change agents use to make sense of their motivations for participation, Susan Iverson's chapter on the underlying discourses of diversity action plans, and Nelly Stromquist's consideration of how the changing priorities of educational institutions today shape the possibilities for change.

Rebecca Ropers-Huilman's chapter focuses directly on students who sought to initiate change in their local, institutional, and/or global environments, and considers the discourses that women and men tapped to explain their involvement in change efforts. Overall, many participants conveyed some understanding of how neoliberal policies characterized students as consumers, rather than as change agents. These policies – such as those associated with financial aid, institutional decision-making processes, and student life – provided a particular way in which students were to engage the institutions. Involvement was possible, but was structured by the institution, rather than by mutual understandings about useful and responsible engagement. Both within and outside of this structuring, students chose to engage in change efforts because of their passion for a cause. Beyond that dominant motivator, though, women were more likely than men to explain their motivation for engagement by drawing on gendered discourses associated with social networks and a desire for personal fulfillment. Students' willingness to get involved in change efforts, then, was shaped by the discourses to which they felt they had access.

While Ropers-Huilman focuses on how student change agents made meaning of their experiences through various discursive constructions, Iverson analyzes diversity policies to understand how those authoring the policies tapped into a variety of discourses that both validate and challenge dominant images of diverse peoples. She identifies predominant images of diversity in diversity action plans, and considers how problems and solutions associated with those images construct particular realities. Discourses associated with access and disadvantage were prevalent, as were marketplace and democracy discourses. Plans informed by these discourses validate or produce complex and even troubling ways of thinking about diversity. For example, language in these plans supports "us vs. them" thinking, as well as a need for accountability and surveillance of "diversity work." Language also fails to identify the lack of connection between the problems as they are articulated (individual and systemic racism, sexism, bias, etc.) and the solutions that are posed (support for victims, training, etc.). Iverson urges that those interested in diversity-related change should work both "within and against" the discourses that frame diversity in current sociopolitical contexts. In this way, they do not become somehow "discourse-free." Instead, they become "discourse-aware" of the terms that shape language, power, knowledge, and difference within their change-oriented policies and practices.

Finally, Nelly Stromquist provides an analysis of how change is both structured and limited by international policies relating to science. In her chapter, Stromquist considers policy documents associated with two of the most powerful international lending institutions, the World Bank and the Inter-American Development Bank. She raises questions about their framing of science and technology, especially as that framing relates to gendered participation in those endeavors. Globalization, neoliberalism, and purposes associated with human agency toward economic development undergird the dominant narrative of educational progress. These focuses tend to highlight the representation of women and girls in education without examining the sociocultural processes which both encourage their participation in some ways, while limiting it in others. The strong masculinist discourse associated with competition so prevalent in neoliberal and marketplace discourses diminishes issues related to gendered experiences or, by focusing merely on women's overall representation in higher education, suggests that gender issues have now been resolved. In this discourse, change is limited because the questions that need to be asked cannot be asked within dominant discourses. Questions can, of course, represent resistances and disruptions. But change strategies that fail to address the ways in which particular discourses do not make sense to certain groups will either fail to meet their policy intentions, or force assimilation and dehumanization of those involved.

Change is a topic that is ubiquitous in postsecondary literature, but whose "progressive" form sits uneasily within poststructural analyses. Are we always changing to get better? That is certainly the dominant narrative associated with postsecondary education, such that the opposite is almost unintelligible. Would a policy ever be constructed to "get worse"? Across which dimensions? Yet, feminist poststructuralism urges an understanding of policies and associated changes that considers power and resistances, unintended effects as well as intended ones, and alternative explanations and framings in addition to those that are "logical" in some way. What are the alternative logics of our thinking in postsecondary education? For example, as Ropers-Huilman asks, "Of the many ways that students can be understood in postsecondary institutions, why is it that we have chosen our current forms?" What will neoliberalism repress and produce in students', faculty members', and administrators' experiences? How will constructions of students as consumers or customers affect teaching and learning and the relationships that we nurture (or prohibit) in educational settings? In focusing on change, then, in this context, we do not mean to imply that feminist poststructuralism will produce something "better" in a structural sense. However, we do mean to suggest that a deeper understanding of the structures and values underlying educational policies and related interpretations (as found in both power and resistance) can help us find both meanings and fissures in the discourses within which we operate. In this way, FPS can also illuminate pathways through which we can change those discourses.

9

Motivated to Make a Difference

Student Change Agents' Gendered Framings of Engagement

REBECCA ROPERS-HUILMAN

> [When I said], "I'm going for Vice President [of my organization]," everyone was OK with that, but as soon as I mentioned "President," it was like, "Oh no, a female would never be elected president." . . . That made me wonder [if] no females had run for president because they had been told that. (Claire, City University Student Change Agent)

Recent scholarship has called on universities to promote social responsibility and civic engagement among their students and in their policies and practices (Colby et al., 2003; Mayhew & DeLuca, 2007; O'Grady, 2000). Professional organizations have likewise underscored the role of higher education in maintaining and informing democracies (American Association of Colleges and Universities, 2006). It is clear from the dialogue among both scholars and practitioners that postsecondary education has a role in helping students contribute to their personal and professional communities. Currently, many students participate in formal curricular and co-curricular leadership development programs, while many others engage in service-learning or volunteer efforts. Policies, initiatives, and programs have evolved to promote many kinds of community–university partnerships, to include student engagement.

In this chapter, I use feminist poststructural perspectives to consider this movement toward increased and purposeful student engagement. A key aspect of feminist poststructuralist perspectives is its emphasis on what is both promoted and omitted in given practices and discourses. Specifically, in terms of this chapter, feminist poststructuralism urges those of us in postsecondary education who are interested in students' development both as students and citizens to consider what has been created and what has been overlooked through our current postsecondary education environments. It questions: How are students positioned within postsecondary education and the broader society by competing discourses, to include gendered discourses? It further foregrounds a consideration of identities, not as static categories, but as developed in the context of discourses in which power relations affect relationships and outcomes.

The analyses in this chapter are taken from a qualitative study with 41 student change agents at two research universities, one in the southern United States and one in New Zealand. My intent was to explore the motivations of students in two institutions that were both experiencing neo-liberal discourses that positioned students as consumers and expressing a desire to encourage both leadership development and engagement in their student population. Overall, student change agents work individually and collectively to initiate change that they believe will be positive for a variety of communities, to include their particular group of affiliation, the entire university, their region or nation, and the global community (Rhoads, 1998). They craft their practices in relation to what they see as viable or options from which they could choose. For the purposes of this discussion, student change agents are characterized in the following way: Change agents are committed to and involved in social and/or institutional change. Following from the literature suggesting that women and men tend to have different experiences in leadership situations (Carli & Eagly, 2001; Gordon, 2008; Ridgeway, 2001), this chapter focuses on the question: How are women and men in different contexts motivated to be student change agents? Understanding students' motivations allows educational leaders to develop policies and practices that support their learning and enhance their abilities to be our communities' next leaders.

Feminist Poststructural Approaches to Understanding Student Engagement

Feminist poststructural approaches to thinking about educational experience were important in this analysis for the following reasons. First, feminist poststructuralism foregrounds the concept of discourse, asserting that:

> Through a concept of discourse, which is seen as a structuring principle of society, in social institutions, modes of thought and individual subjectivity, feminist poststructuralism is able, in detailed, historically specific analysis to explain the working of power on behalf of specific interests and to analyse the opportunities for resistance to it. (Weedon, 1987, p. 41)

Discourse is not static; instead, power influences the contours of a discourse and creates a dynamic set of norms and power relations. However, this fluidity does not render discourse unimportant or without effects. Instead, at any given time, a "snapshot" of a discourse in which people operate can highlight the nature of power and resistance as well as the ways in which "normality" is constructed, understood, and enacted. In this chapter, I particularly focus on the ways in which student change agents were motivated to participate in change efforts. These motivations reflected how they saw their subjectivities (or, in other words, how they understood themselves) intersecting with the discourses they perceived as available to them both in the university and in the larger society. In this context, I also consider how campus rhetoric that encouraged the active engagement of students was situated within those power relations.

Second, feminist poststructuralism suggests that identity and difference are enmeshed and interpreted within various discourses. Further, they create subjectivity in those involved. In other words, discourse provides options for creating oneself and, as discourses and the power relations within them shift, so too do those affected by those discourses. While individuals are clearly not powerless to shape their identities, those identities are always also situated within discourses that affect their shaping. Additionally, those discourses also affect interpretations and perceptions of others' subjectivities. Identities, as variously constructed in communities and contexts, intersect with each other and depend on the global and localized discourses of particular settings. In this chapter, I focus on how men and women students observed and interpreted the various discourses within which they were crafting their identities and actions as engaged participants of their particular academic communities.

Third, feminist poststructuralism urges attention not only to what is repressed by particular power relationships within given discourses. Instead, it also contends that within power, there is always resistance. That resistance can be viewed, in one sense, as what has been produced by that power. Simply, power and resistance are mutually shaping (Weedon, 1987). In this chapter, I consider how student change agents were motivated to respond given their perceptions of the discursive power relations within which they perceived themselves to be lived.

Contextualizing the Questions

In order to situate this analysis within existing research and literature, I present a brief literature review on student activism and the gendered nature of leadership. In this discussion, I propose that student activism has the potential to serve as a powerful educational experience for students. I further discuss how leadership can be gendered, and how the intersection of gender and leadership can have effects on educational and civic engagement.

Student Change Agents

Many scholars have established that college students who choose to be engaged in institutional and community affairs can have powerful effects on their institutions and communities. For example, Boren (2001) illustrates how, beginning in the 1400s, students have been key players in toppling governments and challenging established knowledge, as well as instituting change on more local levels. As he concludes, "In the modern world, student resistance efforts are one of the key forces in social power dynamics" (p. 249). As such, universities need to develop "educated citizens" who understand the importance of their role in enriching their communities (Colby et al., 2003).

A focus on the importance of teaching and enacting civic and/or community engagement in educational institutions is increasingly taken up in scholarly literature (Astin, 1993; Astin & Astin, 2000; Boyte & Kari, 2000; Kezar, 2004; Kuh, 1995; Macgillivray, 2005). Much of this literature has focused on how students themselves develop through their involvement in change, leadership, or activism. Associated policies and practices – such as those related to student representation, support for student initiatives, student interactions with administrators, staff, and faculty, as well as student involvement in financial, educational, and programmatic decision-making – are manifestations of the ways that postsecondary education is perceived in today's societies. In both of the contexts in this study, student involvement is shaped by neo-liberal policies that frame students as economic actors who individually choose, individually pay for, and individually benefit from their experiences. Discourses related to student engagement include emphases on career preparation as well as more general leadership development. These focuses are informed by marketplace discourses aimed to enhance both productivity and graduates' "marketability." However, some of those promoting student involvement hold a strong assumption that:

> schools are important societal institutions where students' democratic identities are shaped and where they learn and practice the citizenship skills that will allow them to participate in a liberal democracy. . . . [And] one of the goals of democracy is to expand the rights of oppressed groups and schools play a large role in this. (Macgillivray, 2005, p. 320)

In order to participate in these change efforts, students need to develop "not only knowledge and technical skills but also facility with many forms of communication and modes of inquiry, integrative capacities, reflective judgment, and cross-cultural competencies" (Colby et al., 2003, p. 43). Institutions must decide how they will employ the various discourses that are available to them when engaging students and, simultaneously, consider the ways in which those discourses both position and serve students, the university, and society.

Given the increasing emphasis on students' civic development and the role of student involvement in promoting that development, how can educators facilitate that involvement? Furthermore, what are the limitations in institutions' abilities to perform that role, and how are particular visions of civic engagement promoted at the expense of others? Who is taken into consideration in the development of initiatives and policies associated with service-learning, for example, or for community–university partnerships? What role does gender play in related efforts?

Gendered Leadership

Like involvement in any social organization, student change agents' experiences are also implicated by gendered expectations. It is important to recognize that leadership is inherently shaped by the context in which leaders are acting (Hartman, 1999; Helgesen, 1995; Rosenberg, 1992; Stake, 2007). Therefore, it is impossible to offer generalized or absolute statements about the nature of women's or men's leadership. At the same time, scholars who have studied leadership have posited that gender plays a part in decisions that women and men make about their leadership efforts. For example, Rosalind Rosenberg's (1992) analysis of women's leadership throughout the twentieth century points out that women, regardless of their political affiliations, tended to involve themselves heavily in issues related to community building, health, welfare, and equality as opposed to business or militaristic efforts. This focus is likewise illustrated in a more contemporary and practical text, *50 ways to improve women's lives: The essential guide for achieving equality, health, and success for all* (National Council of Women's Organizations, 2005).

Contributors to a special issue of *The Journal of Social Issues* presented research that explicitly takes into account the ways in which gender has effects on leadership in multiple contexts (Carli & Eagly, 2001). Their focus on "Gender, Hierarchy, and Leadership" examined leadership styles in a variety of contexts – to include business, military, and educational institutions – and concluded that gender is present in myriad ways in leadership experiences. For example, the authors propose that women and men need to draw on their "agentic" and "communal" roles differently if they are to be perceived as effective (Rudman & Glick, 2001). Specifically, women must balance their active and directing roles with a communal role, whereas men are not expected to tend to the role of community builder. Men are often chosen for leadership experiences based on their perceived potential, whereas women are chosen based on their proven productivity (Ridgeway, 2001). Further, while women are more likely now than in the 1970s to see other women as having similar characteristics to those of managers, men's views of women's traits still contradict the views they have of managers (Schein, 2001). In sum, these authors illustrated that leadership experiences tend to be gendered, both in terms of perceptions and interactions.

A key feminist premise is that gender influences social institutions. As such, without attention to how gender affects students' emerging involvement in political change efforts,

> gender-neutral strategies to engage youth in social justice campaigns will fail by overlooking the particular ways in which girls' and boys' possibilities to emerge as public, political actors are strongly and differently tied to their structural positions in their families, schools, and other institutions. (Gordon, 2008, 32)

"Gender neutrality" does not necessarily lead to similar experiences or outcomes for men and women who wish to be involved as democratic citizens within their educational institutions.

In sum, we know that leadership experiences, like other social interactions, are gendered in a variety of ways. And, we know that involvement in community and co-curricular experiences while in college has the potential to enhance students' civic leadership. These experiences are critical to the development of future leaders for our local, national, and global societies. In this chapter, I present an analysis of the motivations of women and men students who choose to become leaders through their participation as student change agents. Through understanding motivations, we can create policies and paths of engagement that allow colleges and universities to provide opportunities for the civic actors within them to forge more productive and educational relationships with the larger society.

Context of Study

This study was conducted at City University (CU) and Old South University (OSU), two institutions that are similar and dissimilar in many ways. A key difference is the sociocultural environment in which they are situated, as CU is in New Zealand/Aotearoa while OSU is in the southern United States. These institutions were chosen both for their similarities and for their differences. First, OSU and CU are similar in that they share a research orientation that is readily apparent to students. They are both located in urban areas, although CU is located near an active commerce and cultural city center, whereas OSU is located in a park-like setting away from the city's downtown area. They each have a large and ethnically diverse group of students. Perhaps most importantly, at the time of this study, these institutions were actively wrestling with the idea of how they wanted to engage their student populations. This was evidenced by various commissions, offices, or initiatives that had recently taken shape to consider ways of supporting or serving students by promoting engagement. Further contextual information as it affects student engagement is noted in each university's respective section below.

City University is an important social institution within the city and arguably within the entire country. For example, student participants in this study were able to point out current national politicians who had previously served as student leaders at CU. While there is a historical memory of protests and other forms of activism, participants in this study described how the recent shifting of the economic burden for higher education to students has limited student involvement in activities outside academics. This "user pays" model is institutionalized (Peters & Roberts, 1999) but is nevertheless a source of tension for students who believe the government should do more to support their education.

Old South University is one of many universities in the region; however, it is prominent in its state. Activism toward social and/or institutional change at OSU appears to be cyclical. At times, articles appear frequently in the newspaper criticizing the university's approach to various social and institutional issues, such as those associated with socially responsible trade relations and providing a supportive climate for diverse students. However, at other times, student leaders seem squarely within the agenda set by the university. Participants in this study described clear events where students joined together to work toward change; however, they also complained of the overriding apathy among the student population. Rising admissions standards, paralleled by state-supported tuition for high-achieving students at Old South University, likely influenced students' level of involvement. Specifically, if students did not maintain academic excellence, they stood to lose their scholarships and, for many, their ability to stay at Old South.

Methods

Data for this analysis were collected through 41 in-depth interviews with students from two institutions. Of these 41 student interviewees, 29 were women and 12 were men.

This chapter is not meant to suggest that there are uniform experiences or perceptions among women and men at City University or Old South University. Rather, the chapter shows both the commonalities and differences in the ways that women and men who were student change agents in both contexts defined the nature of their motivations.

At both sites, students were selected using criterion and snowball sampling techniques. While my co-researchers, Kathy Barnett and Laura Aaron, and I initially referred to this population of students as student activists, many of the participants, particularly at CU, resisted this definition because of negative connotations associated with that term. "Student leader" and "student politician" were likewise dismissed. As such, we rethought our terminology and instead chose to refer to them as "change agents." We did not limit the participants to people involved in a particular kind of change, so the examples and experiences described in the data reflect multiple views, focuses, and orientations.

Participants in this study had the following characteristics. Of the 26 student interviews conducted at OSU, participants represented a wide variety of

Table 9.1 Interview Participant Characteristics

	City University	Old South University
Women Students	9	20
Men Students	6	6

organizational affiliations. Of these 26 individuals, 20 were women and six were men. Eighteen identified as White, two as Black, two as Hispanic, one as multiracial, and three constructed their own racial category or elected not to respond. The participants' ages ranged from 19 to 25. They represented 20 different academic majors and five different political party affiliations.

Of the 15 interviews conducted at CU, nine were women and six were men. Eight different ethnicities were claimed by participants including "Pakeha" and "European" and "New Zealander" (terms variously chosen by people whose ancestors were originally from Great Britain), as well as Maori, Chinese New Zealander, Taiwanese, Australian, and German. Participants listed ages ranging from 19 to 32 and had chosen to pursue nine different degrees. They were less likely than the United States participants to designate an official political affiliation, with only five people doing so. Four of those five students indicating a political affiliation chose to affiliate with New Zealand Labour.

Interview questions focused on what student activism meant to the students, what motivated them to become involved in change efforts, and what roles student change agents played in university settings. Students were also asked what they had learned from their involvement as student leaders. Additionally, I observed several on-campus events described by participants and interviewed administrators at each institution in order to better understand the contexts in which they were crafting their efforts. All interviews were fully transcribed. I read through each of the interview transcripts and unitized and categorized the data according to the following question: How are women and men in different contexts motivated to be student change agents? In line with feminist analyses that insist that gender, as shaped by social context, will likely shape educational experiences (Bloom, 1998; Middleton, 1993; Ropers-Huilman, 2003), I present the themes using the four groups delineated in Table 9.1 above.

In presenting these data, it is not my intention to essentialize all women or all men in either of the two contexts of my study. Instead, I focus on how women and men with complex identities tap into discourses associated with civic engagement that are accessible and understandable to them. I also consider how they craft their behaviors to lead and, occasionally, resist the power structures within their university contexts. Following the data presentation, I consider implications of this analysis for policies associated with student engagement in postsecondary education.

Motivations of Student Change Agents

In this section, I present data associated with women and men at the City University and Old South University. In each case, I review the predominant themes across the data. These themes indicated that students were motivated by a passion for a cause, by friendships and social networks, and by a desire for personal fulfillment. While the first motivator (passion for a cause) was often expressed in both contexts and for men and women, the second two motivators appeared to be gendered in that women tended to frame their motivations for involvement with a communal discourse related to friendships and social networks as well as a desire for personal fulfillment.

City University Women Change Agents

Passion for a Cause

By far, the largest motivator in all groups in this study was a passion for or commitment to a cause. While this passion was not developed in isolation and instead relates to the other categories, it is important to consider the role of commitment to a cause in motivating student change agents. CU women change agents described their commitments in terms of changing both the university and the surrounding community. Annie-Laurie told us of how her educational experiences abroad motivated her to improve the mentoring and student support at her institution. She decided to initiate a program to facilitate interaction among upper-division and lower-division students in her unit. Sherlene's cause was to educate CU students about the many cultures that were in New Zealand and at CU, in large part because of her experiences as a member of a minority group. And Meina's cause was to ensure that all segments of the CU population were represented when key decisions were made about their educational experiences.

Claire described how her proclivity for positive attention intersected with her passion to improve her surrounding communities. In her words:

> The reason why I'm doing it is because I saw it as the only place to be able to get the things I wanted to do, done. Yeah, I love standing on the stage . . . but [I] also [love] knowing that, we put this on for [students], and they're happy. And that makes me feel brilliant, and so there's of course there's gotta be a sense of self-worth. . . . I'll do anything within my power to make things better.

Collectively, most CU women noted a passion for some cause that motivated their participation as a change agent.

Friends and Social Networks

A strong motivator of involvement in change efforts for women at CU related to friends and social networks. While college students in general benefit from being integrated socially and academically into their institutions (Tinto, 1994), these students were motivated to participate as change agents in their university by their need for integration into identified communities, both within and outside of their college setting. In several cases, women participants at CU told us that the lack of social integration, rather than its presence, was a motivating factor. For example, Diana described that she joined a particular organization in her first year because she thought she would feel "lost" and unable to make friends in "three hundred people lectures."

Others discussed how their friends initiated their mutual involvement in change efforts, or served as models after which they constructed their efforts. In Annie-Laurie's case, her childhood friends continued to be influential in her decisions.

> The [friends] who I've grown up with are . . . very independent and . . . think outside of themselves and they tend to do things very independently and take the initiative themselves. . . . Although they don't have everyday impact in what I do, they do have a lot of impact in philosophy.

Zoe noted that she was motivated because her friend asked her to stand for election with him. As she told us:

> [A friend] just said to me one day, "look, why don't we run for this?" And you know, I like to take up different things and just give it a go. So that was the reason for getting into it, we thought it'd be good fun, and it has been.

Still other City University women recognized that the potential friends and social networks they would gain from particular organizational and personal involvement was worth committing to those efforts.

Personal Fulfillment

The final theme present in the interviews with women student change agents at City University was that participants were motivated by the desire for personal fulfillment. In general, they were motivated to become involved in change efforts because they believed that their efforts would result in a better educational and social experience for them while at the university. For the CU women, this theme included wanting to participate in experiences in which they could derive enjoyment from what they were doing. In one case, Meina described an organization that brought together people similarly situated in the university:

> for an initiative that had a social and professional interaction aspect, a communication aspect, both with the university and with the wider community. . . . [As soon as] I heard [others] saying their idea, I just thought, "Yes, yes, I want that." That's what makes me happier to be here.

And Shara described, "What more appealed to me then was the enthusiasm, and also you could just tell these people were really, really enjoying what they were doing." When asked about her motivations, Sandy seemed puzzled by the question. She eventually articulated that she was simply doing what she loved doing. She briefly described her circuitous route to her current life:

I'm already a qualified [professional]. And absolutely hated it, kind of discovered that being good at something and actually enjoying it were two totally different things. . . . I find that people that are strong organizers and strong leaders aren't happy unless they're organizing or leading. You know, this is their chance to do it. Where they're not taking on the world, but it's enough for them while they're at university.

Finally, Claire articulated the belief that people who were involved in a particular university organization were looking to fill a void in their lives. As she described:

There's always a big joke within [the group] about the fact that the people who make the time to be part of this organization have always got something missing in their life. Like really, they have been adopted or they've got some kind of psychological disorder, or they've got broken families. . . . They're looking for the reason for life; there's this big joke about it. But when you step back and think about it, everybody's got something like that, everybody. So, we're just choosing the thing we got stuck to.

CU women participants expressed that their involvement was motivated by the desire for personal fulfillment, often as it related to developing and learning within an environment they enjoyed.

Old South University Women Change Agents

Passion for Cause

For Old South University women participants, their passion for various causes fueled their desire to be student change agents. In fact, more than half of the OSU women participants articulated that in their belief, they were just doing what was needed as it related to their causes. For example, Lynn described how she felt guilty that she didn't start her activism earlier, since there was so much to do. Ayn said that she was involved in efforts related to recycling because: "I think it needs to be done, and I don't see anyone else doing it." And Helen articulated that, in her view:

Someone has to do it. This stuff is important. Pretty much any issue that we work on is going to have a major lasting impact on society. . . . I don't have a career or family at this time that I have to worry about . . . and this stuff has to be done. . . . If no one else is doing it and it has to be done, I can do it right now. So I am going to do it.

For some student change agents, their capacity to contribute and the perceived need for contributions fueled their efforts.

Other OSU women change agents focused their attention on a variety of issues, most often related to women and minority groups. This was a predominant theme among the OSU women participants. For example, Atalanta talked about how her interactions with diverse others led to her desire to improve the college environment for everyone. Katie talked about her own experience with sexual violence, and how that led to her desire to work against violence directed at women and to take direct action to strengthen OSU's women's center. Laura's efforts focused directly on minority issues, and especially on the "networking of the people who are a lot more liberal to make the climate a lot more tolerable for anyone here who is a minority." Rose framed her work related to African American inclusion as a way to enhance the entire campus. When constructing her efforts, she tried to address the question, "Where can I be most effective and influence ideas of students and administrators and get things done that I think need to get done for the greater good?" And Rachel said that she became active in key leadership positions in student organizations because she wanted to enhance minority representation. As she explained:

> To be completely honest, I ran for government because I felt the need to be a bigger voice for minority rights in student government. . . . I have in mind the needs of the college, and I think that I move forward those needs, but I certainly don't leave behind [segments of the student body]. For example, I get to appoint senators, and we have very few females. Maybe three or four. We have very few Black males or females. We have very few LGBT [senators]. And I mean like one or two. . . . But legislation comes to pass or comes to the table that affects these different groups, and if you don't have that [representation, those voices aren't heard].

The OSU women were largely motivated by their passion for various causes. As illustrated by the data above, most of these causes related to minority rights and fair representation in decision making from all groups of students.

Friends and Social Networks

Several OSU women participants also described how they were motivated by friendships and social networks. For Ayn, a friend who was also a librarian introduced her to progressive and liberal ideas. In Katie's case, she attempted to give herself a break from her heavily involved high school years, but found in her second year of college that "I needed to get involved with somebody or I was going to end up going back home, 'cos I was so homesick at that point that I needed to make friends." Elizabeth noted that the good environment associated with a particular organization drew her to care about those issues. "I felt very welcomed even though I didn't know very much about anything and I didn't even necessarily care about it. . . . I think becoming acquainted with them helped me care about the things that they did." In an amused observation, Christine explained how her friends were motivating – if not long-lasting – factors for her involvement. In her words: "I get started in it because my friends do pull me in, but once I get involved in it, I will go. My friends will have dropped out and quit long before then, and I'll still be in there doing my thing." So, while Christine's motivation to participate emanated from friendships, her continued involvement was fueled by her commitment to the causes in which she had become involved.

Personal Fulfillment

The final theme present in the interviews with the OSU women was that several students were motivated by a desire for personal fulfillment. In Fiona's case, she articulated that she was trying to find out who she was as an individual apart from her family. She said she found what she was searching for in the "environmental social change movement." Holly talked about how she learned to work with others more through her involvement in clubs than through any other experience at the university. She told us that "The route that I am going with my life I learned because I was involved with clubs; nothing else has really helped me at all." Helen echoed this sentiment, saying: "I have learned so much more in my experiences with [my organization] than any class ever taught me. School is important but my experiential education is important also. . . . I think in the long run it's to my benefit."

Finally, Rachel indicated that while it's not always comfortable, her involvement in activism is motivated because:

> Sometimes we think we know more than what we know, and in our everyday lives, we act in a particular way because we think we know how it feels or what it's like [to be someone else], and we don't. So we've got to constantly educate ourselves by exposing ourselves to different things – whatever we're not comfortable with. For example, to go to an all African American event and be the only White person is very uncomfortable, but it's necessary to kind of understand.

Several OSU women were motivated by a desire for personal fulfillment, including seeking learning opportunities that they could not find elsewhere in the university.

City University Men Change Agents

Passion for a Cause

Five of the six CU men articulated that a strong reason for their involvement in their particular change efforts related to their deep belief in a particular cause. While these causes were not uniform, the strength of their conviction was clearly articulated throughout all but one of the interviews.

In Robert's case, his commitment was to the political organization to which he belonged, and his efforts at the university were simply an extension of that ongoing commitment. In two other cases, the students had specific issues that they wanted to work on. In Sam's case, the issues related to student rights and representation. He was particularly interested in ensuring that students' rights were not limited by an increase in fees. In his assessment:

> [The university] wants to increase fees as much as possible. . . . The plan was . . . to hike them up to fees that students pay in America, which is absolutely ridiculous! I am gonna advocate until my last breath so that that never happens here.

Ted's motivation was similar, in that he wanted to ensure adequate representation among all students, especially in the student government. As he told me:

> Previously they were all basically just all the white kids, middle class. And that's how the executive was thinking. They didn't have any involvement with any minority group and didn't participate with them, didn't try to do anything with them. . . . There was one of our goals . . . to represent and then advocate for Asian students' rights. Because we did feel we were being ignored. And Asian students didn't participate in larger student life . . . because they thought that it had nothing to do with them.

In these cases, Robert, Sam, and Ted had particular intentions for their efforts that were shaped by interest in a particular cause.

Christopher and Tamaki's views were similar, with one notable difference. Both of these CU students observed that others on campus were reluctant to address the issues they thought were important. While Christopher and Tamaki were both heavily involved at City University and in their communities, they stressed that they only assumed leadership roles because they weren't satisfied with how their issues were being addressed on campus. In Christopher's case, he wasn't satisfied with his predecessor's efforts and wanted to "make sure that there is an environmental voice on campus." In Tamaki's case, he decided that the only way he was going to strengthen his organization was if he got involved in a more deliberate way. He went on, though, to articulate how his commitment to directly addressing issues related to minority organizations and representation came from his experiences in school as a young child. In his words:

> I came from a lower socio-economic neighborhood. I went to a low socio-economic school. But I partook in activities which were not considered typical of someone who came from that sort of background. And, what I saw when I partook in those activities (such as I was debating team captain, drama, Shakespeare, all those sorts of things) [was] the stereotypes that

people have that someone from my background wouldn't really be into. When I went to those sorts of activities and partook with other schools from higher socio-economic backgrounds, I found there was – it's hard to say this and not sound like I'm bitter – but, I found that they were so much more sheltered to problems in society. They didn't know about all the issues and problems that were at my high school, for instance. And they looked down on us. And, when I see that, it really, really makes me angry, it really does. It makes me really, really angry and that's why I decided that I would always get involved in anything to do with society. Wherever I went, I'd always get [involved].

In these cases, then, a commitment to a cause led even those who were reluctant leaders to get involved in change efforts in their university experience.

Friends and Social Networks

Only one City University man talked about the motivation he derived from friends and other social networks. Graham's words did not echo the enthusiasm and community orientation of those students in other groups. Instead, he described his interest as being developed when "I had nothing better to do in first year than sit around and listen to people, student politicians in the quad, talk about stuff. And that got me interested." Interestingly, Graham was the only CU man who did not articulate a passion for a cause as a motivating factor in his efforts. Instead, his action was motivated by noticing a void in his collegiate experience and deciding to let something fill it.

Personal Fulfillment

Ted was the only CU man who indicated that his motivation to be a student change agent came in part from his belief that he gained personal fulfillment through that involvement. He spoke of a fledgling organization in which he was a member:

I got quite a lot out of the club and I got not only friendships, but the whole cultural identity thing. Before I'd come to university, I didn't view the [specific] culture as one of its own. . . . I got quite a lot out of the club and wanted to put something back into it.

Ted's acknowledgment that he benefited in multiple ways from this organization motivated him to assume a more active role within it. He found in his organizational interactions an opportunity to think reflectively about his own identity, further develop his own beliefs and understandings about himself, and help others do the same.

Old South University Men Change Agents

Passion for a Cause

Several OSU men articulated that they were motivated to be change agents when they encountered situations they believed to be unfair or wrong. In Enrique's case, his surprise at the lack of recycling on campus led him to become a leader in an environmental group on campus. In Joe's case, he had planned to become active within the institutional system but found that "alternative" views were not welcomed there. As he described:

> [A group of us] wanted to form an alternative ticket [to run for student government] and perhaps represent some people who had not been represented. The reason I really got gung ho involved in student government is because they tried to keep us from debating in the main debates for candidates. . . . The cops were called on us, and I had to meet with the dean of students simply for trying to put out my political beliefs. It hardened me to some degree to really want to make changes to where everybody could get their voices heard if they wanted to. . . . Being told that I would not be allowed to express my beliefs and my ideas for change was a major step in making me start questioning some of the system but also to try to work within it to change it.

Keith described himself as a "workaholic of the movement," as a "killjoy who doesn't want to have a good time." He was motivated by a broad-based commitment to enhancing equity and fairness, and this commitment led him to work to limit the university's affiliation with companies that operate sweatshops.

Friends and Social Networks

Several OSU men participants talked about the ways in which friends and social networks were motivating factors for their involvement as change agents. Nick explained that getting involved was "almost a social thing in the beginning – not that it took away from the concerns but my direct joining wasn't because I wanted to fix the world instantly." John Paul expressed how his roommate at the time joined him in an activist lifestyle in which they were overly involved in student activism. In his words, "We both just sort of went off the deep end with organizational involvement, and I was going to about 12 meetings a week and driving myself crazy." Finally, Joe compared his peers on campus as being a family for him, where he felt entirely accepted as a family member. This "family" affiliation has motivated him to continue his participation in change efforts.

Personal Fulfillment

Personal fulfillment was not articulated as a motivator for the Old South University men who identified as change agents.

Discussion

As is clear from the data, men and women perceived their involvement as student change agents similarly in that they were motivated by causes that they deemed important both within and outside the university. Women, though, tended to include in their identification of their motivations a stronger consideration of friendships and social networks and, especially, the personal fulfillment that they desired and experienced. No group spoke with a unified voice. Nor would they be expected to do so, given their multiple and intersecting identities and communities of affiliation. At the same time, these themes illustrate the different ways in which men and women in two different socio-political contexts drew upon a range of discourses to construct meaning about their involvement in change efforts.

Important to remember in this discussion is that the students in this study were people who, regardless of initial motivation, sought or assumed leadership experiences. These are the students who exhibit civic engagement in ways that are promoted in current scholarly literature. Specifically, they have the attitudes, motivation, and skills (Colby et al., 2003) to promote change that they believe is positive in their communities. Considering the views of these students may help postsecondary institutions tap into the energies of students who have the potential to be the civic actors that those institutions claim to develop.

Compelling Discourses

The most clearly and frequently articulated motivator across all groups was students' passion for their cause, however they defined it. This theme was not unexpected, and has been documented in other contexts as well (Boren, 2001; Rhoads, 1998; Thompson, 2004). In some cases, participants told me that they became involved initially because of friendships, but they eventually became motivated by their commitment to the cause. Across the groups, men and women in both contexts spoke of their passions in terms of the need for cultural awareness, support for minority groups and women, and attention to the environment. After identifying those needs – either through personal experience, academic learning, or observation – they believed that someone had to address them. They often framed their motivations using both a liberatory discourse and a rights discourse. In terms of a liberatory discourse, student change agents referred to their desire to make the world a better, fairer place by ensuring that diverse people were treated fairly in terms of representation in governance, adequate focus on and space for student support structures, and visibility in campus programming.

Students were simultaneously motivated by a rights discourse through which they claimed a place at the decision-making table. In all groups, there was a strong undercurrent of the need to have adequate student representation in university decision making that affected students. That need was articulated differently, and the character of that desired participation varied from involvement in nearly all decisions, to limited involvement to determine student services. Yet, student change agents in this study largely believed that it was their right to be involved in shaping their campus environments in some way.

Finally, this research raises questions related to discourses of masculinity and femininity that influence student change agents' motivations. In this study, why were women so much more likely to identify relationships as keys to or catalysts for their involvement in change efforts? What are discourses of femininity and masculinity both limiting and producing in the development of leaders and change agents on campus? And, should institutions identify those discourses and utilize them to more fully engage students, or resist them through their curricular and extracurricular efforts to engage students?

Institutional Response-ability

As policies and practices meant to promote student engagement are developed, efforts to engage students in topics about which they are passionate will provide motivation for their continued involvement. At an individual class level, students can choose how they wish to translate what they are learning into action. At a larger campus level, resources can be established such that students – through organizations or individually – are supported in taking actions that they believe are important to improving their communities. However, institutions must go further.

If institutions promote a climate in which all campus members see themselves as civic actors who are invested in co-creating their broadly multicultural communities, students will be introduced to a discourse which competes with that developed by neo-liberal policies that position students as individual actors who are "products" of the institution. The hierarchies that are endemic in many campus cultures must be open enough to allow students to identify and address issues they believe are important. In this way, civic education could promote a more robust conception of what it means to be a "civic actor," one that includes identification of problems, exploration of options, and an awareness of the ways in which individuals and social institutions can both make differences in their communities. If we enact strict hierarchies among students, faculty members, staff members, and administrators, we communicate a vision of society that replicates hierarchies among groups with more or less power, instead of a vision insisting on the capacity of individuals and groups to make a difference in our world.

Gendered Considerations

In this study, notable differences can be found in the data in particular categories of motivators. Women articulated that friends and social networks were very important motivating factors. Both CU women and OSU women found in change-oriented groups an environment in which they felt cared for and welcomed as motivating. Neither CU nor OSU men spoke a great deal about the role of their friends in motivating them to participate in change efforts. A notable exception to this was Joe's comment that members of his organization have become like a family.

Personal fulfillment was noted as a motivating factor by many women at both CU and OSU but only by one man. Women spoke of the desire to get a better sense of self, to be happy through their involvement, and to learn from experiences that simply weren't available in other contexts. For the one CU man who identified personal fulfillment as a motivating factor, he noted that he gained cultural understanding about himself through his involvement in an organization. Questions remain about men's lack of consideration of these latter two themes, though, in this study. If postsecondary institutions were to explicitly value a discourse centered on the personal fulfillment that can be experienced through connections with community, perhaps it would draw in more women to engage in leadership experiences. Furthermore, it might provide men with an additional discourse through which they can frame their thinking and motivations associated with change efforts and involvement. Are personal fulfillment and friendship networks truly not motivators for men? Or, is it that men have been socialized to see their commitments to particular issues as being more "appropriate" motivators for their behavior?

Summary

It is my intention that this chapter serve as a catalyst for discussion about how to engage women and men with diverse interests and identities in civic engagement while they are in their university experiences. As was pointed out above, people are motivated in different ways to become civic actors and change agents. Participants in this study had different stories. Atalanta told us, "I became an activist because I came to college." Katie dropped out of school for a semester to concentrate on a particular initiative. Sandy found a role that she loved to play through her involvement with student organizations and decided to change her career path. Christopher and John Paul envisioned their university involvement as only one of many significant activist experiences, whereas Ayn confined her involvement to what was happening on her campus. Clearly, activists are not of one ilk. Nor are they motivated in only one way. Indeed, several participants in this study noted that they were motivated in different ways at different times in their efforts. Still, the analysis above illustrates that those of us in postsecondary education can serve as catalysts, allies, or advisors to assist student change agents in their development as civic actors. Likewise, we can learn about our own roles as engaged citizens through our interactions with them.

We know that involvement in activities out of the classroom has the potential to have tremendous educational effects (Kuh, 1995; Pascarella & Terenzini, 2005; Tinto, 1994). We also know that higher education plays a key role in helping to develop leaders for our collective national and global futures (Colby et al., 2003; Gould, 1999). Further, we know that women are severely under-represented in political, educational, and business leadership positions, and that such an under-representation does not serve our society well (Carli & Eagly, 2001). It makes sense, then, to try to better understand both how and why women and men become involved in what is presumably one of the training grounds for future leadership experiences.

While this chapter addresses motivating factors that facilitated students' involvement in change efforts, further research should consider the reasons that many students are not participating in such efforts. Although the most relevant data to address that point would come from a different population than those included here, the interviewees noted that particular university and community structures may serve as disempowering and even prohibitive factors. For example, some participants told us of their inability to understand the "system" of higher education, which therefore led to their inability to work effectively within it (Ropers-Huilman, Carwile, & Barnett, 2005). Others in both CU and OSU told us that financial constraints limited students' abilities to participate in the "extra" effort that is required to be involved in change efforts. This limitation is enhanced by the increasing costs associated with attending postsecondary education today both in New Zealand and the United States.

Further research should also consider more deeply how students' own cultural communities outside the college environment affect their involvement. While many students were motivated by a desire to enhance the ability of minority voices to be heard, this was broadly distributed across diverse categories of identity. Research should examine more explicitly the ways in which students' home communities affect their predispositions to become involved in change efforts. As Carolyn Thompson (2004) points out in her analysis of African American student activism in the 1960s, community net-works can be significant motivators for some students. Additionally, Ellen Broido's (2000) and Keith Edwards' (2006) scholarship on social justice allies could be further engaged in an effort to better understand the multiple motivations and underlying discourses associated with ally behavior and identity.

The change agents in this study resisted becoming a product of the academic factory. Instead, their approach to education mirrors what is evident in the rhetoric around "educating citizens." They wanted to be part of decision making. They wanted to be actively involved in learning for learning's sake. They wanted to ensure that the rights of minority groups were being upheld. And they wanted to be treated as the citizens that current discourses associated with tertiary education in both the United States and New Zealand claim to be educating. It is my hope that this chapter will provide information for university and community members to further our understandings about how we can enact policies and practices to motivate students – both women and men – to become active participants in co-constructing our society.

References

American Association of Colleges and Universities. (2006). American commitments: Diversity, democracy, and liberal learning. http://www.aacu.org/. Retrieved June 1, 2006.

Astin, A. W. (1993). *What matters in college: Four critical years revisited.* San Francisco, CA: Jossey-Bass.

Astin, A. W. & Astin, H. C. (2000). *Leadership reconsidered: Engaging higher education in social change.* Battle Creek, MI: W. K. Kellogg Foundation.

Bloom, L. (1998). *Under the sign of hope: Feminist methodology and narrative interpretation.* New York: State University of New York Press.

Boren, M. E. (2001). *Student resistance: A history of the unruly subject.* New York: Routledge.

Boyte, H. C. & Kari, N. N. (2000). Renewing the democratic spirit in American colleges and universities: Higher education as public work. In T. Ehrlich (Ed.), *Civic responsibility and higher education* (pp. 37–60). Westport, CT: Oryx Press.

Broido, E. M. (2000). The development of social justice allies during college: A phenomenological investigation. *Journal of College Student Development,* 41(1), 3–18.

Carli, L. L. & Eagly, A. H. (2001). Special Issue: Gender, Hierarchy, and Leadership. *The Journal of Social Issues,* 57(4).

Colby, A., Ehrlich, T., Beaumont, E., & Stephens, J. (2003). *Educating citizens: Preparing America's undergraduates for lives of moral and civic responsibility.* San Francisco, CA: Jossey-Bass.

Edwards, K. (2006). Aspiring social justice ally identity development: A conceptual model. *NASPA Journal,* 43(4), 39–60.

Gordon, H. R. (2008). Gendered paths to teenage political participation: Parental power, civic mobility, and youth activism. *Gender and Society,* 22(1), 31–55.

Gould, B. (1999). The future of New Zealand universities. *New Zealand Journal of Educational Studies,* 34(1), 28–34.

Hartman, M. S. (1999). *Talking leadership: Conversations with powerful women.* Piscataway, NJ: Rutgers University Press.

Helgesen, S. (1995). *The female advantage: Women's ways of leadership.* New York: Doubleday.

Kezar, A. (2004). Obtaining integrity? Reviewing and examining the charter between higher education and society. *The Review of Higher Education,* 27(4), 429–459.

Kuh, G. D. (1995). The other curriculum: Out-of-class experiences associated with student learning and personal development. *Journal of Higher Education,* 66(2), 123–155.

Macgillivray, I. K. (2005). Shaping democratic identities and building citizenship skills through student activism: Mexico's first gay–straight alliance. *Equity and Excellence in Education,* 38(4), 320–330.

Mayhew, M. & DeLuca Fernández, S. (2007). Pedagogical practices that contribute to social justice outcomes. *The Review of Higher Education,* 31(1), 55–80.

Middleton, S. (1993). *Educating feminists: Life histories and pedagogy.* New York: Teachers College Press.

National Council of Women's Organizations Staff. (2005). *50 ways to improve women's lives: The essential guide for achieving equality, health, and success for all.* San Francisco, CA: Inner Ocean Publishing.

O'Grady, C. R. (2000). *Integrating service learning and multicultural education in colleges and universities.* Mahwah, NJ: Lawrence Erlbaum Press.

Pascarella, E. & Terenzini, P. (2005). *How college affects students.* San Francisco, CA: Jossey-Bass.

Peters, M. & Roberts, P. (1999). *University futures and the politics of reform in New Zealand.* Palmerston North, New Zealand: Dunmore Press Limited.

Rhoads, R. A. (1998). *Freedom's web: Student activism in an age of cultural diversity.* Baltimore, MD: Johns Hopkins University Press.

Ridgeway, C. (2001). Gender, status, and leadership. *The Journal of Social Issues,* 57(4), 637–655.

Ropers-Huilman, B. (Ed.). (2003). *Gendered futures in higher education: Critical perspectives for change*. Albany, NY: SUNY.

Ropers-Huilman, B., Carwile, L., & Barnett, K. (2005). Working the system: Student activists' characterizations of and desired communication with higher education administrators. *Review of Higher Education*, 28(3), 295–312.

Rosenberg, R. (1992). *Divided lives: American women in the twentieth century*. New York: Hill and Wang.

Rudman, L. A. & Glick, P. (2001). Prescriptive gender stereotypes and backlash toward agentic women. *The Journal of Social Issues*, 57(4), 743–762.

Schein, V. E. (2001). A global look at psychological barriers to women's progress in management. *The Journal of Social Issues*, 57(4), 675–689.

Stake, J. E. (2007). Predictors of change in feminist activism through women's and gender studies. *Sex Roles*, 57(1–2), 43–54.

Thompson, C. J. (2004). The changing role of the village: College student activism in the Post-Brown Era, 1967–1969. *Urban Education*, 39(4), 428–441.

Tinto, V. (1994). *Leaving college: Rethinking the causes and cures of student attrition*. Chicago, IL: University of Chicago Press.

Weedon, C. (1987). *Feminist practice and poststructuralist theory*. Oxford: Basil Blackwell.

10
Producing Diversity

A Policy Discourse Analysis of Diversity Action Plans

SUSAN V. IVERSON

Almost twenty years after the American Council on Education published its handbook for enhancing diversity (Green, 1989), the Association of American Colleges and Universities published *Making a real difference with diversity* (Clayton-Pedersen, Parker, Smith, Moreno, & Teraguchi, 2007), a step-by-step guide for implementing and sustaining diversity work on campus. This publication joins a growing list of publications designed to document the challenges and benefits of diversity, and offer administrators promising practices and practical tools for identifying and assessing diversity on campus, enhancing access and success for historically disadvantaged groups, and strengthening the overall institutional functioning regarding diversity (see Bauman, Bustillos, Bensimon, Brown, & Bartee, 2005; *Does Diversity Make a Difference?*, 2000; Garcia et al., 2003; Kezar & Eckel, 2005; Milem, Chang, & antonio, 2005; *Now is the time*, 2005; Williams, Berger, & McClendon, 2005). The diversity agenda is no longer limited to simply improving the proportional representation of under-represented minorities; "each campus must create an environment that embraces diversity as one of its core values, infusing every aspect of campus life and purpose, and every measure of success" (*Now is the time*, 2005, p. 1; also Milem, Chang, & antonio, 2005, p. 31).

In response to the continued elevation of inequity and diversity on the agendas of most educational practitioners and scholars, "most campuses today have some set of initiatives designed to enhance compositional diversity, create more inclusive communities, or expand horizons" (Clayton-Pedersen, Parker, Smith, Moreno, & Teraguchi, 2007, p. 2). Special committees, charged by senior administrators, typically codify diversity challenges and recommendations into *diversity action plans* – official university policy documents that serve as a primary means by which postsecondary institutions formally advance and influence policy for building diverse, inclusive campus communities.

While recommendations, initiatives, and strategies proliferate, many segments of the national population continue to be grossly under-represented on campus, and equity in education remains a much sought-after goal (Morfin, Perez, Parker, Lynn, & Arrona, 2006). The scholarly literature on the impact and effects of diversity in higher education is growing; however, relatively little research exists investigating institutional policies (e.g., diversity action plans) and their role as a solution to social problems on college and university campuses. This analysis of diversity action plans issued at twenty U.S. land-grant universities investigated how discourses generated by these reports framed diversity in higher education. The findings suggest that the discursive representation of diversity in these policies is neither natural nor neutral. Rather, as Evelyn Hu-DeHart (2000) argues, "the diversity project as we know it on our campuses is complicit in perpetuating the racial order as historically constructed" (p. 42).

Purpose

In order to enhance understanding of diversity policy documents, how they contribute to producing a particular reality on campus, and how they may compromise the achievement of their own goals, this study sought to identify and analyze discourses circulating in diversity action plans. These policy documents are a primary means by which land-grant universities advance recommendations regarding their professed commitment to inclusive access and an equitable climate for *all* members of the campus community. As Schauber and Castania (2001) observe, diversity policies provide a "vision for change" and "the language and goals that can guide our system" (para 16). As such, diversity action plans not only record and reflect organizational culture (e.g., as an archival document), but also construct particular realities for members of the institution (e.g., construct power relations and re/produce dominant ideologies) (Allan, 2003). This is notable when programs and policies are designed "from a dominant cultural perspective, which does not work for most of our under-represented cultural groups" (Schauber & Castania, 2001). Thus, an analysis of the discourses circulating in diversity policies queries and illuminates:

> which groups or institutions have preferential access to various kinds of knowledge, which groups or institutions set the criteria for the very defini-tion or legitimization of knowledge, and which are specially involved in the distribution of knowledge – or precisely in the limitation of knowledge in society. (van Dijk, 2002, p. 88)

Well-intentioned attempts to create a more inclusive institutional culture may unwittingly reinforce practices that support exclusion and inequity. The use of assumptive concepts in diversity planning policies may limit a policy's effectiveness and actually reinscribe the very problem the policy seeks to alleviate (Allan, 2008; Bacchi, 1999; Ball, 1990; Scheurich, 1994).

Conceptual Framework

Policy Analysis

As elaborated in Chapter 2, a variety of approaches to the study of policy exists. Using a dominant, conventional – sometimes called "rational" – approach, policy-makers employ formulaic steps in policy-making, and value decisions are assumed to be "relatively straightforward" and are "clearly formulated in advance" – meaning the problem which the policy seeks to resolve is accepted as an unquestioned, objective fact, and attention is instead focused on identifying solutions to the given problem (Bacchi, 1999, p. 18).

Critiques of conventional approaches to policy analysis (Bacchi, 1999; Ball, 1990; Marshall, 1999, 2000; Scheurich, 1994) posit that such policy approaches are guided by a technical-rational evaluation of what makes effective policy – meaning they want to offer ways of "doing it better" (Bacchi, 1999, p. 20) – and serve to legitimize some socially constructed norm of behavior that functions to categorize people, things, and ideas. Policy problems, studied using rational approaches, are typically uncritically accepted, naturalized in the individual, and ignore the social construction of the policy problem (Allan, 2003; Bacchi, 1999; Baez, 2002; Scheurich, 1994). From this perspective, policy implies consensus and risks "ignoring and creating silences on the contradictions of lived experience and social ideals" (Ball, 1990, p. 139). Such approaches to policy-making and analysis often fail to examine underlying and often taken-for-granted assumptions about solutions embedded within how a problem is represented and the implications for these representations (Allan, 2003; Bacchi, 1999; Baez, 2002).

Blending critical approaches to policy analysis with methods of textual analysis invites researchers to focus on silences and exclusions, giving voice to those at the margins (Baez, 2002; Reinharz, 1992; Roe, 1994). Specifically, the use of a feminist perspective on policy helps to raise important questions about the control and production of knowledge, and the ways policy can be used to empower individuals to act upon/in their environment to challenge dominant ideology (Blackmore, 1999; Marshall, 1999, 2000). Eyre (2000), for instance, utilizing discourse analysis in her investigation of one case of sexual harassment on a university campus, investigated how policy administrators at one institution framed sexual harassment and raised awareness of how these discursive constructions may benefit some while marginalizing others. The researcher's basic suppositions with this approach are to make visible and critique the social relations of power that normalize sexual harassment; to reveal the conditions that make sexual harassment possible; and to transform the institution through this awareness (Eyre, 2000).

Power

Multiple conceptualizations of power exist. A dominant view is evident in articulations of power as a force that can be controlled, used to influence, possessed, and deployed as "weapons" that through "their tactical use" administrators can "influence policies" (Baldridge, 1971, p. 154; also Fisher, 1984; French & Raven, 1959; Pfeffer, 1981). From this perspective, which some conceptualize as "power-over" (Allen, 1999; Beckwith, 1999), power is causative, intentional, and purposeful, but not predictive; one event triggers the next, but power does not consist of a discrete set of actions or stages, nor can we predict the outcome of any one event or action (Burns, 1978).

Another view defines power as the "ability of a collectivity to act together for the attainment of an agreed-upon end or series of ends" (Allen, 1999, pp. 126–7). Such power is "an expandable resource that is produced and shared through interaction" (Astin & Leland, 1991, p. 1; also Beckwith, 1999; Blackmore, 1999). Redefined as "power through and with others," such power is exercised rather than possessed, illustrating its transformative potential (Blackmore, 1999, p. 161; also Anderson & Grinberg, 1998; Sawicki, 1991). This perspective is captured by a participant in Blackmore's (1999) study of women and leadership who redefined power as "being at the centre of the spokes of a wheel rather than out in front pulling the wagon" (p. 161).

In contrast to traditional views of power as possessive, coercive, and controlling, this study of the discursive framing of diversity draws upon the work of Foucault (1978/1990), who articulates a theoretical conception of power that is produced and transmitted through knowledge and discourse at the micro-levels of society. The "macro-level" of society focuses on power located in ideologies, structures, and institutions (Gore, 1998, p. 278), whereas a "micro-level" analysis of power relations examines specific (discursive) practices, such as those codified in diversity action plans that discipline individuals' ways of thinking and acting through self-regulation (Anderson & Grinberg, 1998). From this perspective, policy, itself a form of disciplinary power, "both constrains individuals by subjecting them to regulation, control, and normalization and, at the same time, enables or empowers individuals by positioning them as subjects who are endowed with the capacity to act" (Allen, 1999, p. 51; also Sawicki, 1991). Different from theorists of power who view individuals as oppressed by power relations, "Foucault sees [individuals] as the effects or instances of power relations" (Mills, 1997, p. 22).

Policy, a form of institutional knowledge and site of power relations, has the power to define what is normal (and thus abnormal); this power derives from its location at the top of the institutional hierarchy – that is from senior administration who legitimize policy with their official status. Institutions act, through policy, with the authority to classify, objectify, and normalize persons. Additionally, policies attempt to "represent the world in factual terms so that certain kinds of practices flow 'naturally' from them" (Knight, Smith, & Sachs, 1990, p. 133). This investigation of the discursive framing of diversity involves an examination of the forces and relations of power connected to discursive practices. It illuminates "the ways in which arguments are structured, and objects and subjects are constituted in language" (Bacchi, 1999, pp. 40–1).

Methods

This investigation utilized the method of *policy discourse analysis* to investigate university diversity policies to understand how these documents frame diversity and what reality is produced by diversity action plans. A hybrid methodology, policy discourse analysis focuses on written documents; it is a strategy for examining policy discourses and the ways they come together to make particular perspectives more prominent than others (Allan, 2003). The use of assumptive concepts in language may limit a policy's effectiveness and actually reinscribe the very problem the policy seeks to alleviate (Allan, 2003; Bacchi, 1999; Stein, 2004). For example, a university's diversity action plan may construct a world for racial minorities that disqualifies them from participation, even as it strives to include them as full participants.

In order to examine the discursive framing of diversity in diversity action plans, the following questions guided this study:

- What are the predominant images of diversity in diversity action plans?
- How are problems related to diversity represented in diversity action plans?
- How are solutions related to "diversity problems" represented in diversity action plans?
- What discourses are employed to shape these images, problems, and solutions?
- What realities do these problems, solutions, and images construct?

The data for this investigation consisted of 21 diversity action plans issued at 20 U.S. land-grant universities from 1999–2004 (see Table 10.1).[1] The process of data analysis was informed by established methods of coding and categorizing to identify broad themes and predominant images of diversity (Marshall & Rossman, 1999; Miles & Huberman, 1994). The first phase of the analysis involved deductive coding in reply to the research questions. Through the use of NVivo, computer software designed for qualitative data analysis, I conducted line-by-line analysis of each report to identify and code *images* of diversity, the *problems* related to diversity described in diversity action plans, and the proposed *solutions* to these problems. Once all documents were coded, I used NVivo to generate "reports" for each category – images, problems, and solutions – across all diversity action plans; these reports were then analyzed using both

198 • Susan V. Iverson

Table 10.1 Sample

State	Institution	Diversity Action Plan(s)
Alabama	Auburn University	Strategic Diversity Plan, 2004
Arizona	University of Arizona	Diversity Action Plan, 2003–2004
Arkansas	University of Arkansas	Diversity Plan, 2002–2005
California	University of California, Berkeley	Report of the Chancellor's Advisory Committee on Diversity, 2000
Connecticut	University of Connecticut	Diversity Action Plan, 2002
Georgia	University of Georgia	Institutional Diversity Strategic Plan, 2002–2005
Idaho	University of Idaho	Diversity and Human Rights at the University of Idaho: Comprehensive Plan for Action and Accountability, 2004
Illinois	University of Illinois at Urbana-Champaign	Final Report of the Diversity Initiatives Planning Committee, 2002
Maine	University of Maine	Diversity Action Plan, 1999; 2003–2005
Maryland	University of Maryland, College Park	Report and Recommendations of the President's Diversity Panel, 2000
Nebraska	University of Nebraska, Lincoln	Comprehensive Diversity Plan, 1999 (revised draft)
Nevada	University of Nevada, Reno	Strategic Plan for Diversity Initiatives, 2002
New York	Cornell University	The Cornell University Story: A Holistic Approach to Diversity and Inclusiveness, 2004
North Carolina	North Carolina State University	Diversity Initiative, 1999 (revised and final)
Ohio	The Ohio State University	Diversity Action Plan, 2000
Oklahoma	Oklahoma State University	Institutional Diversity Strategic Plan, 2003
Pennsylvania	Pennsylvania State University	Framework to foster diversity, 2004–2009
Texas	Texas A&M University	Report by the President's Ad Hoc Committee on Diversity and Globalization, 2002
Virginia	Virginia Tech	Diversity Strategic Plan, 2000–2005
Wisconsin	University of Wisconsin, Madison	Plan 2008: the campus diversity plan (1999)

deductive and inductive processes, which served as the second phase of coding. These codes were then clustered according to common themes to generate image categories and identify identity positions that emerged from these images. All 21 documents were then re-analyzed inductively, listening for silences (Pollock, 2004; Stein, 2004) and with a focus on what is taken-for-granted or accepted as given, and analyzed deductively, using the following research question as a guide: what discourses are employed to shape the predominant images? In this phase of the analytic process, I also examined the identity positions that emerged in phase one of the analysis to identify discourses that were most prominent in constituting these positions.

The Discursive Representation of Diversity in Educational Policy

The goal of this investigation was to understand how university diversity policies frame ideas about diversity and what discourses are employed to shape the images, problems, and solutions related to diversity. In this section, I will provide an overview of the research findings as context for a discussion of what realities are produced by the discourses carried in these documents.[2]

Analysis of 21 diversity action plans revealed a dominant discourse of *access*, evident in attention to and improvement of recruitment, retention, and advancement practices to enhance entrée and representation, and create a campus culture which would affirm diverse individuals (see Figure 10.1). Three distinct strands were evident within the access discourse: a discourse of *entrée*, clear in calls for diverse persons to be permitted to enter and participate in the

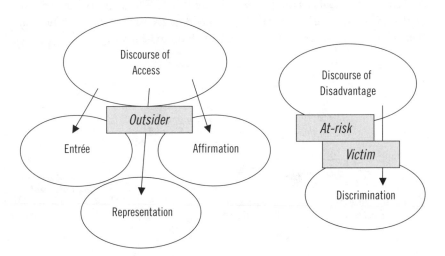

Figure 10.1 Discourses of Access and Disadvantage

university; a discourse of *representation*, apparent in attention to greater involvement, full participation, and increased retention and advancement; and a discourse of *affirmation*, visible in calls for diverse persons to be valued, welcomed, and celebrated by the campus culture. These discourses coalesce to produce the diverse individual as an *outsider* to the university, particular arenas within the institution, and the dominant culture.

Analysis also revealed descriptions of diverse individuals as *at-risk* for educational failure before entering institutions of higher education, and remaining at-risk once a member of the university – at-risk for educational failure, non-promotion, no advancement, no tenure, attrition, discrimination, and harassment, among other things. These characterizations are made visible by a discourse of *disadvantage*, along with a discursive strand of *discrimination* that constructs the diverse individual as an at-risk *victim* (see Figure 10.1). Framed in this way, differences in educational outcomes are generally attributed to lack of academic preparation, deficiencies in skills, and inadequate support. The diverse individual, constituted as at-risk before and after entering the university, is also dependent on the university – represented by an administration that is predominantly white and male – for access to and success in higher education, as well as for remediation, skill development, safety, and support.

Further analysis revealed a *marketplace* discourse, characterized by fierce competition and rapidly changing market conditions and the need for multicultural competence in the global marketplace. Two distinct strands emerged within this discourse: a discourse of *excellence*, evident in a focus on success and reputation, quality and performance; and a discourse of *managerialism*, apparent in the emphasis on effectiveness, accountability, monitoring of costs and effects, and quality assurance (see Figure 10.2). These discourses contribute to shaping the diverse individual as a *commodity*: possessing economic value that can enhance the university's status, and an object to be managed.

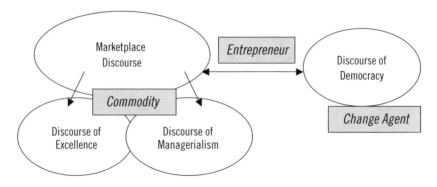

Figure 10.2 Discourses of Marketplace and Democracy

Finally, analysis of diversity action plans revealed a discourse of *democracy*, evident in calls for inclusion and opportunity, civic responsibility, commitment to equity and equality, and open, participatory, and deliberative dialogue (see Figure 10.2). This discourse contributes to shaping a *change-agent* identity, visible in individual and collective efforts to produce social change and equality as a result. The discourse of democracy emerges as an alternative to the marketplace discourse; however, the dominance and greater weight of the marketplace discourse undermines the systemic change-making possibilities of the discourse of democracy. Instead, out of the tension evident between the discourses of democracy and the marketplace, images of the change agent give way to images of entrepreneurial endeavors: individuals encouraged and rewarded for initiative and the development of innovative programs that ensure the university a competitive edge in the marketplace.

What Has Been Produced?

In this section, I will offer a reply to the final research question, what realities do these problems, solutions, and images construct? First, however, I will punctuate the significance of Foucault's work (1977/1995, 1978/1990) for this investigation, in order to foreground my discussion. As noted above, this inquiry draws upon the work of Foucault and others who reconceptualize power as a productive force, meaning – through discourse – it constructs social identities (subjectivities) and produces particular realities. Foucault describes this form of power as "disciplinary power," because it disciplines individuals' ways of thinking and acting through self-regulation; in part, through "an increase of obedience and allegiance" to a perceived norm, but more so through "ordering and organizing" practices and relationships (Simola, Heikkinen, & Silvonen, in Popkewitz & Brennan, 1998, p. 68). This "disciplinary power," according to Foucault, is deployed through "techniques of power," such as surveillance, (self)regulation, normalization, and classification, among others (in Gore, 1998).

For the purposes of this discussion, I define these terms as follows. *Surveillance* is evident in the use of experts (e.g., senior administrators, presidential commissions) to supervise, oversee, and monitor diversity efforts, and through the dissemination of knowledge by those who are senior in rank, authority, or expertise. While surveillance can be seen to have regulating effects, *(self)-regulation* focuses on the explicit use of regulation to invoke a rule, often through use of rewards and punishment; through training, the rule "occupies" individual bodies who self-regulate and discipline, are compliant and obedient (Foucault, 1977/1995). *Normalization* is apparent in comparisons between "minorities" and "the majority," sometimes framed as "them" and "us" respectively; these comparisons serve to invoke or require conformity to a standard (that which is "normal"). Related to normalization is *classification* which is evident in the ways in which groups and individuals are differentiated from one another through sorting and ranking of identity statuses. Next, I present a discussion of the use of these "techniques of power" in diversity action plans.

Surveillance

A predominant solution described in diversity action plans is what I refer to as the use of expert hierarchy. Diversity action plans propose the appointment of senior administrators, faculty, and presidential commissions (e.g., diversity councils) to serve as monitors of diversity efforts, possessing instrumental knowledge. This view reinforces assumptions that anyone not endowed with privileged knowledge, expertise, or organizational stature (e.g., those in lower ranks) is dependent upon those who are.

An illustration of this use of expert hierarchy is the pronounced use (or proposed development) of mentoring programs. The goal of such programs is to pair "knowledgable" and typically senior persons as guides and to provide counsel and advice to diverse persons who are described as at-risk and in need of support. This strategy serves to help diverse persons with their "adjustment" and to ease their "transition"; this approach acculturates the diverse person to institutional policies and practices that may otherwise appear foreign. Exemplified by one report: "junior faculty ... immediately upon his or her arriving on campus, [will be assigned] a senior faculty mentor, and advocate, who will offer both encouragement and useful advice" (University of Maryland, 2000). Another report, describing a peer mentoring program for international students, identifies its goal as "to help students assimilate into the university community" (Texas A&M University, 2002).

Overwhelmingly, the mentor is senior to the mentee (e.g., senior faculty mentoring junior faculty or upper-class students mentoring first-year students). On a few occasions peer-to-peer partnerships were described; however, these relationships are usually still hierarchic. For instance, a current staff person will be assigned to mentor a new staff person. Each is a peer to the other, but the current staff person has greater length of employment, and thus, more knowledge to offer the new employee. No documents propose "bottom-up" mentoring, which would assume that those in "subordinate" positions might possess knowledge that could benefit or inform senior persons. This surveillance, or more specifically hierarchical observation (Foucault, 1977/1995), provides for the (possibility of) supervision of inferiors by superiors (or even by peers).

A few diversity action plans consider the ways in which existing practices may benefit some more than others. For instance, one policy asserts that:

> New approaches to evaluating diversity scholarship must acknowledge the scholarship inherent in research, teaching, and service without relying on narrow and unquestioned rubrics. ... Diversity-related research and teaching initiatives [should] be supported and appropriately valued in

tenure and promotion decisions. (Pennsylvania State University, 2004; also Texas A&M University, 2002; University of Idaho, 2004; University of Illinois, 2002; University of Maryland, 2000; Virginia Tech University, 2000)

However, diversity action plans are devoid of specific interventions to "trouble" the ways existing practices advantage some and disadvantage others. Instead, experts "clarify criteria," helping diverse "others" to navigate existing practices. Thus, the criteria remain unchallenged. The documents, focused primarily on diverse populations' needs and challenges, construct white males as the normative standard against which to measure "minority" progress and success. This standard or criteria (white, male), and thus advantage or privilege, remains largely unacknowledged and unquestioned in the documents.

Diverse individuals, discursively constructed as at-risk outsiders, do not possess the knowledge of the knower; are likely disempowered; and are dependent upon experts from whom they acquire essential knowledge "in order to gain a foothold in mainstream postsecondary education" (Tierney, 1992, p. 109). Further, the use of expert hierarchy fails to challenge universalizing systems and dominating social structures (Tierney & Dilley, 1998). While diversity action plans seek to contest monocultural perspectives and disrupt assimilationist approaches, they may inadvertently reinscribe such views through surveillance (e.g., mentoring programs).

(Self)Regulation

Linked with the use of expert hierarchy, or rather Foucault's hierarchic surveillance, is the explicit use of regulation – the invocation of rules – that "occupies" individual bodies that self-regulate, ensuring compliance. Regulation is pronounced in solutions made visible by the discourse of managerialism that contributes to (self)regulatory behaviors. This discourse is characterized by efficiency, productivity, accountability, and coordination. Managerial practices serve to monitor, supervise, watch, and regulate. Individuals are deferent to the authority of "superiors" – whether mentors, administrators, faculty, or even an ombuds-person, and subjected to surveillance. Aware of the consequences and motivated by incentives, individuals are regulated by others and ultimately self-regulate their behaviors to achieve a diverse and inclusive community.

Regulation is clearly evident in calls for accountability. Most reports recommend specific strategies to ensure compliance with the goals of the plan, including the creation of overseers to "monitor implementation" (University of Idaho, 2004), e.g., committees or the appointment of "someone who sits on the President's cabinet" (University of Maryland, 2000). One document identifies "specific individuals . . . to serve as 'point persons' [who are] responsible for taking the lead or overseeing implementation of and reporting the progress on the key strategies" (University of Connecticut, 2002). Resonating with Foucault's illustrative use of the Panopticon as a surveillance mechanism, enabling an observer to watch and monitor without individuals being able to tell if they are being observed, another diversity action plan proposes to "squarely beam the accountability spotlight on individuals and units who are ultimately responsible for meeting the diversity challenge" (Auburn University, 2004).

A prominent regulatory strategy is the use of performance evaluations. Diversity action plans assert that employees are expected to "demonstrate helpfulness, consideration, and flexibility ... with respect to all foreign students" and their performance will be evaluated (at least annually) on "progress toward achieving diversity goals" (University of Idaho, 2004). More specifically, one report delineates elements of "a diversity and inclusiveness component" to be added to the annual performance review that includes "show respect for differences" and "promote cooperation and a welcoming environment" (Cornell University, 2004). "Skills in managing diversity" are also considered "standard qualifications for all leadership positions" (University of Idaho, 2004).

Regulation occurs on an institutional level, a departmental (or unit) level, and on a personal level. Personally, it is most evident through the use of performance evaluations, which, notably, form "the basis for annual salary increases" (North Carolina State University, 1999). Through an emphasis on "personal accountability" (University of Idaho, 2004), individuals, then, are not only observed by "experts" (e.g., supervisors, senior administrators), but also self-regulate to ensure compliance with diversity goals. Regulation, requiring conformity to a standard, is linked with normalization, which is discussed next.

Normalization

Normalization is most pronounced in the use of a "majority" in diversity action plans as the standard for success, progress, and quality. For instance, climate assessments differentiate white male responses from their "diverse" counter-parts, e.g., white males don't perceive the campus as sexist or racist, whereas women and African-Americans do (Virginia Tech University, 2000). Similarly, numerous plans use retention and graduation rates for whites as the bench-mark of achievement by which to measure the progress of "minority students." Diverse individuals, "them," are compared with and measured against a standard, "us," that is implicitly defined as normal. This "normalizing judgment" that "hierarchizes qualities, skills and aptitudes" (Foucault, 1977/1995, p. 181) is most prominent in characterizations made visible by discourses of access and disadvantage, which produces the at-risk outsider and enables comparisons to be made between "us" and "them." The use of training (e.g., professional development) and correction (e.g., programs designed to compensate for deficiencies) – predominant solutions to problems of disadvantage

– ensure conformity to a standard "that is at once a field of comparison, a space of differentiation and the principle of a rule to be followed" (Foucault, 1977/1995, p. 182).

Throughout the diversity action plans, diverse individuals (them) are discursively constructed in binary opposition to a majority (us). One report observes: "Diversity is the recognition, value, and acceptance of . . . how we are similar to or different from others" (University of Arizona, 2003). Another document states: "the campus community [must] learn how best to interact with and support LGBT people" (University of Illinois, 2002). The solution to this us–them divide is through inclusion and integration, while affirming and celebrating difference. The diverse individual must shed "otherness" in order to conform to the norm, "so that they might all be like one another" (Foucault, 1977/1995, p. 182). However, a seemingly paradoxical conclusion is that while diverse individuals must be the same as the majority, in order to be included and achieve insider status, they must also sustain their difference, an exotic otherness that enables the majority and the institution to benefit from their presence. This illustrates the tension that exists between the discourse of access that demands the acculturation of the outsider to an insider (emphasizing sameness) and the marketplace discourse that commodifies the value of the diverse individual (emphasizing difference); this is exemplified by one report that recommends facilitating "learning opportunities available through interaction with international students," adding that "through these efforts, U.S. students will begin to understand the importance of having international students on campus and why they [U.S. students] should be part of the welcoming process for incoming international students" (Texas A&M University, 2002).

Classification

In addition to producing norms, differentiating "us" from "them" is also a form of classification. Nearly every diversity action plan defined diversity early in the document, sorting individual identities in component parts: race, gender, sexual orientation, age, disability, among other identity statuses. Some examples of this classification in diversity action plans follow:

> Women are still not well represented in some colleges that have been traditionally dominated by men, and a significant disparity in graduation rates persists between undergraduate students of color and white students. (Pennsylvania State University, 2004)
>
> For African American and Latino/Chicano students, the Berkeley freshman class of 1999 was less representative of the California high school graduate population than the freshman class of 1997. . . . The African American work force declined from 17.1% to 14.9% . . . Latinos and American Indians made only modest gains. (University of California at Berkeley, 2000)

An optional Franco American designation . . . has now been added to the UMS application. Beginning with the Class of 2004, we will have an indication of the number of Franco American students, in addition to the numbers of federally designated minority students, on campus. (University of Maine, 2003)

The classification of individuals and groups reinforces an "us–them" binary. It also serves to arrange, separate, and rank diverse groups from each other. Further, the diverse individual who achieves insider status is described in exceptional terms, thus ranked as unique from other diverse individuals. Some diverse individuals who the reports describe as having achieved insider status (e.g., Asian-Americans) are also classified as different. Finally, the attention to identity statuses occupied by diverse individuals implies that the majority are without race, gender, sexual orientation, enabling those who occupy privileged identity categories (e.g., straight white males) to remain oblivious to their complicity in the systems and structures that produce and maintain (dis)advantage (Johnson, 2005).

A Foucauldian analysis helps to reveal the assumptions of goodness embedded within most of the solutions represented in diversity action plans, and even the acceptance of the "naturalness" of diversity itself. Diversity, and all the solutions (e.g., mentoring programs) recommended to produce "more diversity," are assumed to be good and valuable. Yet, the inherent goodness of these solutions demands suspicion. Who determines "best" practices? In what ways are the criteria for benchmarking culturally projected? How are individuals "constituted and regulated with the claims of appropriate practice and learn to judge themselves as 'good' or 'bad'" (Grieshaber & Cannella, in Rhedding-Jones, 2002, p. 107)? My point is not to deny the growing scholarship on the educational benefits of diversity or the positive contribution many of the proposed solutions will have for a university toward achieving its diversity goals. Rather, my intent is to illuminate the unquestioned assumptions of goodness and challenge practitioners to interrogate the very taken-for-grantedness of the assumption of what is good. An acknowledgment of embedded value bias can lead practitioners and scholars to ask different questions.[3]

Implications for Policy

The goal of this research is to enable individuals engaged in the policy-making process (e.g., drafting diversity action plans) to be more aware of the discursive effects of their efforts to inform change and achieve equity in U.S. higher education. The findings of this study offer a particular perspective that invites an opportunity for thinking differently about diversity policies and the discourses carried by them. I will offer a few suggestions for how educational administrators might engage new possibilities for thinking to improve practice.

Reframe the Problem, Influence Discursive Shifts

Generally, institutions approach educational policy-making as a process of problem-solving, and thus every policy proposal contains within it problem representations and an explicit or implicit diagnosis of the problem (Bacchi, 1999). How the problem is framed determines the range of solutions available; in turn, it also conceals from view an array of options that could emerge from alternate conceptions of the problem. Awareness calls for an interrogation of the assumptions that ground the construction of the policy problem – the "assumptions about the causes of the 'problem'" (Bacchi, 1999, p. 109).

What does it mean to initiate "an interrogation of assumptions"? Practitioners are challenged to consider how the articulation of "solutions" in policy corresponds with the stated "problems." For instance, in this investigation, the problems made visible by a discourse of discrimination are harassment, bias, racism, sexism, homophobia; solutions include to offer support services to those who are victims, deliver training and education, and facilitate inter-group dialogue. These solutions are important, but fail to sufficiently address the "source" of the problem: the individuals or systems that are discriminatory, racist, sexist, and homophobic. Examining the (in)congruence between problems and solutions articulated in policy, coupled with an awareness of the discursive construction of diversity, can provide a different lens through which to view diversity. Such a "cognitive shift" (Bensimon, 2005) may inspire discussions about different solutions and deploy the tactical use of discourse.

Practitioners, then, have the potential to influence discursive shifts. Notably, individuals do not "stand outside of discourse and choose when, where, and how to take up particular discourses to produce some intended and predictable effect" (Allan, 2003, p. 65). Thus, policy-makers cannot write discourse into a policy recommendation to produce different effects; they cannot simply rewrite policy by finding and replacing certain words with others, such as searching a document for "disadvantage" and replacing it with "equality" in order to shift from a deficit to an equity focus. However, practitioners can be more informed and critical of the ways in which policy documents are discursively constituted and inspire opportunities for different discourses to be taken up. For instance, as noted above, the marketplace discourse undermines the change-making potential of the discourse of democracy. Diversity councils could take up strategies made visible by a discourse of democracy to facilitate difficult dialogues; suspend a rush to affirm and unite across difference; and "lean into" conflict and dissonance.

Working Within and Against

Drawing upon alternative discourses will likely bump up against dominant power structures. Fuller and Meiners (2005) describe this problem in their reflective essay on their decision-making process while writing a grant proposal. They observe that successful grant proposals originate "from a positivistic and a (mythic) politically neutral epistemological terrain" (p. 169). Thus, they determine that in order to acquire funding, they must "eliminate language that could be perceived as postmodern . . . to pass with a 'neutral ideology'" (p. 169), adding that "nonconformity with no money [is] unproductive" (p. 170).[4] Individuals, then, working for social change must consider the consequences of deploying particular discourses, both alternative discourses (*This policy may not be approved by legal counsel*), and dominant discourses (*I am more likely to acquire grant funding*). Further, individuals must consider how participation in "mainstream discursive and epistemological paradigms" may constrain possibilities for change; and determine how to access the resources to fuel social change yet also resist the power of dominant discourses (Fuller & Meiners, 2005, p. 174). Applied to this analysis of diversity action plans, the current diversity planning process may better serve the existing structures and constrain efforts to enact social change. Individuals who serve on diversity councils and engage in the policy-making process, then, face a dilemma of how to work within the system they are trying to change.

One strategy is to educate diversity councils on privilege and power through reading, training, and discussion. Such education and training should not divert attention from the material realities of oppression and disadvantage, but rather extend discussion to include awareness of the privileging conditions that construct both oppressive and empowering realities for individuals. Further, this awareness may offer insights on how discourses can both constrain and liberate. An expanded focus from diversity, disadvantage, inequality, and deficiency, to include privilege, power, and individual and institutional oppression may also lead to a renaming of these councils; rather than councils on diversity, they could serve as councils on privilege and disadvantaging systems, or a diversity council could be charged with developing an action plan for equity, rather than diversity.

Conclusion

This investigation of discourses circulating in diversity action plans identified dominant discourses of access, disadvantage, the marketplace, and democracy as most prominent in conveying images of diverse individuals. These discourses contribute to shaping perceptions of diversity and constructing particular social identities for diverse individuals to assume. Discursive practices, carried by diversity action plans, produce individuals' ways of thinking and acting, meaning these discursive practices construct (at times competing) possibilities and constrain, even conceal, alternatives. For example, diverse individuals constructed as at-risk outsiders by the discourses of access and disadvantage are dependent upon the university for access to and success in higher educa- tion. Also, constituted as victims by the discourse of discrimination, diverse individuals are situated as needy and vulnerable, requiring institutional intervention to ensure their safety and provide support. This discursive framing of diverse persons positions individuals as objects being acted upon. Intersecting with the marketplace discourse that constitutes the diverse person as a com- modity, the at-risk outsider appears more like a chess piece moved strategically to achieve a competitive edge. However, multiple discourses circulating in diversity action plans construct multiple subject positions (social identities) which individuals may inhabit, including alternatives, such as the change agent produced by the discourse of democracy, which endow diverse individuals with the capacity to act.

In sum, I am hopeful this study of the discursive framing of diversity enhances understanding of diversity policy documents, how policy discourses come together to make particular perspectives more prominent than others, how they contribute to re/producing a particular cultural reality. I also expect these findings to inspire new questions and further research about discourses of diversity, and how diversity action plans, in their current form, may (unwit- tingly) compromise the achievement of their own goals.

Notes

1   For a full explication of sampling procedure see Iverson, 2005, 2007.
2   A fuller description of these findings can be found in Iverson, 2005, 2007, 2008.
3   Eccles (1994), in her analysis of gender and achievement-related choices, illuminates these taken-for-granted assumptions: "too many social scientists have adopted a male standard of ideal achievement when judging the value of female achievements. . . . [which] inevitably leads us to question 'why aren't the women selecting the same occupational fields as the men?' instead of the question 'why do women choose particular occupations?'" (pp. 586–587).
4   Fuller and Meiners do note, however, that some language required in the grant proposal, such as non-discrimination statements, "comes from the work of earlier paradigm changers" (p. 169) illuminating that change does occur (see also Johnson, 2005).

References

Allan, E. J. (2008). *Policy discourses, gender, and education: Constructing women's status*. New York: Routledge.

Allan, E. J. (2003). Constructing women's status: Policy discourses of university women's com- mission policy reports. *Harvard Educational Review*, 73(1), 44–72.

Allen, A. (1999). *The power of feminist theory: Domination, resistance, solidarity*. Boulder, CO: Westview Press.

Anderson, G. L. & Grinberg, J. (1998). Educational administration as a disciplinary practice:

Appropriating Foucault's view of power, discourse, and method. *Educational Administration Quarterly*, 34(3), 329–353.

Astin, H. S. & Leland, C. (1991). *Women of influence, women of vision: A cross-generational study of leaders and social change.* San Francisco, CA: Jossey-Bass.

Auburn University. (2004). *Strategic Diversity Plan.* Auburn, AL: Auburn University Office of the President, with Clayton and Associates.

Bacchi, C. L. (1999). *Women, policy and politics: The construction of policy problems.* Thousand Oaks, CA: Sage.

Baez, B. (2002). *Affirmative action, hate speech, and tenure: Narratives about race, law, and the academy.* New York: RoutledgeFalmer.

Baldridge, J. V. (1971). *Power and conflict in the university: Research in the sociology of complex organizations.* New York: John Wiley & Sons.

Ball, S. J. (Ed.). (1990). *Foucault and education: Disciplines and knowledge.* New York: Routledge.

Bauman, G. L., Bustillos, L. T, Bensimon, E. M., Brown II, M. C., & Bartee, R. D. (2005). *Achieving equitable educational outcomes with all students: The institution's roles and responsibilities.* Washington, DC: Association of American Colleges and Universities. Retrieved June 5, 2007 from http://www.aacu.org/inclusive_excellence/documents/Bauman_et_al.pdf.

Beckwith, J. B. (1999). Power between women. *Feminism and Psychology*, 9(4), 389–397.

Bensimon, E. M. (2005). Closing the achievement gap in higher education: An organizational learning perspective. *New Directions for Higher Education*, 131, 99–111.

Blackmore, J. (1999). *Troubling women: Feminism, leadership and educational change.* Buckingham, UK: Open University Press.

Burns, J. M. (1978). *Leadership.* New York: Harper & Row.

Clayton-Pedersen, A. R., Parker, S., Smith, D. G., Moreno, J. F., & Teraguchi, D. H. (2007). *Making a real difference with diversity: A guide to institutional change.* Washington, DC: Association of American Colleges and Universities.

Cornell University. (2004). *The Cornell University Story: A Holistic Approach to Diversity and Inclusiveness.* Ithaca, NY: Cornell University Office of Workforce Diversity, Equity and Life Quality. Retrieved August 9, 2004 from http://www.ohr.cornell.edu/commitment/publications/Cornell_Story_2005.pdf.

Does diversity make a difference? Three research studies on diversity in college classrooms. (2000). Washington, DC: American Council on Education and American Association of University Professors. Retrieved May 31, 2005 from http://www.acenet.edu/bookstore/pdf//diversity_report/2000_diversity_report.pdf.

Eccles, J. S. (1994). Understanding women's educational and occupational choices. *Psychology of Women Quarterly*, 18, 585–609.

Eyre, L. (2000). The discursive framing of sexual harassment in a university community. *Gender and Education*, 12(3), 293–308.

Fisher, J. L. (1984). *Power of the presidency.* New York: Macmillan Publishing Company and American Council on Education.

Foucault, M. (1978/1990). *The history of sexuality: Volume 1: An introduction.* New York: Vintage Books.

Foucault, M. (1977/1995). *Discipline and punish: The birth of the prison*, 2nd ed. Trans. by Alan Sheridan. New York: Vintage Books.

French, J. R. P. & Raven, B. (1959). The bases of social power. In D. Cartwright (Ed.), *Studies in social power* (pp. 150–167). Ann Arbor, MI: Institute for Social Research.

Fuller, L. & Meiners, E. (2005). Reflections: Empowering women, technology, and (feminist) institutional changes. *Frontiers*, 26(1), 168–180.

Garcia, M., Hudgins, C., Musil, C. M., Nettles, M., Sedlacek, W., & Smith, D. (2003). *Assessing campus diversity initiatives: A guide for campus practitioners.* Washington, DC: Association of American Colleges and Universities.

Gore, J. M. (1998). On the limits to empowerment through critical and feminist pedagogies. In D. Carlson & M. W. Apple (Eds.), *Power/Knowledge/Pedagogy: The meaning of democratic education in unsettling times* (pp. 271–288). Boulder, CO: Westview Press.

Green, M. (1989). *Minorities on campus: A handbook for enhancing diversity.* Washington, DC: American Council on Education.

Hu-DeHart, E. (2000). The diversity project: Institutionalizing multiculturalism or managing differences? *Academe*, 86(5), 39–42.

Iverson, S. V. (2005). *A policy discourse analysis of U.S. land-grant university diversity action plans.* Unpublished doctoral dissertation. Orono, ME: University of Maine.

Iverson, S. V. (2007). Camouflaging power and privilege: A critical race analysis of university diversity policies. *Educational Administration Quarterly*, 43(5), 586–611.

Iverson, S. V. (2008). Capitalizing on change: The discursive framing of diversity in U.S. land-grant universities. *Equity and Excellence in Education*, 41(2), 1–18.

Johnson, A. (2005). *Privilege, power and difference*, 2nd ed. Boston, MA: McGraw Hill.

Kezar, A. & Eckel, P. D. (2005). *Leadership strategies for advancing campus diversity: Advice from experienced presidents.* Washington, DC: American Council on Education.

Knight, J., Smith, R., & Sachs, J. (1990). Deconstructing hegemony: Multicultural policy and a populist response. In S. J. Ball (Ed.), *Foucault and education: Disciplines and knowledge* (pp. 133–152). New York: Routledge.

Marshall, C. (1999). Researching the margins: Feminist critical policy analysis. *Educational Policy*, 13(1), 59–77.

Marshall, C. (2000). Policy discourse analysis: Negotiating gender equity. *Journal of Education Policy*, 15(2), 125–156.

Marshall, C. & Rossman, G. B. (1999). *Designing qualitative research*, 3rd ed. Thousand Oaks, CA: Sage.

Milem, J. F., Chang, M. J., & antonio, l. a. (2005). *Making diversity work on campus: A research-based perspective.* Washington, DC: Association of American Colleges and Universities. Retrieved June 4, 2007 from http://www.aacu.org/inclusive_excellence/documents/Milem_et_al.pdf.

Miles, M. & Huberman, A. M. (1994). *Qualitative data analysis: An expanded sourcebook of new methods*, 2nd ed. Newbury Park, CA: Sage.

Mills, S. (1997). *Discourse*. New York: Routledge.

Morfin, O. J., Perez, V. H., Parker, L., Lynn, M., & Arrona, J. (2006). Hiding the politically obvious: A critical race theory preview of diversity as racial neutrality in higher education. *Educational Policy*, 20(1), 249–270.

North Carolina State University. (1999). *Diversity Initiative.* Raleigh: North Carolina State University Office of the Provost. Retrieved August 10, 2004 from http://www.ncsu.edu/provost/diversity/initiative.html.

Now is the time: Meeting the challenge for a diverse academy. (2005). Washington, DC: National Association of State Universities and Land Grant Colleges and American Association of State Colleges and Universities.

Ohio State University. (2000). *Diversity Action Plan.* Columbus: Ohio State University Office of University Relations. Retrieved July 12, 2004 from http://www.osu.edu/diversityplan/index_1.php.

Oklahoma State University. (2004). *Institutional Diversity Strategic Plan.* (2004). Stillwater: Oklahoma State University Office of Institutional Diversity. Retrieved July 15, 2004 from http://avpma.okstate.edu/strategic.pdf.

Pennsylvania State University. (2004). *Framework to foster diversity, 2004–09.* University Park: Pennsylvania State University Office of the Vice Provost for Educational Equity. Retrieved August 9, 2004 from http://www.equity.psu.edu/Framework/assets/framework_to_foster_div.pdf.

Pfeffer, J. (1981). *Power in organizations.* Marshfield, MA: Pitman Publishing.

Pollock, M. (2004). *Colormute: Race talk dilemmas in an American school.* Princeton, NJ: Princeton University Press.

Popkewitz, T. S. & Brennan, M. (Eds.). (1998). *Foucault's Challenge: Discourse, knowledge, and power in education.* New York: Teacher's College Press.

Reinharz, S. (1992). *Feminist methods in social research.* New York: Oxford University Press.

Rhedding-Jones, J. (2002). An undoing of documents and other texts: Towards a critical multiculturalism in early childhood education. *Contemporary Issues in Early Childhood*, 3(10), pp. 90–116.

Roe, E. (1994). *Narrative policy analysis: Theory and practice.* Durham, NC: Duke University Press.

Sawicki, J. (1991). *Disciplining Foucault: Feminism, power, and the body.* New York: Routledge.

Schauber, A. C. & Castania, K. (2001). Facing issues of diversity: Rebirthing the Extension Service. *Journal of Extension* [on-line], 39(6). Available at http://www.joe.org/joe/2001december/comm2.html.

Scheurich, J. J. (1994). Policy archaeology: A new policy studies methodology. *Journal of Education Policy*, 9(4), 297–316.

Stein, S. J. (2004). *The culture of education policy*. New York: Teachers College Press.

Texas A&M University. (2002). *Report by the President's Ad Hoc Committee on Diversity and Globalization*. College Station: Texas A&M University Office of the President. Retrieved August 10, 2004 from http://www.tamu.edu/provost/documents/reports/Div-global.pdf.

Tierney, W. G. (1992). *Official encouragement, institutional discouragement: Minorities in academe – the Native American experience*. Norwood, NJ: Ablex Publishing Corporation.

Tierney, W. G. & Dilley, P. (1998). Constructing knowledge: Educational research and gay and lesbian studies. In W. F. Pinar (Ed.), *Queer theory in education* (pp. 49–71). Mahwah, NJ: Lawrence Erlbaum Associates.

University of Arizona. (2003). *Diversity Action Plan, 2003–04*. Tucson, AZ: University of Arizona Office of the President. Retrieved August 23, 2004 from http://diversity.arizona.edu/pdf/diversity%20action%20plan.pdf.

University of Arkansas. (2002). *Diversity Plan, 2002–05*. Fayetteville: University of Arkansas Office of the Provost and Vice Chancellor for Academic Affairs. Retrieved July 12 2004 from http://pigtrail.uark.edu/diversity/diversity_downloads/diversityplan.pdf.

University of California at Berkeley. (2000). *Report of the Chancellor's Advisory Committee on Diversity*. Berkeley: University of California Office of the Vice Chancellor for Diversity and Equity. Retrieved August 9, 2004 from http://evcp.chance.berkeley.edu/documents/Reports/documents/archived/DIVERSITYREPORT.pdf.

University of Connecticut. (2002). *The Report of the Diversity Action Committee to the University of Connecticut Board of Trustees*. Storrs: University of Connecticut Office of the Vice Provost for Multicultural and International Affairs.

University of Georgia. (2002). *Institutional Diversity Strategic Plan, 2002–05*. Athens: University of Georgia Office of Institutional Diversity. Retrieved August 21, 2004 from http://www.uga.edu/diversity/strategicplan.pdf.

University of Idaho. (2004). *Diversity and Human Rights at the University of Idaho: Comprehensive Plan for Action and Accountability*. Moscow: University of Idaho Office of the President. Retrieved August 19, 2004 http://www.webs.uidaho.edu/hrco/DivPlanFinal4–20–04.pdf.

University of Illinois. (2002). *Final Report of the Diversity Initiatives Planning Committee*. Urbana: University of Illinois Office of the Provost. Retrieved August 8, 2004 http://www.provost.uiuc.edu/programs/diversity/committee/initiatives/Final%20Annual%20Report%2001–02.pdf.

University of Maine. (2003). *Diversity Action Plan, 2003–05*. Orono: University of Maine Office of Equal Opportunity and Diversity. Retrieved August 23, 2004 from http://www.umaine.edu/diversity/Publication/Diversity%20Action%20Plan%202003-%202005.htm.

University of Maine. (1999). *Diversity Action Plan*. Orono: University of Maine Office of Equal Opportunity and Diversity.

University of Maryland. (2000). *Report and Recommendations of the President's Diversity Panel*. College Park: University of Maryland Office of the President. Retrieved August 13, 2004 from http://www.inform.umd.edu/CampusInfo/Departments/PRES/divrpt.pdf.

University of Nebraska. (1999). *Comprehensive Diversity Plan*. Lincoln: University of Nebraska-Lincoln Office of the Chancellor. Retrieved August 9, 2004 from http://www.unl.edu/svcaa/priorities/diversity/diversityplanI.shtml.

University of Nevada. (2002). *Strategic Plan for Diversity Initiatives*. Reno: University of Nevada Office of the President. Retrieved August 13, 2004 from http://www.unr.edu/planning/0203-cycle/diversity-initiative.0212.pdf.

University of Wisconsin. (1999). *Plan 2008: The campus diversity plan*. Madison: University of Wisconsin Office of the Provost. Retrieved July 13, 2004 from http://www.provost.wisc.edu/docs/plan2008.pdf.

van Dijk, T. (2002). The discourse–knowledge interface. In G. Weiss & R. Wodak (Eds.), *Critical discourse analysis: Theory and interdisciplinarity* (pp. 85–109). Basingstoke, UK: Palgrave Macmillan.

Virginia Tech University. (2000). *Diversity Strategic Plan, 2000–05*. Blacksburg: Virginia Polytechnic Institute and State University Office of Multicultural Affairs. Retrieved August 9, 2004 from http://www.dsp.multicultural.vt.edu/pdfs/DSP-All.pdf.

Williams, D. A., Berger, J. B., & McClendon, S. A. (2005). *Toward a model of inclusive excellence and change in postsecondary institutions.* Washington, DC: Association of American Colleges and Universities. Retrieved February 5, 2007 from http://www.aacu.org/inclusive_excellence/documents/Williams_et_al.pdf.

11

Knowledge Capital and Excellence

Implications of a Science-Centered University for Gender Equity

NELLY P. STROMQUIST

The economic and technological developments that constitute much of what we call globalization are fostering a conception of the university as producer of knowledge for the benefit of the economy and learners as producers and consumers. Not surprisingly, a referent with growing application to the university today is the knowledge society, which intimately links knowledge to an efficient and effective labor force (Simons & Mosschelein, 2007). In the new scenario, education emerges as a major tool for economic success and individual advancement.

Knowledge today appears primarily in two different forms: as a tool for social actors who must make rational choices and thus should have the ability to process the information, and as an asset, which can take the form of input (worker competence) and output (innovation) in the production process (OECD, 2000). Prevailing discourses contribute to sustaining a highly competitive climate within and between universities by defining higher education systems as contributing to the well-being of countries and seeking to incorporate the business sector as a key financial supporter of higher education (Maila, 2007).

Accompanying the technological features of globalization is a rapid circulation of ideas. The prevailing discourses circulating among Northern governments and their international funding agencies are reflected in the popular press as well as in their own publications. The Organization for Economic Cooperation and Development (OECD), the World Bank, the regional development banks, and other large international institutions influence higher education through the studies they conduct or commission, their publications, the conferences they organize, and the reports from such conferences. The events and materials present an instrumentalist vision of education by emphasizing the preparation of students for a global economy. The semi-official U.S. report entitled *A Nation at Risk* (published in 1983) was very influential in Europe, particularly in OECD countries (Henry et al., 2001). Now that diffusion of ideas has been accelerated, the rates of policy borrowing – or to put it into more conventional terms, of policy convergence – have grown rapidly.

The dominant paradigm of globalization is based on neoliberalism, which resides in the principles of knowledge and free trade as essential to any successful endeavor. Accompanying such principles are the assumption of rationality and the norms of individuality and self-interest (Peters, n.d.). The purpose of human agency is framed as problem-solving or as the practical needs of society, which is often translated as giving individuals the skills they will need for gainful employment. Links between university and economy are becoming strengthened with a premium on global economic competitiveness. Firms in industrialized countries make demands on universities to produce the innovations they need to become successful in the international marketplace (Bernasconi, 2008). Functions of a social and humanistic nature are being sidelined; the formation of a well-rounded person, with conceptions of participatory democracy, social justice, solidarity, and ecological sensitivity, is not part of the prevailing discourse on human capital. In the circulation of these ideas, attention to gender issues is reduced to its minimum expression, to primarily mean access and often to mean access to basic education.

This chapter explores the discursive shaping of ideas regarding S&T by international institutions and their subsequent legitimation. It centers on the analysis of two important policy documents on higher education with global implications. They derive from the World Bank (WB) and the Inter-American Development Bank (IDB).These institutions exert pervasive influence on policies in the developing world (Bernasconi, 2008; Bradford & Linn, 2007) and they present their recommendations as based on research and thus scientific knowledge. About the World Bank it has been written: "Its universal membership, its comprehensive and cross-sectoral focus, its experience with a large array of financing instruments, and its high professional and technical capacities in the analytical and advisory areas are unmatched by any other institution of the globe" (Bradford & Linn, 2007, p. 4). IDB is a highly influential organization in Latin America and the Caribbean.

Conceptual Approach

The selected policy documents were examined from poststructuralist and feminist perspectives. Poststructuralism has multiple facets; one of them seeks to analyze the power relations reflected in communication, including the messages conveyed in the modern forms of mass media (Peters & Burbules, 2004). Poststructuralism shares with feminist critical analysis a focus on issues of bias, power, and the values that drive the identification, labeling, and legitimation of a problem (Hennessy, 1993; Hirschmann & Di Stefano, 1996; Marshall, 1997).

Poststructuralism owes many of its foundational premises to Foucault, for whom power is constantly produced by and between social actors. For Foucault, knowledge and power are intimately tied because one serves to produce and protect the other. From Foucault's perspective, nodes of power/knowledge operate throughout the social system. However, contrary to most interpretations of his work, Foucault recognizes that not all these nodes have the same degree of influence, and that some have a strong capacity to monitor and punish (Pringle & Watson, 1998). Foucault pays attention to the status and institutional setting in which particular statements are embedded (Williams, 1999). While Foucault shifts attention away from the intentionality of the state, his focus on the localized and specific mechanisms and technology of power (Pringle & Watson, 1998) is a welcome shift in the analysis of the creation and deployment of power. Relying on this logic in this chapter, I consider that official documents that enjoy great diffusion and are presented with much authority create undisputed realities. Their examination, therefore, serves both to explain and to challenge this power.

Poststructuralism recognizes the importance of language, not merely in describing the world but also in constructing social reality (Pringle & Watson, 1998; Lee, 1992). As Peters and Burbules note (2004), by paying close attention to the way narratives are constructed, poststructuralism fosters the integration of the social sciences and the humanities. So I consider not only the processes and logics of social action but also how meaning is manufactured through narratives, texts, symbols, and text analogues. Foucault calls for an examination of discursive formations, which he sees occurring through: types of statements, systems of concepts, theoretical orientations, and reference to common objects of analysis (Peters & Burbules, 2004).

Foucault defines discourse as a particular way of organizing meaning and hence of ordering the world (Lee, 1992). Another elaboration of discourse sees it as the body of ideas, concepts, and beliefs that become established as knowledge and are generally expressed in texts (Doherty, 2007). Endorsing the importance of discourse, feminist theoretician Cixous (1981) argues that political analysis begins with consideration of the language being used. Discourse combines knowledge and power by presenting itself as authoritative, while selecting what is worth discussing and what is not. The importance of discourse, therefore, is paramount and it is crucial that those who analyze the social world be attentive to how language is used. The construct of discursive field – defined as a set of discourses that are systematically related (Kenway et al., 1994) – constitutes the unit of analysis in poststructural analysis.

A key tool of poststructuralism, which it shares with postmodernism, is deconstruction. Deconstruction enables us to probe the production and reception of texts, to examine the key elements of any rhetorical situation: interlocutor, conceptions of the real, audience, and language. Further explaining what deconstruction is, Ninnes and Burnett (2003) state that while discourses are ways of thinking, talking, and writing about an issue, deconstruction of such discourses involves "exploring what is said, what is not said, and what cannot be said; the particular conditions under which discourses arise; and their effects" (p. 282; see also Kenway et al., 1994).

Content analysis, which preceded by far the process of deconstruction, bears some similarities to and differences with it. While both look at the written text, content analysis considers documents as simple transmitters of information and thus as unequivocal representations of the social subjects to which they refer (Williams, 1999). Deconstruction, instead, can be used to detect not only what is said but also to "reveal subtext and textual silences" (Atkinson, 2002, cited in Cole, 2003, p. 493). Archaeological methods, an approach also pioneered by Foucault, assume that systems of thought and knowledge are governed by rules, beyond those of grammar and logic and function to create a system of "conceptual possibilities that determines the boundaries of thought in a given domain and period" (Foucault, n.d.). Moreover, deconstruction, when coupled with governmentality, becomes a solid analytical tool. Governmentality is of constant interest to Foucault. One definition of it is the multiple use of "techniques, schemas, structures and ideas *deliberately mobilized* in attempting to direct or influence the conduct of others" (Doherty, 2007, p. 196, emphasis added).

Poststructuralism has its own critics, who assert that it and postmodernism "are not concerned with structural and modern problems nor do they have solutions for them" (Cherryholmes, 1994, p. 204). There are several weaknesses in poststructuralism. First, while its suspicion of metanarratives or "great truths" serves as a pivot to challenge uncontested knowledge, it must also be recognized that not all claims to truth are equally invalid or weak. Hennessy (1993) highlights a second weakness when he states: "Reducing social relations to language is problematic . . . because it closes off signification and discourse from the nondiscursive – from relations of property, of labor, state control" (p. 123). Third, poststructuralism has been accused of a lack of analytical closure. Building on Derrida's concept of "supplementarity," according to which "no voice is suppressed, displaced by, or privileged over another, but rather, each voice complements, enhances, and at the same time undercuts the other" (Baxter, 2002, cited in Cole, 2003, p. 493), poststructuralism seeks to decenter the voice of dominant actors. This was meant to allow the views and experiences of marginalized people, but it remains crucial to recognize the powerful voices of hegemonic institution (Hennessy, 1993). Another, fourth, weakness of poststructuralism lies in its treatment of the state. Some poststructuralist writers hold that "the state should be seen as erratic and disconnected rather than contradictory" and that "it is not an object or an actor so much as a series of arenas" (Pringle & Watson, 1998, p. 213). These authors also argue that "The state is too diverse, divided and contradictory to evoke as an entity" (pp. 213–214). But comprising a multiplicity of arenas does not make the state necessarily contradictory. On the contrary, the state represents a concentration of power and, through the use of international vehicles, it may be successful in achieving goals that any one country could not have attained independently. In this chapter, I argue that the two development banks which are the object of this chapter exist under the close tutelage of states and thus do not represent policies entirely free of the economic and political interests of their member states. To recapitulate, I consider that a modified version of poststructuralism, one that recognizes the virtues of its methods and is less willing to accept a fluid and changeable state, has potential for an understanding of global policies.

I also employ a feminist lens in the analysis by considering the asymmetry between women and men that is created through the current definition of and emphasis upon science. This lens leads me to observe the discourse about women and men and about gender, and how and when these referents appear in influential public discourse. Traditional gender expectations for men and women continue to influence them in the selection of field of study and, subsequently, in the occupations they select. The exaggerated view of science as the key motor of change is particularly detrimental to women and to advances in the social relations of gender. S&T are supposedly gender-neutral but in fact both are closely associated with masculinity (Harding, c.1991 and c.1998; Fox Keller & Longino, 1996). Cultural images of technology are associated with hegemonic masculinity although there is a lack of congruence between image and practice (Faulkner, 2001). At the same time, given the increasing importance of science in contemporary society, it is unlikely that gender relations may change without first a critical examination of the role of S&T in society (Faulkner, 2001).

The Importance of Science Today

The knowledge economy, a commonly invoked mantra, treats people as human resources and is designed to turn out flexible, multiskilled knowledge-workers for the twenty-first century. And, as societies become more technologically developed, the importance of science is growing exponentially. It is presented as being unambiguous, precise, and non-subjective; moreover, it is proposed as the solution to all kinds of problems. So highly ranked is the position of science that Habermas (1971) has argued that science and technology are modern substitutes for ideology, securing compliance with a depoliticized and administered social order by ministering to private "needs" (cited in Crook et al., 1992; see also Harding, c.1998, 2008; Hubbard, c.1990; Keller & Longino, 1996; Lather, 1991)

While much is to be gained through scientific advances, there are several negative consequences of the uncontested importance of science. In the view of Santos (1987), these are: (1) the belief that that which is not quantifiable is not scientifically relevant, (2) mathematics supplies modern science not only the privileged analytical tool but also its research logic, and (3) the laws of modern science center on how certain things operate rather than on considering who the agents are or what the end is of certain things. In contrast to the "scientific" view of the social world, it can also be argued that insofar as humans are complex beings, conditioned both by history and culture, the social *sciences* cannot produce universal laws but rather approximations of truth (Lather, 1991, 2007)

Poststructuralism questions the "apparent naturalness" of such concepts as knowledge, education, research, and policy (Peters & Burbules, 2004) and maintains that rationalist conceptions can themselves disguise power positions so that "reason is treated as the converse of the arbitrary and violence" (Williams, 1999, p. 19).

Women and Gender in Higher Education

Throughout the world, women have been increasing their representation in higher education. Today, in all developed countries (with the exception of Switzerland) and in eight of 12 developing regions, the female/male ratio favors women (UNESCO, 2007). National statistics for tertiary education are not strictly comparable because they sometimes include all levels of postsecondary education and at other times only one or two of the three levels established by UNESCO. Nonetheless, at first glance, it would seem that women's representation in tertiary education is problematic only in a few regions, particularly South and West Asia and Sub-Saharan Africa. We do not know with precision what fields of study men and women follow in each country. Data from the industrialized countries, however, highlight the low presence of women in fields with high components of science and technology (UNESCO, 1999). Gender is implicated in many aspects of S&T but not always visibly and explicitly. To examine these ties requires discussion of elements seemingly independent of such issues or peripheral to them. Within the university, new hierarchies are being created through academic capitalism, competition, and entrepreneurial behaviors. Fields that receive research contracts and grants and thus status are those in the sciences and technologies, while most women are located in the social sciences and the humanities.

The World Bank and Higher Education

What are the effects of deploying a particular version of truth about education (Ninnes & Burnett, 2003)? In what spaces is this truth presented? There is a convergence today around neoliberal policies in which education is framed as human capital investment and development. Who are the actors fostering such convergence and through what means do they accomplish it?

Modern mass media are capable of supplying us with constant and wide-reaching messages on many issues. To the role of modern communications we must add the use of research reports and policy papers distributed freely by a number of international agencies. It can be argued that official reports function as technologies of domination insofar as they carry discourses that present truth and frame solutions to problems from perspectives that serve to solidify the status quo. The WB's annual publication, the *World Development Report,* is a glossy publication, with numerous tables and charts, distributed free of charge among government ministries and agencies in the developing world, international organizations, and bilateral development agencies. It is clear that the power of the WB enables it to distribute a particular type of knowledge and such knowledge is displayed as scientifically valid because it is the product of a major think tank (Peters, n.d.). In discussing WB products, this analysis will focus on two documents, one a quasi-policy document, *Higher education in developing countries: Peril and promise* (hereafter *HEDC*; World Bank, 2000); the other, used in a supplementary fashion, is a report dealing specifically with knowledge, *Knowledge for development* (World Bank, 1999). The back of the first page of the HEDC document states, "The World Bank encourages dissemination of its work and will normally grant permission promptly." At the same time, and countering previous WB assertions that knowledge is free, the WB sells its products to readers not linked to government units. Thus, the HEDC document notes: "Permission to photocopy for internal or personal use, for the internal or personal use of specific clients, and for educational classroom use, is granted by the World Bank, *provided that the appropriate fee is paid* directly to the Copyright Clearance Center" (emphasis added).

HEDC was written by a Task Force on Higher Education and Society, comprised of 14 experts appointed by the World Bank, four of whom were women. It is a glossy publication, with 102 pages of text and a statistical appendix of 31 pages. The report asserts its authority by noting that it was "based on discussions and hearings conducted over a two-year period" (p. 9), was elaborated with the assistance of 94 "task force supporters" and counted on the financial support of three bilateral agencies and five philanthropic agencies in addition to in-kind support of ten agencies (including UNESCO), the international agencies formally in charge of the education sector. The word "policy" is never used to describe the document, but it declares early on that it has the "purpose of exploring the future of higher education in the developing world" (p. 9) and that it identifies "a number of areas where immediate, practical action is needed" (p. 11). *HEDC* also announces that it is "aimed at higher education policy makers, including educational ministers, members of governing boards, and others, *who need to understand* the special needs and opportunities that higher education faces in the new century" (p. 20, emphasis added). This, in the words of a major lending organization such as the World Bank, makes the report assume a unique claim to truth and acquire a strong policy dimension. It claims further authority by assuring the reader that "The report proceeds by reasoned argument, relying heavily on experience and belief. Some empirical support is provided from case studies and statistical analysis, although further data analysis would certainly be useful" (p. 21).

HEDC consists of six chapters: higher education's long-standing problems and the new realities it faces, the nature of public interest in higher education, how focusing on higher education as a system will yield the benefits of planned diversification, the improvement of standards of governance, how to satisfy the acute requirements in science and technology education, and a call to develop imaginative general education curricula for certain students. *HEDC* asserts that knowledge has supplanted capital as a source of wealth and that the quality of knowledge generated in higher education is "critical to national competitiveness" (p. 9). The report, further, upholds the existence of a meritocratic society that is pluralistic and accountable. It also calls for "tolerance rather than discrimination" and for "free and open search for truth, rather than secrecy and deception" (p. 45). Such declarations do not identify for whom the society is supposed to be meritocratic nor do they identify those discriminated people for whom the search for truth is to be conducted. There is an absolute lack of referents in this narrative.

Chapter III of the *HEDC*, on Systems of Higher Education, invokes the need for a differentiated system of higher education, with both private and public education institutions. When the report makes categorical recommendations, the text does not say "The World Bank believes," but rather "The Task Force believes," thus presenting a strong point of view while deflecting the source of such messages – a strategy that presents the recommendation as less linked to a particular institution and thus masks the institutional source of power. The Task Force recommends a "stratified system [of higher education], one that comprises one tier that is oriented toward research and selectivity and another that imparts knowledge to large numbers of students" (p. 50). Such an approach is defended as a "hybrid that marries the goals of excellence and mass education" (p. 50). There is no analysis of the implications this combined system might have for gender and social class. Outside the discussion at this point are potential contradictions between meritocracy and access to quality higher education for those who lack the means to enter prestigious institutions and those who encounter pervasive social discrimination in society. The report recognizes that "an important downside to private financing" is that "it may preclude the enrollment of deserving students who do not have the ability to pay, and often evokes resentment among students who do" (p. 57). At least two observations can be made about this statement. First, such a "downside" is identified but far from discussed. The same statement combines two very different reasons for the "downside" of private financing: the question of social equity for the potentially large number of poor students who will not have access to private higher education, and the rather trivial observation that those students who have to pay for their education will resent such payment. It proposes means-tested scholarships and loan programs for the poor students, but fails to examine to what extent such measures would be able to reduce inequities in private higher education.

Increasingly, the search for sources of revenue calls more attention to private funding (Slaughter & Leslie, 1997; Mohanty, 2003). This makes universities more vulnerable to consumer demand and pressures to serve the economy, with the consequence that consideration of social issues (equity, social justice, the redistribution of wealth) is diminished (Marginson, 1997; Stromquist, 2002). The inevitable tension between attending commercial needs and maintaining a distance from them – so that the university may provide constant critique of society's path and evolution – does not constitute an object of examination in the WB policy paper. Habermas has expectations for the university and assigns it an "integrative consciousness," meaning that research, education, and critique belong together (Simons & Mosschelein, 2007). According to current dynamics, it remains unlikely that this tripartite objective will hold.

HEDC treats women as one among a number of disadvantaged groups, as they are identified along with "racial, linguistic and religious groups that suffer discrimination" (p. 41). In so doing, it does not acknowledge the role of gender in society. Chapter V of the report, entitled "Science and Technology" (pp. 75–76), notes that women are "still under-represented" in those fields and states that the widest gaps by gender occur in South Asia, the Middle East, and Sub-Saharan Africa. It also observes that women are "disproportionately enrolled in alternative forms of higher education such as distance education, teacher training colleges, nursing schools and non-university tertiary-level institutions" (p. 75). The situation of gender in science is reduced to the under-representation of women; thus, the document calls for special measures to be put in place to advance the condition of women: "mentoring programs in math and science, increasing scholarship assistance and loans, actively recruiting women for graduate study and developing supportive networks" (p. 76). Yet, a subsection of Chapter V, labeled "Strategies for Scientific Development" (pp. 79–80), concentrates on arguing that universities in developing countries should not conduct research in "every field" but rather "consider the types of scientific and technological research that can directly contribute to its development" (p. 79). The provision of special measures to help women, even within the under-representation argument, is simply not present among the recommended strategies. In all, the chapter on S&T fails to discuss contributions by feminist theorists who argue that science operates within gendered frameworks and that it needs to be reconceptualized. A crucial opportunity to question gender is missed.

The word "sex" appears twice, to refer to safe sex and sexually transmitted diseases such as HIV. "Gender" appears 19 times, in references to gender equality, gender balance, gender gaps, gender data, gender discrimination, and gender indicators. There is no sustained discussion of gender, except for the text in Box 8, entitled Gender Agenda. Close examination of this text reveals that the discourse limits itself to events in the World Science Conference in Budapest[1] in which an Indonesian educator stated that gender issues "have entered the science agenda" and another Indonesian delegate announced that "gender indicators such as participation, education, and career structures would be developed" and that while "OECD have carried comparative studies of scientific efforts," "hitherto [they] have not collected gender data." UNESCO is said to have recently "announced its intention to fund a science and technology network for Arab women" (p. 76). It is to be noted that the discussion of gender appears as an insert, anecdotal to the primary content rather than integrated in the text as part of the experts' deliberations. When gender is mentioned, it appears in the words of two participants to the Budapest conference, not stated by any governmental authority. Likewise, when the OECD is criticized in the text for not collecting gender data, the critique comes from a conference participant, not a source in a formal position of authority, thus avoiding the possibility that powerful institutions may challenge one another and thus question the importance of what is recognized as knowledge. While UNESCO is reported to be interested in helping women in S&T, the actual promise is "the intention to create a network" and this network is further limited to "Arab women," implying that only women in the Middle East need support. The discussion of gender issues in the report is very limited and fails to put S&T in the context of broader issues affecting men and women as users and producers of technology. The persistently low representation of women scientists is captured by a sentence in Box 8, which states that "women's role in science has come under increased scrutiny of late." Yet there is no subsequent development of what this role entails and what lines of action are to be taken by higher education.

In another section of the text that makes reference to women, it is stated, "In many societies women study subjects that conform to their traditional roles, rather than courses that will maximize their opportunities in the labor market" (p. 24). This statement is followed by another that argues that "better information on the labor market is needed, combined with policies that promote economic growth and labor absorption" (p. 24). The problematic conditions of women are thus portrayed as caused by their poor choices (they do not select courses that will maximize their employment opportunities) and by poor labor market information. The assumption is that if these two obstacles could be overcome, women's conditions would improve. These arguments fail to locate gender asymmetries in a wider and more complex socio-cultural context, contrary to an extensive body of gender-sensitive research (e.g., Acker, 1994; Blackmore, 2006; Gaskell, 1983). So, from a shallow diagnosis of gender, follows a shallow prescription for its reformulation.

Chapter IV of *HEDC*, on Governance, discusses such issues as financial stability, accountability, regular testing of standards, and accreditation, noting that they can be "an important tool for monitoring institutional performance and promoting the responsible exercise of authority" (p. 67). The reference to accreditation comprises significant messages. First, it defines accreditation as "visiting committees, consisting of recognized national or *international* experts" (emphasis added); second, it states that "*international* standards of accreditation

– for example, those used by external examiners – also promote institutional quality" (p. 67); in other words, what is proposed here is a recommendation to use international standards and international experts, something that moves the definition of quality toward a transnational criterion. This carries two implications: first, since science and technology are recognized as omnipotent, excellence may be linked only to science and not to the humanities and the social sciences (in this respect, see Iverson, 2008), and, second, gender issues may be assigned a low priority as universities compete for excellence.

The concluding section of *HEDC* offers a large number of recommendations. Among them, the most tangible in the promotion of equity is the provision of scholarship programs or the facilitation of access to textbooks, computers, or other equipment. In other words, calls for equity, inclusive of gender, prescribe the allocation of more (but meager) resources instead of drawing upon alternative discourses to renegotiate the sociocultural systems that create and sustain gendered power relations. In a subsection addressed to donor agencies, the report chastises them for the "tendency for financial concerns to sideline the principle of equal opportunity" (p. 96). So, when a criticism is expressed, it is not toward any particular state but rather toward donor agencies, as if they have the strongest responsibility for equality issues. Further, the criticism is limited to equality of opportunity, not equality of outcomes, which would call for very specific and complementary equity measures.

Examining *HEDC* in conjunction with another WB document, *Knowledge for Development*, illuminates additional issues for discussion. This document states in its opening sentence, "Knowledge is like light. Weightless and intangible, it can travel the world, enlightening the lives of people everywhere. Yet billions of people still live in the darkness of poverty – unnecessarily" (1999, p. 1). This message, widely quoted by various authors and authorities in the field of education, presents knowledge as a public good readily available to those who seek it. Although the document goes on to clarify that "Knowledge can be costly to create" (p. 1), the first sentence prevails and shapes the tone of the document. This style of communication – the presentation of strong assertions followed by qualifiers that render the earlier assertions elusive if not discarded – seems to be the preferred style of the WB. This approach enables it to send explicit messages while at the same time claiming that it recognizes any particular issue to be more complicated than seems at first sight.

The International Development Bank and Higher Education

The main document from the IDB on the question of higher education is entitled *Higher education in Latin America and the Caribbean: A strategy paper* (IDB, 1997). In this document, the IDB declares that it "favors projects with strong and sensible reform components because they improve efficiency, raise benefits, and/or improve equity" (p. 3). What exactly constitute "strong and sensible reform components" is not defined, thus giving IDB ample discretion in determining when a project is worthy of funding or not.

The IDB document chastises countries in the region for their "cultural indifference to science and research" (p. 8) and recognizes the "unsurpassed" role of universities for the study of science (p. 12). Curiously, it does not set an agenda for scientific endeavors at the university but only for technical training.

The IDB document identifies three critical policy issues: (1) equity and public subsidization, (2) incentives, firms, and governance, and (3) quality enhancement and control. Although equity appears prominently, the document goes on to argue that it supports cost recovery, noting that "Subsidization means that the poorer citizens who lack access to higher education support the more privileged" (citing the World Bank, 1994, 1995 and others; IDB, p. 21). The document then recommends providing "loans that improve equity," that are given in direct and indirect ways, and that "stimulate serious student performance and competition among institutions" (IDB, 1997, p. 21). This last assertion is presented as factual although no evidence is cited in its support. Further, the assertion is made independent of any analysis of how women and minorities may be disadvantaged (or not) by moving into a loan and cost recovery scheme. Here, IDB combines in its recommendation some unproven assertions (that loans "improve equity" and "stimulate serious student performance and competition among institutions") with administrative procedures ("can be given in direct and indirect ways"), clouding the issue of how equity can be attained.

Gender issues are recognized only in terms of women's participation in higher education. Thus IDB (1997) observes that by 1980 women accounted for more than 40 percent of the enrollment and that by the mid-1990s they accounted for over half in the "institutions of higher learning" (IDB, 1997, p. 5). The IDB statement correctly states "institutions of higher learning" and not "universities" because women indeed comprise the majority in the former. The implications of women's over-representation in vocational and technical schools, and their concentration in only a few fields, are not problematized in this assertion.

The final section of the document is entitled "The Quest for Equity." It states that loans are to be more accessible to the less privileged. Again, how this will benefit them is merely assumed. The same section emphasizes that improvements in quality and efficiency are needed and that to that end, systems of "information, evaluation, certification, testing, development and updating of curricula and training materials" are essential (p. 34). It is crucial to note the complexity of this statement. In a single stroke it combines the recommendation for testing, evaluation, and certification – all of which move universities toward accreditation systems of debatable benefit – with the need to update curricula and training materials – with which most people would agree. Here the juxtaposition of a recommendation that is questionable with one that is easily acceptable obfuscates the issue and makes all of these measures appear as equal tools to achieve equity. Both sets of recommendations, however, simultaneously link quality to measurement and delink quality from any specific social concern, and thus are subject-free: they do not refer to individuals or groups but to a generalized, high abstract "all." In this way the dominant discourse defines quality as an entirely neutral feature, and not as a socio-political construction linked to specific power configurations.

Common Patterns in WB and IDB Policies

Three main patterns emerge from the policies under this analytical lens.

The Premium on Quality

A persistent trait of globalization efforts in education is the exaltation of competition, which in turn brings the issue of quality to the fore. Sachs (quoted in Henry et al., 2001) distinguishes two competing models of quality: a quality improvement model, which is negotiated, consensual, and has an internal locus of control operating through peer reviews (see Bensimon, 1995, for a critical analysis of the TMQ model), and a quality assurance model, which follows government directives, external audits, and quantitative indicators of performance centered on accountability (citing Sachs, in Henry et al., 2001).

At elementary and secondary levels of schooling, prevailing accountability procedures – like the second of Sachs' models – as exemplified by the No Child Left Behind policies in the U.S., focus on student performance, for which teachers are mainly held responsible. When the notion of accountability is transferred to higher education, government-imposed student testing is not utilized because a variety of factors and situations affect the learning performance of adults, and their "learning" occurs in a multiplicity of disciplines and specializations. Since the early 1990s, quality assurance has become the dominant management ideology in the higher educational systems of all OECD countries, in particular those in which they have moved into massive provision. Consequently, what has emerged as the key means to approximate accountability at this level of education is the concept of accreditation, which can be obtained either at the program/department level or at the institutional level. Accreditation pushes quality into that which is readily measurable, such as productivity in terms of publications (books and articles), amount of research funds attracted, and selectivity ratios in the admission of undergraduate students. There are measures regarding reputation that are more subjective in nature but in fact they amount to overall assessment of numerical indicators.

In the Latin American context, accreditation is producing a convergence of universities into the U.S. model, moving them to adopt such features as smaller departments, a discrete cadre of administrators, compressed programs of education, putative faculty governance (as opposed to the Latin American model where students and administrators participate in governance), and rewards for research and publication (Bernasconi, 2008).[2] I contend that accreditation is increasingly moving universities throughout the world toward a convergence characterized by structures, rules, and procedures that cut across countries. Accreditation criteria are very clear in this respect: what is rewarded has to do with the amount of research funds attracted, the productivity of professors in books and articles in prestigious journals that will elevate the reputation of the university and thereby increase its possibility of attracting more research funds and more applicants from who to select from admission. Most accreditation exercises link excellence with research and research has been connected primarily with science and technology, both fields that receive priority for their ability to respond to market needs (Rhoads & Torres, 2006; Slaughter & Leslie, 1997)

Although often invoked, left out of accreditation is the concept of democratic governance. Such discussions seldom consider the persistent increase of part-time faculty, with little or no institutional identification, who typically serve as "knowledge workers" rather than as members of an academic community. Also reduced to secondary importance is the contribution of the university's mission and vision to society at large. Out of the picture as an element of accreditation is the pursuance of a social mission in which equity and inclusion of previously marginalized groups may be important objectives. As Bernasconi notes (2008), with the growing emphasis on accreditation, there is a disregard for concerns that should be present in all universities, but particularly in those of developing countries where inequalities of all types are so prevalent. These features are political awareness, social critique, and outreach to the underprivileged.

The Erosion of Social Equity

The dominant discourse on the importance of science and technology does not acknowledge that employment will not be exclusively in high technology and that a large number will be menial, low-paid jobs. Some university graduates, therefore, may not find the jobs they seek and the successful ones may be those graduating from the more prestigious universities. Further, recent research conducted in the U.S. reveals the growing income disparities since 1980 are due to the rise of salaries among professional occupations and the stagnant wages among non-professional jobs (Weeden et al., 2007). This is being caused by the increased credential, licensing, certification, and training requirements of the high-skilled jobs. The rapidly exploding income disparities present two features, peculiar to the new market circumstances. First, these high-skilled jobs are relatively small in number. Second, they command much higher salaries than non-menial jobs. So, here we encounter both the positive and negative features of education: higher levels of education do result in greater income and good jobs will be few and increasingly out of reach to disadvantaged groups.

Given the manner and speed in which education, the traditional tool for social mobility, is behaving to increase the rewards of those with more advanced levels of formal schooling, equity as a common good needs to be heeded. At present, the notion of "equity" is invoked in global policies. It suffers, however, from a lack of definition and effort to trace it to specific policy interventions. Moreover, challenges to the emergence of equity are seldom probed. So *HEDC*, along with other global policies, touches lightly on equity and mentions it devoid of any concrete referent. Equity as fairness, if not erased, has become secondary to the imperatives of reshaping universities toward greater responsiveness to the market. Universities are consequently growing increasingly detached from the issues of social redistribution (Henry et al., 2001).

The Notorious Absence of Gender

The quasi-policy documents produced by the WB and the IDB do not deal with gender as a social construction that permeates everyday life and that, consequently, is deeply engaged in the definition and uses of S&T. The feminist literature on theoretical, political, and practical aspects of gender is patently ignored in the works circulated by these major banks. It would appear that when attention is paid to central issues affecting higher education in the developing world, gender disappears as a core problem linked to social, political, and economic advancement. By recognizing gender only in terms of women's uneven access to higher education and to scientific fields, these documents contribute to maintaining the gender status quo by not foregrounding discourses that would serve to challenge the gender structures and ideologies that caused the uneven access to S&T in the first place.

The policy documents produced by WB and IDB also fail to make reference to policies on higher education drafted by UNESCO, the UN agency responsible for education matters. This signals the increased marginalization of UNESCO in crucial educational decisions and, conversely, the assertion of hegemony by the lending organizations.[3] In 1998 UNESCO sponsored a World Conference on Higher Education, which produced – as is customary in these meetings – a declaration and a framework for action. Its *World Declaration on Higher Education* identifies the following as missions and functions of higher education:

1. Produce highly qualified graduates and educated citizens.
2. Expand opportunities for higher education and learning throughout life.

3. Advance, create, and disseminate knowledge through research.
4. Help understand, interpret, preserve, enhance, promote, and disseminate national and regional, international and historic cultures, in a context of cultural pluralism and diversity.
5. Protect and enhance societal values by training young people in the values which form the basis of democratic citizenship.
6. Contribute to the development and improvement of education at all levels, including through the training of teachers (UNESCO, 1998).

This *Declaration* is attentive to social and cultural values, especially the formation of citizens. Quality education is invoked but in the broader context of social usefulness. A second document from the conference, the *Framework for priority action for change and development in higher education*, in its Point 1(i), admonishes states to:

> define and implement policies to eliminate all gender stereotyping in higher education and to consolidate women's participation at all levels and in all disciplines in which they are under-represented at present and, in particular, to enhance their active involvement in decision-making.

It is after referring to gender issues, in paragraph (f), that the *Framework* calls upon states to "set relations with the world of work on a new basis involving effectiveness partnerships with all social actors concerned." Next, in paragraph (g), it calls upon states to "ensure high quality of international standing, consider accountability and both internal and external evaluation, with due respect for autonomy and academic freedom" (UNESCO, 1998). The *Framework* puts issues of equity before economic production, mentioning explicitly the need to address gender issues. It does not invoke the importance of science and technology. And its reference to quality considers the validity of *national* accreditation (now a practice of low prestige) and juxtaposes the use of accountability and evaluation to "due respect for autonomy and academic freedom." These principles are at odds with the discourse in higher education prevailing in the major lending institutions.

Conclusion

Rallying the university to meet the needs of the economy presents an inauspicious time to explore structures of power, social inequality, and inadvisable forms of development. The most substantial efforts are going into making the university globally competitive and influential vis-à-vis external markets.

If an informed and interdisciplinary-based humanities and social sciences component in the university is seen as a burden, and perhaps even as an obstacle, how can the formation of an "enlightened and humanitarian being" (Thompson, 2000) occur? Simons and Mosschelein (2007) argue that competitiveness makes institutions forget core values, as they constantly have to adjust to what produces success, and since what produces success is linked to the labor market rather than to aesthetic or ethical values, universities become institutions with no defining principles.

There is interplay of power and institutions. Institutions such as the World Bank, the Inter-American Development Bank, and the OECD use their policy documents as instruments of social influence and control. The notions of the knowledge society and the knowledge economy are deployed to justify a stronger university–market nexus. To do so, the situation is presented not as one imbued with neoliberal economic ideology but rather as the inexorable outcome of scientific and technological development. The answer proposed therefore is one that embraces science with strong resolve, while making rationality, individualism, and self-interest emerge as values that both justify and benefit from the current situation. That the two banks defend neoliberalism is not surprising given the strong hegemony of the U.S. and OECD countries in their membership; consequently, what is at work reflects the will of states and is not just a random endorsement.

The competitive university endorses masculinist strategies, solidly based on competition and marked hierarchies. In these strategies, quality is paramount but it is a quality with narrow parameters: those that generate revenue and prestige for the university. The path is clear but the final destination point is negotiable – whatever helps to win the competition. Accreditation surfaces as a scientific and objective requirement for excellence. Invisible in this process are serious examinations of how social equity may be affected by the emergence of selective research universities and the parallel set of marginal institutions of higher education that attend to the massification of higher education. Gender issues are rendered mute or invoked to argue that they have been resolved.

Through poststructural and feminist analysis I have worked to identify and disrupt the discourses used by powerful institutions such as the WB and the IDB. Their policy papers create an implicit binary system that opposes scientific vs. non-scientific approaches, high-quality vs. low-quality education, accredited vs. non-accredited institutions, objective vs. equity-insensitive policies, and gender-free vs. gender-sensitive logics. I argue that the deconstruction of such discourses can serve to show the political nature of many assertions; it can serve also as a preliminary step toward the creation of subversive politics by recognizing the multiple terrains where political truths are created and by high-lighting both what they assert to be truths and what they fail to acknowledge as distortions and erasures.

Notes

1   The Declaration of this conference, which took place in 1999, argued that "women should participate actively in the design of science and technology policies" and that "governments and NGOs should sustain traditional knowledge systems … and fully recognize the contribution of women as repositories of a large part of traditional knowledge" (UNESCO, 1999, Annex II, p. 12), but also seems to assign the role of science *user* rather than science *producer* to women. This is evident in the assertion that "It is essential that the fundamental role played by women in the application of scientific development to food production and care be fully recognized, and efforts be made to strengthen their understanding of scientific advances to these areas" (Appendix II, p. 5).

2   The U.S. model was introduced to Latin America in the 1920s and emphasized in the 1960s through grants by the Ford Foundation, the Inter-American Development Bank, and USAID, which are recognized as "key actors in the modernization of the region's universities" (Bernasconi, 2008, p. 41). Now grants for the region have significantly decreased but the influence of globalization intensifies the model even more.

3   Curiously, HEDC indicates that the Task Force was convened both by WB and UNESCO (p. 9). It is not clear exactly what UNESCO's role was in the production of the report. Certainly, no UNESCO expert is listed among the contributors to it.

References

Acker, S. (1994). *Gendered education.* Buckingham, UK: Open University Press.

Bensimon, E. (1995). Total quality management in the academy: A rebellious reading. *Harvard Educational Review,* 65(44), 593–611.

Bernasconi, A. (2008). Is there a Latin American model of the university? *Comparative Education Review,* 52(1), 27–52.

Blackmore, J. (2006). Localization/globalization and the midwife state: Strategic dilemmas for state feminism in education? In H. Lauder, P. Brown, J. A. Dillabough, & A. H. Halsey (Eds.), *Education, Globalization & Social Change* (pp. 212–227). Oxford: Oxford University Press.

Bradford, Jr., C. & Linn, J. (2007). *Reform of global governance: Priorities for action.* Policy Brief No. 163. Washington, DC: The Brookings Institution.

Cherryholmes, C. (1994). Pragmatism, poststructuralism, and socially useful theorizing. *Curriculum Inquiry,* 24(2), 193–213.

Cixous, H. (1981). Castration or decapitation. *Signs: Journal of Women in Culture and Society,* 7, 41–54.

Cole, M. (2003). Might it be in practice that it fails to succeed? A Marxist critique of claims for postmodernism and poststructuralism as forces for social change and social justice. *British Journal of Sociology of Education,* 24(4), 487–500.

Crook, S., Pakulski, J., & Waters, M. (1992). *Postmodernization change in advanced society.* London: Sage.

Doherty, R. (2007). Critically framing education policy: Foucault, discourse and governmentality. In M. Peters & T. Besley (Eds.), *Why Foucault? New directions in educational research* (pp. 193–204). New York: Peter Lang.

Faulkner, W. (2001). The technology question in feminism: A view from feminist technology studies. *Women's Studies International Forum,* 24(1), 79–95.

Foucault, M. (n.d.) Foucault. *Stanford Encyclopedia of Philosophy.* Retrieved April 4, 2008 from http://plato.stanford.ed.entries/foucault.

Fox Keller, E. & Longino, H. (Eds.). (1996). *Feminism and science.* New York: Oxford University Press.

Gaskell, J. (1983). The reproduction of family life: Perspectives of male and male adolescents. *British Journal of Sociology of Education,* 4(1), 19–38.

Harding, S. (c. 1991). *Whose science? Whose knowledge? Thinking for women's lives.* Ithaca, NY: Cornell University Press.

Harding, S. (c. 1998). *Is science multicultural? Postcolonialism, feminisms, and epistemologies.* Bloomington, IN: Indiana University Press.

Harding, S. (2008). *Sciences from below: Feminism, postcolonialities, and modernities.* Durham, NC: Duke University Press.

Hennessy, R. (1993). *Materialist feminism and the politics of discourse.* New York: Routledge.

Henry, M., Lingard, B., Rizvi, F., & Taylor, S. (2001). *The OECD, globalisation and education policy.* Amsterdam: Pergamon.

Hirschmann, N. & Di Stefano, C. (1996). Introduction. In N. Hirschmann & C. Di Stefano (Eds.), *Revisioning the political: Feminist reconstructions of traditional concepts in Western political theory* (pp. 1–25). Boulder, CO: Westview Press.

Hubbard, R. (c. 1990). *The politics of women's biology.* New Brunswick, NJ: Rutgers University Press.

IDB. (1997). *Higher education in Latin America and the Caribbean. A strategy paper.* Washington, DC: Inter-American Development Bank. Retrieved February 28, 2008 from http://www.ladb.org/sds/doc/edu-101e.pdf.

Iverson, S. (2008). Capitalizing on change: The discursive frame of diversity in U.S. land-grant universities. *Equity and Excellence in Education*, (41)2, 1–18.

Kenway, J., Willis, S., Blackmore, J., & Rennie, L. (1994). Making "hope practical" rather than "despair convincing": Feminist post-structuralism, gender reform and educational change. *British Journal of Sociology of Education*, 15(2), 187–210.

Lather, P. (1991). *Getting smart: Feminist research and pedagogy with(in) the postmodern (critical social thought).* New York: Routledge.

Lather, P. (2007). *Getting lost: Feminist efforts toward a double(d) science.* Albany, NY: State University of New York Press.

Lee, A. (1992). Poststructuralism and educational research: Some categories and issues. *Issues in Educational Research*, 2(1), 1–12. Retrieved February 28, 2008 from http://www.iier.org.au/iler2/lee.html.

Maila, M. W. (2007). Quality provisioning and accountability in Africa higher education. *South African Journal of Higher Education*, 21(4), 694–705.

Marginson, S. (1997). *Markets in education.* St. Leonards, Australia: Allen & Unwin.

Marshall, C. (Ed.). (1997). *Feminist critical policy analysis.* London: Falmer Press.

Mohanty, C. (2003). *Feminism without borders: Decolonizing theory, practicing solidarity.* Durham, NC: Duke University Press.

Ninnes, P. & Burnett, G. (2003). Comparative education research: Poststructuralist possibilities. *Comparative Education*, 39(3), 279–297.

OECD. (2000). *Knowledge management in the learning society: Education and skills.* Paris: OECD.

Peters, M. (n.d.). Poststructuralism and education. Retrieved May 5, 2008 from http://www.ffst.hr/ENCYCLOPEDIA/poststructuralism.htm.

Peters, M. & Burbules, N. (2004). *Poststructuralism and educational research.* Lanham, MD: Rowman & Littlefield.

Pringle, R. & Watson, S. (1998). "Women's interests" and the poststructuralist state. In A. Phillips (Ed.), *Feminism and politics* (pp. 203–223). Oxford: Oxford University Press.

Rhoads, R. & Torres, C. (Eds.). (2006). *The university, state, and the market: The political economy of globalization in the Americas.* Stanford, CA: Stanford University Press.

Santos, Boaventura de Sousa. (1987). *Um Discurso sobre as Ciências.* Porto: Afrontamento.

Simons, M. & Mosschelein, J. (2007). Only love for the truth can save us: Truth-telling at the (world)university? In M. Peters & T. Besley (Eds.), *Why Foucault? New directions in educational research* (pp. 139–161). New York: Peter Lang.

Slaughter, S. & Leslie, L. (1997). *Academic capitalism: Politics, policies, and the entrepreneurial university.* Baltimore, MD: Johns Hopkins University Press.

Stromquist, N. (2002). *Education in a globalized world: The connectivity of economic power, technology, and knowledge.* Lanham, MD: Rowman & Littlefield.

Thompson, G. (2000). Toward a relegitimation of higher education: Reinvigorating the humanities and social sciences. In R. Brown & J. D. Schubert (Eds.), *Knowledge and power in education: A reader* (pp. 150–163). New York: Teachers College Press.

UNESCO. (1998). *World declaration on higher education for the twenty-first century: Vision and action and framework for priority action for change and development in higher education.* Paris: UNESCO. Retrieved January 3, 2008 from http://www/unesco.org/education/educprog/coahe/declaration-eng.htm.

UNESCO. (1999). World Science Conference. *Declaration of science and framework for action.* Budapest: UNESCO.

UNESCO. (2007). *EFA global monitoring report 2008. Education for all by 2015: Will we make it?* Paris: UNESCO.

Weeden, K., Kim, Y., Di Carlo, M., & Grusky, D. (2007). Social class and earnings inequality. *American Behavioral Scientist*, 50(5), 702–736.

Williams, G. (1999). *French discourse analysis: The method of post-structuralism.* New York: Routledge.

World Bank. (1999). *World development report: Knowledge for development.* Washington, DC: World Bank.

World Bank. (2000). *Higher education in developing countries: Peril and promise.* Washington, DC: World Bank.

12
Questions and Complexities in Feminist Poststructural Policy Analysis

REBECCA ROPERS-HUILMAN, SUSAN V. IVERSON,
AND ELIZABETH J. ALLAN

Purposeful Policies?

The chapters included in this volume represent a range of feminist post-structural approaches to understanding the social contracts that are reified in policies. These policies posit norms and expectations for both individual behaviors and institutional practices. The approaches found in this book, unique from other approaches to policy analysis, foreground the underlying discourses that not only guide behavior, but also constitute the terms or frameworks through which educators, policy-makers, students, and community members structure their thinking. That thinking can relate to the characterization of students, faculty, community members, or administrators. It can also influence perceptions of the social (to include economic, legal, political, and environmental) responsibilities of organizations. In either case, how educators and policy-makers view what is available to us within perceptible discourses matters a great deal.

As co-editors, we had the privilege to see ideas emerging within complex frameworks and to engage with contributors' passion around their chosen topics. We encouraged authors to craft analyses that critically examined policies that shape particular groups of people's access to and involvement with educational experiences. In our hearts, we hoped both to learn from this experience and offer this text to colleagues and students as one path toward change.

We acknowledge the complexities of our intentions. Poststructuralism is highly suspicious of efforts to uncritically "improve" policies because improvement is always constructed along axes that in themselves represent what is powerful and valuable within a given context. In this sense, poststructuralism resists the "naturalness" assumed in hierarchies and dichotomies that frame educational relationships and the terms that define them, such as "quality," "rigor," "student," and "teacher," in addition to socially ascribed identities such as gender, race, ethnicity, sexual orientation, and socio-economic status.

Feminism, however, has insisted on a social justice framework that acknowledges how identities shape experience, to include educational experience, and foregrounds how power and privilege align with those identities. The combination of a poststructural analytic lens that pushes toward deeper understandings of what policies both suppress and produce, with a feminist insistence that identity matters and that our current terms of engagement are imbued with uneven power–knowledge relations that can do harm, undergirds our intentions for this volume.

We chose to organize this book by themes associated with FPS. Namely, our sections considered: (1) Productions of Power through Presence within Absence; (2) Subjects and Objects of Policy; and (3) Discursive Constructions of Change. In this final chapter, we consider these themes through our own lenses as members of personal and professional communities, all of which hold a stake in the processes and outcomes of higher education policy.

Rebecca

Knowledge is produced; knowing is produced; production is knowledge; producing is knowing. Where is power? Where is community? Must I know to produce? Am I producing students or knowledge any more than they are "producing" me? What am I, as a faculty member or community member, trying to produce? Is that my function? It is not how I see myself.

In working collaboratively on this book over the past several years, I have been perplexed by several questions related to how power, knowledge, and community have been shaped in academic settings. Feminist poststructuralism for me is a way to retain my political and ethical commitments to equity, while continuing to acknowledge the complex contexts in which power relations form inequitable situations for those involved.

Yet, policy often seems inaccessible both to me and to the students with whom I teach and learn. What exactly is policy and who gets to engage it or avoid its effects? Who are the "producers" and "consumers" of the policies that structure educational experience in various contexts today? After working on this book, I am left with better understandings of dominant discourses that are (often subconsciously) employed to structure policy. I am also better aware of the need to notice those discourses and question our own assumptions about what constitutes "fairness" in educational experience. Simultaneously, I am frustrated by the lack of movement toward equity that has occurred when we consider economic and social disparities that remain in the United States and in many other places around the world. I am also confused that our best efforts in postsecondary education have not "produced" more equitable outcomes. If higher education is to fulfill its urgent task of enriching our collective society, isn't equity a necessity? Isn't equity inextricably linked with educational excellence? Through this volume, I better recognize specific instances wherein policy-makers' and educators' multi-faceted visions of our ideal collective society would yield different answers to those questions.

I continue to have great faith in the potential of education to build bridges that span wide gorges of identity, ideology, disposition, and experience. This paradox – the great potential of education and the slow, slow change of society – leads me to believe that we need to continue to look inward to our own institutions and our own practices. How and why do we replicate and (re)produce the gendered, racial, economic, and heterosexist norms that many of us claim to be working against? How can we work on both micro- and macro-levels to counteract dominant norms that perpetuate the status quo? Though not sufficient, I believe the discursive analyses offered by feminist poststructuralism are useful in helping those of us interested in making deep-seated changes to academic environments.

Susan

Within and against. As I reflect on the thinking and writing process for this book, I am struck by my/our struggle of working within and against rules, guidelines, and structures that provide us the space and opportunity to do our work while simultaneously constraining some of its possibilities. It is through discourse that possibilities for agency are enacted; that structures and conventions are produced and through which we are able to act. To write, or act, outside of the dominant discourses, those that make one visible and give one voice, risks being rendered unheard, invisible, or at the edges.

Concepts and terms – language – *signify* certain understandings, and consequently constrain our struggle to deconstruct and reconstruct alternatives. In this text I faced this challenge, frustrated with the fixed meanings that alternatives signified. For instance, we sought to illuminate the ways in which FPS is deployed. Initially referred to as a "continuum," we quickly recognized the structural image this evoked. Language, and the ways that words once put on a page reflect a static position, seems to betray efforts to write FPS. I find/found myself compromised/ing by/with words, negotiating with the limits of language.

This negotiating must not be an either/or dilemma (work within or be relegated outside); I can adopt a within/against approach (work within in order to work against). I am discursively produced and situated; I take up and perform identities discursively constituted. For instance, in Chapter 5, we analyzed the ways that gender discourses shape realities for men and women as leaders. These gender discourses shape my experience and the ways that I perform my role as a tenure-track female faculty member in higher education. Through an FPS lens, I can examine how the rules of tenure are discursively constituted, better serving men than women; yet, I risk not getting tenure if I fail to conform to the rules of this system. I do not stand outside of and am powerfully shaped by discursive practices. This does not, however, mean that FPS lacks practical utility. When

I am teaching, for example, student development theory, I challenge students to interrogate the inherent goodness of identity development as an upward, linear trajectory, and our belief in the essential goodness of (higher) education for generating a productive citizenry.

Through awareness of the ways in which discourse reflects, shapes, and produces reality and my sense of myself I can work within and against. I am reminded of Audre Lorde's "the master's tools will never dismantle the master's house." I don't know that we can abandon or discard the tools, but we can understand how their use better serves existing structures and constrains efforts to enact change. An FPS lens can illuminate their use and appropriation, the potential to use them differently, and other tools that are available. My hope is that this concourse of words, ideas, images, stories, and analyses in this text affords readers a point of entry to re/thinking about policy, practice, and the ways in which they (policies and practices) are socially constituted and sites of/for constructing meaning.

Elizabeth

In reflecting on the work of this volume, I am drawn to thinking about the "conditions of possibility" for this project and the complex web of places, spaces, practices, and people from which it emerged and took form over time. From an FPS perspective, these contexts, subjectivities, and discursive practices are *produced by* and also share in actively *producing* systems of meaning, or networks of intelligibility, that render what is thinkable, understandable, and doable. So, what were some of the forces that coalesced to shape this text? And, in the process, what has been produced, enabled, and also constrained by our work? I offer some thoughts on these questions from my dynamic and evolving vantage points as a member of personal and professional communities for whom educational policy has consequences.

I do not pretend to know all the forces that converged to produce this volume, for that would be impossible. However, it is possible to speak from experience in an effort to move toward exposing motivations, influences, desires, and bodies that are often eclipsed by the end product, yet actively shape (and are shaped by) the making of any text. To begin, I circle back to our shared motive for this work – that is, a desire to make a difference in struggles toward social justice. Given this desire, our feminist commitments, as well as our shared view of the non-innocence of policy discourses, we forged this collaboration in an effort to make a difference by exposing and interrupting dominant systems of meaning that frame and constrain traditional approaches to understanding and enacting policy-making and analysis. This work was motivated by our desire to open up spaces that might be fertile ground for more promising approaches toward equitable social relations, including, but not limited to, gender equity. This project then embodies ironic tensions produced by the methodological hybrid of FPS – an approach that engages with postmodern/poststructural perspectives, yet also maintains a commitment to agency and the liberatory goals of feminism.

This project was also motivated by the ways in which FPS has served to help each of us unthink and think differently about the inherent "goodness" of policy-making, policy analysis, and policy practices in the context of higher education. This is not to say that nothing good can come of policy. Rather, it is a shared recognition that policy problems and solutions are made intelligible through dominant systems of meaning (discourses) that foreground particular perspectives. When hegemonic meaning systems are employed via policy to solve problems, they are rarely transformative and can contribute to under-cutting attempts to promote social justice. As faculty members and teachers in graduate programs of higher education, we believe this is an important perspective to share. We have frequently found ourselves engaged in describing FPS to students and colleagues who express a desire to learn more about these perspectives.

We have also often been reminded of the marginality of these perspectives. For instance, I recall when a number of the authors who wrote chapters for this text gathered to provide a symposium of FPS papers for the Association for the Study of Higher Education conference. During the discussion period following the paper summaries, some graduate students voiced concern that FPS methodologies are not taught by their faculty. Another attendee wondered what kind of message was being sent by conference planners, noting that our session was scheduled for the last day of the conference, during the last time slot, and placed at the farthest end of an obscure hallway in the convention center. The marginality of FPS and our desire to promote more widespread understanding and use of these perspectives drives another dilemma for us in assembling this volume. How do we re/position and amplify FPS within the academy and yet avoid contributing to a successor grand narrative? These kinds of questions gave us much to consider throughout the process of writing and editing this book, and will continue to challenge us in necessary ways, as we employ FPS perspectives in our work.

Summary

We hope that this book both facilitates and interrupts policy conversations, therefore drawing forth multiple ways of making sense of the policies that guide our relationships with each other and structure access to resources. These policies make some behaviors and expectations "normal," while determining that other ways of being – those that fall out of the constructed discourse – are "strange," "deviant," or at least "unexpected." With their contributions in this book, the authors are not trying to work their way "out" of discourse, for that is not possible. Instead, the compilation of diverse chapters points out the ways in which power is represented, produced, and resisted. Most importantly, perhaps, the chapters provide analyses that suggest the possibility of shifting discourses, perhaps to ones that will allow for more inclusivity in ways of thinking and doing.

We hope that through the conversations generated by this book, readers will be compelled to look at policies in new and different ways. Yet, we are aware of what is represented and absent in this book. For example, financial aid policies would benefit from further analyses that focus on gendered, as well as raced and classed, experiences. Additional studies are needed from those who foreground the construction of race, ethnicity, and citizenship, especially in terms of institutional policies that affect different groups' access to and involvement in postsecondary education. Multiple considerations of promotion and tenure policies have already been conducted, to include a focus on "family-friendly" campus practices. Additional work in this area, such as that evidenced in Elizabeth Allan and Susan Iverson's work on policy discourse analysis, is warranted to better understand not only promotion and tenure policies, but how those policies shape women's and men's experiences in caring for their families and communities. Higher education has witnessed a broad-scale shift to part-time or non-tenure track faculty. These policies do not have gender-neutral effects, and our understandings of them would benefit from critical analyses.

The silences and emphases illustrated in this book come from our own positioning as well. Researchers are multicultural subjects and in this case, like any other academic project, the motivations, subject positions, and sociocultural locations of its makers matter. As editors, we are white, middle-class, able-bodied, professional women working in universities and benefiting from identity privilege associated with each of these, as well as our perceived (hetero)-sexual identities. Recognizing this, as we journeyed through this project together, we were committed to working against, destabilizing, and interrogating discursive formations and practices that enable identity privilege and oppression. Indeed, this was an ongoing theme in nearly every conversation as we planned for and worked to bring this text to fruition; we desired to produce a text that reflected diversity in its treatment of topics. In many respects, we met this objective. Yet, despite our best efforts, we remain conscious of the inevitability of partial perspectives, and the need for reflexivity in all feminist work. We believe that the silences we have identified here – as well as those identified by readers – are opportunities for important analyses of the policies that shape both the potential for and character of educational experience at all levels.

Index

Page references in **bold** refer to figures.